HAROLD DIETERLE'S

Kitchen Notebook

HAROLD DIETERLE'S

Kitchen Notebook

HUNDREDS OF RECIPES,

TIPS, AND TECHNIQUES FOR COOKING

LIKE A CHEF AT HOME

Harold Dieterle and
Andrew Friedman

Photography by Daniel Krieger
Illustrations by Eve Hammer

GRAND
CENTRAL
L&S
LIFE & STYLE
NEW YORK · BOSTON

Grand Central Life & Style

Hachette Book Group

1290 Avenue of the Americas

New York, NY 10104

www.GrandCentralLifeandStyle.com

Printed in the United States of America

Q-MA

First Edition: October 2014

10 9 8 7 6 5 4 3 2 1

Grand Central Life & Style is an imprint of Grand Central Publishing.

The Grand Central Life & Style name and logo are trademarks of Hachette Book Group, Inc.

The Hachette Speakers Bureau provides a wide range of authors for speaking events. To find out more, go to www.HachetteSpeakersBureau.com or call (866) 376-6591.

The publisher is not responsible for websites (or their content) that are not owned by the publisher.

Library of Congress Cataloging-in-Publication Data

Dieterle, Harold.

   Harold Dieterle's kitchen notebook: hundreds of recipes, tips, and techniques for cooking like a chef at home / Harold Dieterle and Andrew Friedman.

     pages cm

   Includes index.

   ISBN 978-1-4555-2863-9 (hardback) — ISBN 978-1-4555-2864-6 (ebook)   1. Cooking, American.   I. Friedman, Andrew, 1967–   II. Title.   III. Title: Kitchen notebook.

   TX715.D58185 2014

   641.5973—dc23

2014002849

To Meredith, my dear and loving wife

Making Connections

When you get right down to it, cooking is all about making connections. From a creative standpoint, this notion is especially true for chefs like me. We devise our own dishes, from tried-and-true signature combinations to spontaneous nightly specials that take advantage of a burst of inspiration, kitchen leftovers, or an ingredient we suddenly discovered was in season during a morning market visit.

The act of cooking also depends on a series of connections—on combining bits of knowledge and skill in different ways to produce different results. For home cooks and professionals alike, the progression is the same: you pick up one ability and technique after another, from knife skills that enable you to properly slice and shape ingredients to cooking methods such as sautéing, roasting, braising, and so on. Whether played out in a culinary institute with a chef-instructor scowling over you, or in the much safer, calmer sanctuary of a home kitchen, almost all Western culinary developments follow the same path: slicing garlic, onions, celery, and carrots, then heating oil in a pan, sautéing the vegetables, and building a dish on that foundation. Or maybe the process begins with the cleaning and preparation of raw vegetables, the whisking and seasoning of a vinaigrette, and then the tossing of the two together to make a salad.

That's how we *all* begin, even the best chefs who ever lived. From there, we grow and expand, our culinary abilities snowballing as we acquire recipes for the building blocks of cooking: stocks, sauces, soups, potato and egg preparations, and so on. Once we've mastered the basics, we are equipped to cook just about anything.

For aspiring professional cooks, the next steps are usually to work in a restaurant, then go to culinary school, and then work in *more* restaurants. As we continue to gain knowledge and experience, we learn what we most enjoy cooking and eating, and we follow our palates on a path of development. We choose a succession of jobs based on cuisines and styles we want to emulate or build on when the time comes for us to create our own menus. One budding young chef might stick to the classics, working in nothing but French restaurants before opening his or her own bistro; another might gravitate toward Spanish cuisine, even taking a year or two in Madrid; yet another might decide that a particular American region excites him or her, spending some time in New Orleans learning

the nuances of Creole cooking, or in St. Louis mastering the fine art of barbecue.

Whether they realize it or not, the same is true for many home cooks, who, by and large, gravitate to a particular type of food—French or Italian, Western or Eastern, classic or contemporary—or combine one or more types into a personal taste profile and sensibility.

THE SECRET WEAPON

Just about every chef I know uses a notebook to track his or her advancement and development. From the time we are students and line cooks, each of us maintains a notebook in which we scribble recipes for everything from stocks, sauces, and vinaigrettes to spice rubs, marinades, and braising bases. Notebooks are our culinary diaries—a record of what we've learned and how to apply it.

Every cook has his or her own type: some use a spiral pad; others have beautiful leather-bound versions. I bought my first notebook when I was a student at Western Suffolk BOCES at Wilson Technical School, in Central Islip, New York, which I attended during my junior and senior years in high school, spending half my day learning the basics of food preparation. At some point, to keep track of all the information that flew around the room—too much, too quickly to be memorized—I bought myself a royal blue Mead spiral notebook, one of those basic ones with the thin, glossy cardstock cover. In it I kept basic information, like how to make an emulsified dressing, such as for a Caesar salad, or the makeup of a Caprese salad.

Following technical school, I landed my first professional kitchen job, at The Gull restaurant in Babylon, Long Island. I actually started as a dishwasher, then was promoted to line cook. I worked there for two summers, during which I confirmed that this career path was for me, and expanded my notebook with some vintage fish-house recipes, such as for crab cakes. After my second summer there, I attended the Culinary Institute of America (also known as the CIA) in Hyde Park, New York. As a student there, I continued to record daily lessons in my notebook—everything from classic French preparations such as duck à l'orange to how to make different potato and egg standards. One thing I *stopped* doing after a while was making sketches: during my externship at the Island Mermaid restaurant in Ocean Beach, Long Island, we had to present a list of recipe ideas along with informal illustrations. Mine were abysmal, including a three-clawed lobster that has become legendary among my friends. When our sketches were unveiled, everybody in the kitchen, including the chefs, burst out laughing at mine. I never sketched again.

I graduated from the CIA in 1997. After that, I started working as a sous chef at Della Femina, a pair of restaurants with locations in New York City and East Hampton, and my notebook really took off. The chef, Kevin Penner, was the first person I worked for who brought a distinct "voice" to the plate; rather than just following a playbook of standards, he created his own combinations and compositions. I kept track of the elements he called on to stitch together dishes like his signature pan-roasted halibut with Yukon Gold potato purée, wild mushroom broth, truffle oil, and frizzled leeks, or veal tarragon ragù with lobster and mushrooms. In the New York City restaurant, we did a riff on Jean-Georges Vongerichten's legendary molten chocolate cake, and I wrote the recipe for that in my notebook, even though I wasn't a pastry chef. In time, I used the morning commute from West Babylon to Manhattan to dream in my notebook, scribbling down ideas for dishes of my own, borrowing from preparations I had picked up at work as well as dishes I'd read about in restaurant reviews, articles, and even cookbooks. The notebook became a repository for both my knowledge and my imagination.

Once in a while, Chef Penner would let me try out one of my own dishes as a daily special. Occasionally these dishes found their way onto the menu, which for me was like graduating from the minor leagues to the majors. The first one that made it into print was foie gras sausage with pickled vegetables, grilled bread, and mustard, which drew from several notebook entries. It made it into print in another way, too, when it was mentioned in the *Daily News* review of the restaurant—a big moment for me.

A series of gigs followed: I became sous chef at Red Bar, a New York City spin-off of a Hamptons restaurant. With the chef mostly stationed in Long Island, I essentially ran the city outpost, which was a valuable learning experience. Then I spent a summer working as sous chef to Chef Penner at the 1770 House restaurant in East Hampton. After that, returning to New York City, I was executive sous chef at The Harrison in Tribeca, first to chef Joey Campanaro, then to Brian Bistrong.

While I grew as a chef, so did my notebooks. Even now, they inform the recipes at my restaurants Perilla, where the menu is defined by an Asian-inflected New American style, and Kin Shop, where I offer my own spin on Thai dishes and flavors. (I actually keep a special notebook with an ornamental leather cover from a few formative trips I've taken to Thailand.) Over the years, I've also used my notebooks to help me explore the two cultures that defined my childhood: Italian American (my mother) and German (my father), creating or re-interpreting dishes in those styles.

Every cook—including adventurous home cooks—has a distinct approach to what he or she wants to make and serve. For some, the starting point is the protein (the meat or fish) they'll use. For others, it's the accompaniment, or side dish. For me, it's usually the protein—or main vegetable if I'm preparing a vegetarian dish—or the sauce, with a strong focus on what's in season. When it's time to devise a new menu, I sit at a big table with lists of what's available from all my purveyors arrayed before me, and I think about how to use each ingredient. I rummage through my notebooks—both physical and mental—and call on what's there, mixing and matching different ingredients, subrecipes, and techniques to come up with something new.

HOW TO USE THIS BOOK

This book blends elements of a traditional cookbook with the kind of information found in a chef's notebook in order to enable you to make fully fleshed-out dishes and to apply the examples and lessons of those recipes to other cooking. My goal is for you to be able to use the Notebook section the same way a chef uses a notebook, drawing on it to cook an ingredient you love in new and exciting ways; to access a repertoire of preparations to bring ideas you have to life; or just to use whatever's on special in the market—or awaits attention in your fridge—in a way you never thought of before.

This might sound obvious, but nothing makes you a better cook than actually cooking. *A lot*. I want this book to be a constant presence in your kitchen life—one that you turn to for everything from dinner party fare to quick and simple weeknight meals inspired by the Notebook entries. If you read, think about, and call on these Notebook entries frequently, I really believe that you will become a more intuitive, improvisational cook—and maybe even find yourself keeping your own notebook before you know it.

STRUCTURE

The chapters that follow are organized according to the courses of a meal: salads, starters, soups, pasta and risotto, fish and shellfish, poultry and game birds, meats and game, and desserts. There are recipes for one hundred dishes, each preceded by a headnote that shares a little bit about it. After each dish, you'll find my Notebook entry, which isolates one component of the dish, explains why I like and value it, then offers a number of ways to use or adapt it. The topics of the Notebook entries could be just about anything, but they break down into a few main categories:

- **Raw Ingredients:** Many of the Notebook entries discuss a recipe's prominent or supporting raw ingredient and then offer different uses, preparations, and dishes for it.
- **Preparations:** Some Notebook entries are built on recipes that produce condiments such as remoulade, sauces such as tomato sauce, versatile elements such as preserved lemons, and even cooked meats such as braised rabbit leg, as well as a wide range of other preparations, then offer additional ways to use or adapt them.
- **Combinations:** A few Notebook entries focus on combinations such as chiles and citrus or eggplant and basil, then show how else to use them.
- **Techniques:** Other Notebook entries describe techniques such as brining or grilling that can be applied to your everyday cooking.

While the primary dish recipes in this book are fully fleshed out, as they would be in any cookbook, the advice in the Notebook entries is presented in shorter form and assumes a certain amount of comfort in the kitchen. Many of the applications described in the Notebook entries leave precise ingredient amounts and ratios up to your personal taste or offer only approximate amounts as a guideline. Some are more complex than others, but if you aren't comfortable with the judgment calls that some applications require, you can still avail yourself of most of the Notebook suggestions regardless.

Many of the recipes in this book call on *other* recipes or techniques from elsewhere in the book, for maximum value. For example, the pasta on page 145 features a tomato sauce and toasted bread crumbs that have multiple applications throughout these pages and offers you the choice of buying pasta or really going for it and making your own from yet another recipe provided in this book. Assembling these building blocks of cooking in different ways is how professionals like me get better at our craft, and the same is true at home.

A FEW KITCHEN BASICS

Below I've gathered some important information to guide you as you read and cook from this book.

RECIPES

I strongly recommend that you read the recipes from start to finish before making them, just to be sure you have the ingredients and necessary tools, equipment, and supplies on hand, and to be ready for any special timing requirements, such as preparations that need to rest for several hours or even overnight.

TOOLS, EQUIPMENT, AND SUPPLIES

I don't have a lot of idiosyncrasies or quirks in the kitchen. For the most part, the recipes in this book can be made with standard home equipment. That said, to help you be prepared, here's a list of just about all the tools, equipment, and supplies I call for in my recipes—most of which I'd guess you already have in your kitchen.

KNIVES, SLICERS, AND PEELERS: The two knives every home cook should own are a large (8 inches or longer) chef's knife and a paring knife. While there is a wide variety of other knives on the market, each intended for a specific task—deboning meat, for example—these two are all you really need for almost any cooking. (If you will be shucking oysters, though, as for the recipe on page 65, the only really safe way to do it is with a sturdy oyster knife.) I also recommend a mandoline for when paper-thin slices are desired, although a sharp chef's knife and a steady hand are a passable alternative. And you will need a vegetable peeler; I prefer the T-shaped European-style peeler, which affords the greatest control.

MEASURING SPOONS AND CUPS: For gathering accurate amounts of ingredients, a set of measuring spoons and a heatproof measuring cup are essential. I suggest having a small (1- or 2-cup) measuring cup and a larger (4-cup) one, both spouted, which are also handy for holding sauces and other preparations, especially those that might need to be poured at some stage in a recipe.

MIXING BOWLS: You will need a set of bowls of varying sizes, at least two each of small, medium, and large. They should be heatproof as well as capable of being transferred to the refrigerator or freezer while holding hot liquid without cracking.

IMPLEMENTS: The implements I call for most often in this book are a wooden spoon, a slotted spoon, a rubber spatula, a ladle, a whisk, and tongs. If you don't own all of them, I recommend you obtain them, because they all perform different tasks, are relatively inexpensive, and come in handy on a daily basis if you do a lot of cooking. I also suggest having a rolling pin for dough, although in a pinch you can use the side of a bottle or a similar cylindrical kitchen item. One recipe in the book calls for a meat mallet, but the bottom of a heavy pan can be used instead.

POTS, PANS, AND BAKING SHEETS: A complete set of pots and pans, in various sizes and with lids, is essential for all cooking. I don't insist on exact capacities in my recipes, and saucepans and soup pots can generally be replaced by other types of cooking vessels, but you should have small, medium, and large options available, as well as a Dutch oven, baking dish, cast-iron pan, grill pan, and roasting pan with a rack. Your pots and pans should be of a high quality, with a good heft, and ideally be made of stainless steel or copper, which conduct heat the best and most evenly. You will also need baking sheets, preferably rimmed to catch any liquid or drippings, for many recipes; a few call for two sheets, and one calls for three. It's also a good idea to have at least one large nonstick sauté pan, one oven-proof sauté pan, one stovetop-safe baking dish, and one nonstick baking sheet.

WRAPS, LININGS, AND OTHER MATERIALS: A number of recipes call for aluminum foil, plastic wrap, and parchment or waxed paper for wrapping foods, lining baking sheets, and so on. For some baking, a silicone baking mat, or Silpat, is a must. For trussing poultry, you will need kitchen twine.

GRATERS: Every home kitchen should have two types of graters: a microplane for zesting citrus rinds, ginger, and finely grating hard cheeses, and an old-fashioned box grater for larger grating, especially of hard cheeses.

CUTTING DEVICES AND MOLDS: A good set of ring cutters, ranging in size from ½ inch to 4 inches, will help you shape some pastas and baked preparations such as homemade oyster crackers and roti dough. These can usually be replaced with an openmouthed vessel of the right diameter, such as a glass or cup. A fluted pasta cutter is also helpful for achieving a classic effect on some pasta shapes. A 6-inch ring mold is required for some dessert recipes.

COLANDERS AND FINE-MESH STRAINERS: You will need a colander for draining cooked items of their liquid and a strainer for the same purpose, as well as for passing purées and other preparations through to eliminate small particles of food. I never insist on it, but in a few recipes a conical strainer, or chinois, is recommended in order to obtain the most silken result possible.

STEAMING BASKET AND DOUBLE BOILER: For steaming foods, there's no substitute for a basket sized to fit a pot with a lid. For keeping certain foods warm or for melting some ingredients, a double boiler is useful, although a similar effect can be achieved with two pots or bowls, one, slightly larger and filled with boiling water, below the other.

THERMOMETERS: A meat thermometer is necessary for determining doneness of a variety of proteins as they cook. For some pastry preparations, such as making marshmallows, you will need a candy thermometer. For other pastry applications, and for the sea urchin dish on page 76, where exact temperatures are required, a digital thermometer is the most accurate way of measuring.

BLENDERS, PROCESSORS, JUICERS, AND GRINDERS: A number of recipes ask you to process foods in different ways. A blender and food processor are musts. I also suggest investing in an immersion blender, also known as a stick blender, for blending right in the pot or bowl, which is very convenient, although never mandatory. One recipe requires a juicer, and a few recipes, especially for homemade sausage, call for a meat grinder, although you can always have your butcher do that work for you. (A related piece of equipment, a sausage stuffer, is required if you want to make one of the homemade sausages on pages 214–15.) A few recipes call for a food mill, which is often the best tool for processing cooked potatoes or tomatoes. You will also want a spice grinder or a coffee grinder.

GRILL, GRILL PAN, SMOKERS, AND ACCESSORIES: Whether one uses a gas or charcoal grill is matter of personal taste and is discussed on pages 274–75, along with equipment needs that are specific to charcoal grills. In some cases, a grill pan can be a viable alternative to the real thing, and appropriate recipes indicate so throughout the book. For outdoor grilling, you will need a pair of long tongs and a heat-proof spatula, preferably one with a long handle as well. For the related technique of smoking, you may want to have a brûlée torch or stick-style barbecue lighter for igniting wood chips. (For more on smoking, see page 304.) The torch is also called on to brown marshmallows in the s'mores dessert on page 355.

DEEP FRYER: There are a lot of deep-fried dishes in this book, and using a deep fryer is the easiest method because you can simply set the desired temperature for the oil. You can also use a pot, preferably at least 12 inches deep, and a clip-on thermometer.

PASTRY BAG AND TIPS: You will need a pastry bag for a few recipes that require you to pipe certain elements. While it's good to have a set of pastry tips for different uses, a number 3 plain tip will work for the recipes in this book. If you don't own a pastry bag, you can put the food to be piped in a large, resealable plastic bag, squeeze the top so the bag is tightly filled, and snip off a bottom corner of the bag to simulate a piping tip. The higher up you cut the bag, the wider the "tip" will be.

ICE CREAM MACHINE: To make your own homemade ice cream, as is called for by many of the dessert recipes, there's no substitute for an ice cream machine. There are many inexpensive models on the market that produce about a quart of ice cream per batch.

PASTA MAKER: If you plan to make your own pasta, as recommended in several recipes, you will need a pasta maker—a hand-crank mechanism that clamps onto the side of your counter is fine, although a special device is required to make your own cavatelli.

CO_2 CANISTER: One recipe in the book, the sea urchin dish on page 76, calls for a CO_2 canister, a device used to aerate preparations, rendering them extraordinarily light, and pipe them into dishes.

A NOTE ON INGREDIENTS

When it comes to basic ingredients, I have a couple of strongly held personal preferences that are reflected in the recipes in this book.

PEPPER: I use white pepper in almost all my cooking and encourage you to do the same. White pepper brings a more gentle, nuanced heat to dishes, rather than overpowering the other flavors as black pepper can. In white or light-colored preparations, white pepper also doesn't interfere with the natural beauty of the other ingredients, whereas black pepper can be distracting. White pepper is easy to find in the spice section of any supermarket and can be put in a mill and ground just like black pepper. Of course, if you like, you can use black pepper in place of white, but I really urge you to try keeping some white pepper on hand and see if you don't notice a difference in your cooking. I also recommend having black pepper on hand because I use it to season red meat, some mushrooms, and grilled vegetables, and in certain dishes where it's traditional, such as the HD Caesar Salad on page 45.

BLENDED OIL: In many of the recipes in the book, such as those for vinaigrettes, I call for blended oil, which means a 90/10 percent blend of neutral oil and olive oil. (It is not sold this way; you need to combine it yourself.) Blended oil is used in many professional kitchens and brings balance to dishes with a little, but not too much, olive presence. As with white pepper, I urge you to try using blended oil at home, but if you choose not to, all recipes that use it give you the choice of using just a neutral oil, such as canola or grapeseed, instead.

SPECIAL INGREDIENTS AND SOURCES

Throughout the recipes, if you encounter an unfamiliar ingredient, look in the back of the book, where you'll find a compilation of some of the harder-to-find ingredients, mostly Asian in origin, used throughout the book, as well as sources where they're available for order. I also encourage you to seek out a good local Asian market, where you will be able to find most of these ingredients in person. There's also a list of a few other ingredients and specialty items, such as sausage casings, that you may need to purchase online if you don't live near a specialty store or an especially well-stocked supermarket.

BASIC RECIPES AND TECHNIQUES

At the back of the book, you'll find appendices featuring a few techniques that are called on often in the recipes, such as toasting nuts and blanching vegetables, as well as recipes for a few basics, such as homemade stocks and pastas. Where applicable, recipes indicate when making your own is not essential. Homemade basics will always make your cooking better—and preparing them is easier than most people think—but store-bought versions, especially high-quality, low-sodium options, are often viable substitutes.

* * *

As you cook from this book, I hope that it adds many dishes to your repertoire and that the Notebook entries encourage you to try new things, helping you develop greater confidence and creativity. The book's structure and recipes track my own growth as a cook, and then as a chef, so I know that you will find much here to draw on and build upon. Nothing would make me happier than if you started keeping your own grease-spattered notebook along the way, a diary of *your* evolution and ideas—and, yes, maybe even your own signature dishes—inspired by the recipes and information in these pages.

1

Salads

Roasted Tristar Strawberry Salad
with Wild Mushrooms, Peas, and Balsamic Vinegar

Strawberries are my second-favorite berry after blueberries (page 339). I'm especially crazy for Tristars, because they are so insanely sweet and extremely seasonal, but any small, local strawberry makes a fine stand-in. When they're around in June and July, I eat them as much as possible, and I especially love pairing them with wild mushrooms; it sounds illogical, but the contrast between the sweet fruit and earthy mushrooms works, and the balsamic vinegar and crunch of pea-shoot leaves help pull it all together. You can make this salad with just about any wild mushrooms—chanterelles, morels, black trumpets, hedgehogs—or even cultivated mushrooms. (If you ever find yourself wondering if a mushroom is wild or cultivated, here's a surefire way to tell: if they're expensive, they're wild!)

¼ cup extra-virgin olive oil

1 cup wild mushrooms

Kosher salt

Freshly ground black pepper

2 cups wild strawberries (about 8 ounces), stems removed

¼ cup balsamic vinegar, preferably a sweet variety

1 cup (loosely packed) pea-shoot leaves or baby spinach

½ cup blanched and shocked English peas (see page 362)

½ cup finely diced pecorino Romano cheese

Heat the oil in a wide, deep sauté pan over high heat. When the oil is shimmering, add the mushrooms, season with salt and pepper, and cook, stirring, until golden brown, 5 to 6 minutes. Remove the pan from the heat, add the strawberries and vinegar, and toss to integrate the ingredients and warm the strawberries.

▷ Transfer the contents of the pan to a heatproof bowl. Add the pea-shoot leaves, peas, and pecorino Romano, and gently toss.

▷ Divide the salad among 4 small plates and serve warm.

Small Wild Strawberries

One of my favorite childhood memories is of picking strawberries at Lewin Farms on Long Island. My mother used them to make strawberry shortcake—strawberries macerated with sugar, served over white cake, and topped with whipped cream—and strawberry preserves. When shopping, try to find the ones with no bruises or green spots on the stem end or bottom, which indicate they are underripe and flavorless. If you can get them from a farm stand or pick your own, you should; there's nothing like fresh-picked strawberries.

SNACKING: Unadorned wild strawberries make an amazingly easy between-meals treat that's as sweet and satisfying as candy. You can also dip them into melted chocolate and either let them harden on a rack or eat them right out of the chocolate, like fondue.

STRAWBERRY PRESERVES: The difference between store-bought and homemade preserves is massive, and it's very easy to make your own: Cook 2 cups stemmed strawberries and ½ cup granulated sugar in a medium pot slowly over low heat, stirring often, until the strawberries break down, about 30 minutes. (You may need to season with additional sugar depending on the sweetness of your strawberries; this can be done toward the end of the cooking.) Allow to cool and serve right away, or refrigerate in an airtight container for up to 1 week.

PICKLED GREEN STRAWBERRIES: Just as young, green tomatoes are terrific for pickling, prematurely picked strawberries that show a shade of green have their own ideal uses. I like to pickle them (see page 100 for pickling guidelines) and toss them into salads featuring goat cheese; serve them alongside fried shellfish, especially soft-shell crab and shrimp; and even add them to sandwiches.

STRAWBERRY BUCKLE: Substitute stemmed, quartered strawberries for the blueberries in the recipe on page 337.

MACERATED STRAWBERRIES WITH WHIPPED CREAM: Toss 1 cup strawberries with 1 tablespoon granulated sugar. Cover and refrigerate for 1 to 3 hours. *Do not drain.* Serve, topped with whipped cream. (For the best contrast between berry and cream, do not add sugar to the cream.)

Apple and Bibb Lettuce Salad
with Shaved Fennel, Maytag Blue Cheese, and Spiced Walnut Vinaigrette

SERVES 4

I grew up in a home of mixed Italian and German heritage, and the Italian side ruled the roost on Sunday nights, when we always came together for a family supper. My mother (that's the Italian side) had a touch with salads, often making them with shaved fennel, an Italian American staple. In the fall they sometimes featured a combination of apples, blue cheese, and nuts—though the exact varieties and types changed all the time: the cheese might be Gorgonzola dolce or even a generic blue, and the nuts could be anything from walnuts to cashews to pecans. This is my take on that salad. It has near-universal appeal because the primary ingredients bring to mind everything from the classic French pear, endive, and Roquefort salad to the quintessentially American Cobb and Waldorf salads. The main innovation here is the nut vinaigrette, which combats the problem of nuts getting lost in a salad and ending up in the bottom of the bowl. Nut vinaigrettes underscore the nut flavor and ensure that you get a little bit in every bite. If possible, make this salad with heirloom apples for their nuanced flavor and with "Hydro-Bibb" lettuce, which has a clean flavor and sturdy, well-shaped leaves, though regular apples and Bibb will still be delicious.

¼ cup champagne vinegar

⅓ cup walnut oil

Kosher salt

Freshly ground white pepper

2 cups thinly sliced red apples, such as Honeycrisp or Fuji (about 2 apples)

3 heads Bibb lettuce, or 2 heads "Hydro-Bibb" lettuce, cleaned, leaves separated and left whole

1 bulb fennel, thinly shaved, ideally on a mandoline

1 shallot, minced

½ cup crumbled Maytag Blue cheese or other blue cheese such as Gorgonzola dolce or Roquefort (see Note at right)

Spiced Walnuts (see Notebook, page 22)

To make the vinaigrette: Whisk together the vinegar and walnut oil in a medium bowl. Season with salt and pepper.

▸ To make the salad: Put the apples, lettuce, fennel, and shallot in a large bowl, drizzle with the vinaigrette, and scatter the blue cheese and spiced walnuts over the salad. Toss gently to coat the salad with the vinaigrette. Season with salt and pepper, toss again, and serve family-style or divide among 4 salad plates.

NOTE: In this age of readily available European cheeses and the rise of the artisanal American cheese producer, a mass-produced warhorse like Maytag Blue doesn't get much respect. But Maytag is actually a remarkable blue cheese. For starters, many blue cheeses have such a high fat content that you can't manipulate them, not even to crumble them; they're hopelessly gummy and messy. Maytag, on the other hand, can be cut or crumbled and has a high vein content and strong flavor. I also love Gorgonzola, Gorgonzola dolce, and Roquefort, especially for small hors d'oeuvres that require the cheese to be melted; and Cabrales from Spain and Kikorangi from New Zealand, which I'd categorize as falling between Gorgonzola and Maytag—nicely creamy and slightly sweet, with relatively small blue veins. Any of these can be used in this recipe.

Spiced Walnuts

Cooking walnuts creates a compelling contrast between the crunchy exterior and their soft, almost creamy insides. At my restaurants I sometimes fry nuts, but this home-cook-friendly technique tosses the nuts with a spice mixture and egg whites, then bakes them to create more of a crust than frying them would.

MAKES ABOUT 1 CUP

2 tablespoons egg whites
    (about 1 large egg white)
½ cup (packed) dark brown sugar
2 tablespoons cayenne
Kosher salt
Freshly ground white pepper
1 cup walnuts

Preheat the oven to 300°F. Line a baking sheet with parchment paper, waxed paper, or a Silpat and set aside.

▸ Put the egg whites, sugar, and cayenne in a medium bowl, season with salt and white pepper, and whisk to incorporate. Add the walnuts and toss to coat. Spread the walnut mixture on the prepared baking sheet and bake, shaking the pan occasionally to prevent scorching and to ensure even cooking, until the walnuts are crisp and golden brown, about 40 minutes. Remove the baking sheet from the oven and set it aside to cool completely, about 12 minutes. Use right away or store in an airtight container at room temperature for up to 1 week.

COCKTAIL SNACK: The nuts are an addictive homemade snack that goes well with cocktails, especially gin or vodka martinis. They can also be enjoyed by themselves.

CREAMY WALNUT VINAIGRETTE: For a variation on the vinaigrette in the Apple and Bibb Lettuce Salad, put ¼ cup of the spiced walnuts in a blender and blend with 1 large egg yolk, ¼ cup champagne vinegar, and 1 tablespoon Dijon mustard. While continuing to blend, slowly add ¾ cup walnut oil to make an emulsified vinaigrette. Season with salt and pepper. Serve over the salad on page 20 or as a dip for crudités, especially cauliflower and celery.

STREUSEL TOPPING: Add a small amount of chopped spiced walnuts to the streusel recipe on page 336 or use them in streusel made to top cobblers or crisps made with apple, pear, peach, or other stone fruits.

SPICED WALNUT SUNDAE: Top ice cream sundaes such as banana splits and mango parfaits with these nuts. They also elevate a simple bowl of vanilla ice cream topped with chocolate sauce or hot fudge to something extraordinary.

Artichoke and Fava Bean Salad

with Ricotta Salata, Red Oak Lettuce, and Marcona Almond Vinaigrette

SERVES 4

I came up with this spin on a classic springtime Italian salad while working on a new seasonal menu one day. An elusive missing ingredient was driving me crazy until I realized the answer was right in front of my nose: the Marcona almonds I had been snacking on. When I added them, they provided the texture and saltiness that had been missing.

1½ pounds fava beans in the pod

½ cup white wine vinegar

¾ cup almond oil (sunflower oil can be substituted)

Kosher salt

Freshly ground white pepper

2 heads red oak lettuce, leaves separated, cleaned, dried, and coarsely chopped

1 artichoke, turned (see Note below) and shaved or thinly sliced, ideally on a mandoline

½ cup chopped roasted, salted Marcona almonds

1 shallot, minced

½ cup diced ricotta salata cheese

1 tablespoon minced chives

1 tablespoon minced flat-leaf parsley

Fill a medium pot halfway with water and bring to a boil over high heat. Fill a medium bowl halfway with ice water and set aside. Snap the fava bean pods in half and remove the "string" that runs along the seam of the pods. Remove the individual favas. Blanch them in the boiling water for 1 minute, then drain in a colander and "shock" in the ice water. Drain again and peel the individual favas by gently tearing off the end of their outer white shells and pushing the fava out with your thumb. Dry the bowl that held the ice water and collect the shelled favas in the bowl. Set aside.

▸ To make the vinaigrette: Whisk together the vinegar and oil in a medium bowl. Season with salt and pepper.

▸ To make the salad: Put the red oak lettuce, artichoke, almonds, fava beans, shallot, ricotta salata, chives, and parsley in a large bowl. Drizzle the vinaigrette over the salad, season with salt and pepper, and toss well to coat.

▸ Serve family-style or divide among 4 salad plates.

NOTE: To prepare artichokes for cooking, cut off the top inch or so of the artichoke with a large, heavy knife.

For whole artichokes, trim the fibrous end of the stem and peel the stem with a vegetable peeler. Snap off the small leaves closest to the stem. Use kitchen scissors to snip off the thorny tips of the remaining leaves.

For artichoke hearts, take a paring knife in one hand and the artichoke in the other, hold the knife at a sharp angle against the base of the artichoke, and carefully but firmly turn the artichoke, cutting away the leaves until you are left with just the heart. Use a tablespoon to scoop out and discard the fibrous portion inside. Hold prepared artichokes in acidulated water until ready to use, then drain.

Artichokes

Like sunchokes (page 292), artichokes are a very meaty vegetable, especially their hearts. The irony with artichokes is that so many people cut off and discard the stem, which is actually the second-best part of the vegetable, after the heart; it's not to be eaten raw, but if you peel it with a vegetable peeler, it can be braised, marinated (see Marinated Artichokes, below), or prepared as a confit in olive oil.

FRIED ARTICHOKES: The mineral flavor of artichokes stands up well to frying. Turn and fry baby artichokes, or turn, shave, and fry larger ones. Serve with Caesar dressing (page 45) for dipping, or use the fried artichokes to garnish salads and main courses.

BOILED ARTICHOKES WITH TARRAGON-MUSTARD VINAIGRETTE: Trim the stems off large artichokes, gently poach them in simmering water until tender, about 30 minutes, then drain and let cool. Serve warm or chilled with a whisked-together vinaigrette of ½ cup white wine vinegar, 1 teaspoon chopped fresh tarragon, 1 tablespoon Dijon mustard, 1 cup extra-virgin olive oil, salt, and pepper.

MOM'S STUFFED ARTICHOKES: For a quick and easy version of my mother's stuffed artichokes, simmer 4 large globe artichokes (cut off the stems so they stand up) in about a gallon of water seasoned with 2 smashed garlic cloves, salt, and pepper for about 5 minutes. Drain, reserving a few tablespoons of the cooking liquid, allow to cool, and snip off the prickly tops. Push down on the tops to spread out the leaves. Stir together 1 cup dried bread crumbs, 1 teaspoon minced garlic, 1 tablespoon dried oregano, and 1 tablespoon dried basil. Season with salt and pepper and push the mixture between the leaves of the artichokes. Set the artichokes side by side in a heavy pot without crowding, and top with ½ cup each of grated provolone, mozzarella, and pecorino cheeses. Season with salt and pepper, and drizzle with extra-virgin olive oil. Drizzle 1 tablespoon of the artichoke's cooking liquid over the artichokes. Add water to come three-quarters of the way up the sides of the artichokes, just below where the cheese is. Cover and gently simmer for 2 hours, basting every 20 minutes. You will know they are done when the leaves pull away easily. Remove the artichokes from the liquid and serve.

MARINATED ARTICHOKES: To make marinated artichokes that riff on the flavor of jarred artichokes, put 4 turned globe artichokes, 1 quart extra-virgin olive oil, 2 garlic cloves, and 1 oregano sprig in a heavy pot and season with salt and pepper. Cook slowly over medium heat until the artichokes are soft to a knife tip, about 40 minutes. Use a slotted spoon to remove them from the oil and set them aside to cool. When cool enough to handle, cut them into 6 wedges each. Place in an airtight container, cover with about 2 cups of the oil, and stir in 2 cups white wine vinegar. Let marinate, refrigerated, for at least 24 hours or up to 1 week.

Red Romaine and Hearts of Palm Salad
with Manchego, Mango, and Macadamia Nuts

I first had a version of this dish alongside the Mediterranean Sea when visiting the legendary Rock of Gibraltar. I was struck by how well the unlikely combination of mango and cheese got along. It's a simple salad that's made immensely satisfying by the interplay of those ingredients and the macadamia nuts; my touch is the use of the nuts' frying oil in the vinaigrette.

¾ cup blended oil or canola oil

½ cup macadamia nuts

Kosher salt

¼ cup sherry vinegar

¼ cup champagne vinegar

1 shallot, minced

Freshly ground white pepper

2 heads red romaine lettuce, core removed, leaves torn into large pieces

2 cups (about 8 ounces) thinly sliced fresh hearts of palm (see page 84)

¾ cup diced mango (see Notebook, page 26)

½ cup diced Manchego cheese

To cook the nuts: Line a large plate with paper towels and set aside. Heat the oil in a wide, deep sauté pan over high heat. When the oil is shimmering, add the nuts to the oil and pan-fry until golden brown, 3 to 4 minutes. Drain the oil through a fine-mesh strainer or chinois into a heatproof bowl. Transfer the nuts to the prepared plate to drain, and season immediately with salt.

▷ To make the vinaigrette: Measure out ½ cup of the strained macadamia nut oil, allow it to cool for about 10 minutes, and transfer to a medium mixing bowl. Whisk the sherry vinegar, then the champagne vinegar, into the oil. Whisk in the shallot and season with salt and pepper.

▷ To make the salad: Put the romaine, hearts of palm, mango, and cheese in a large bowl. Drizzle the vinaigrette over the salad and gently toss, taking care not to break up the mango and cheese.

▷ Divide the salad among 4 plates, scatter the nuts over the top, and serve, or present the salad in a serving bowl, with the nuts scattered over, and serve family-style.

NOTE: Leftover macadamia nut oil may be saved in an airtight container at room temperature for up to 3 days. Use it for other vinaigrettes, or in a brown butter sauce, but not as a cooking medium.

Mango

Mango is a tropical fruit that I've always appreciated for its bright, beautiful color and powerful flavor. I came to like it even more during trips to Thailand, where it's used in curries, sticky rice, and desserts. It's incredibly versatile, comfortable in every part of a meal, from cocktails to salads to sweets. When shopping for mangoes, seek out those that are soft but not mushy to the touch. If you can't find any ripe ones, put them in a brown paper bag with tomatoes, an old trick for speeding the ripening process.

DRIED MANGO WITH CHILI: The intense flavor of mango survives the drying process very well, making it one of my favorite fruits to dry. Dried mango slices can be snacked on, stuck into a sundae as a garnish, or served as an accompaniment to tropical cocktails and frozen drinks. To prepare, toss slices of peeled mango with dried ground chili powder, and dry in a food dehydrator or on a baking sheet in an oven at its lowest setting (200°F or lower) for about 10 hours, until the fruit is dry and slightly shriveled.

For a variation on this theme, put wedges of fresh, peeled mango in lime juice (about 1 tablespoon juice per mango), and toss with salt, sugar, and ground chili powder. Eat as a snack or thinly slice and dehydrate, per the previous instructions.

MANGO SUMMER ROLL: Make a summer roll by adding peeled, diced mango to your favorite crab salad and wrapping it in rice summer roll paper or in any other wrap of your choosing.

MANGO COULIS: A simple puréed mango sauce that is a useful component of dessert making, this is especially good in sundaes. To make a cup of coulis, simmer 2 cups peeled, diced mango, ¼ cup granulated sugar, ¼ cup water, and ¼ teaspoon kosher salt in a pot over medium heat until the mango is soft to a knife tip, about 15 minutes. Purée, strain, chill, and serve.

MANGO STICKY RICE: To make this traditional Thai dessert, cook 2 cups sticky rice in a steamer (after soaking it overnight in cold water and draining) until soft, about 40 minutes. Transfer the rice to a heatproof bowl and stir in 1 cup coconut milk. Wrap the rice in a banana leaf or place in a microwavable vessel and reheat in a microwave or steamer until hot. Make a sauce by cooking 1 cup coconut milk and ¼ cup palm sugar, dark brown sugar, or turbinado sugar over medium heat, stirring, until the sugar dissolves, about 5 minutes. Serve the rice warm, topped with the sauce, sliced ripe mango, and toasted white sesame seeds (see page 362). You can also garnish with shredded coconut.

Crispy Calamari and Watercress Salad
with Peanuts, Mint, and Chile-Lime Dressing

I first tasted a version of this salad in Thailand, where I sampled water spinach (aka Siamese watercress) that had been deep-fried in tempura batter in a wok, tossed with a green papaya dressing, and finished with herbs and peanuts. The coming together of crunchy vegetables and tangy sauce is addictively delicious, and the herbs lift the whole thing into the stratosphere. This is my freestyle spin on that dish, with crispy fried calamari added. You can serve the salad without the calamari, or replace the calamari with shrimp.

1 tablespoon minced shallot

1 tablespoon minced chives

2 tablespoons hand-torn mint leaves

Canola oil or other neutral oil, for frying

1 pound calamari, tentacles and tubes, cleaned and sliced (about 1 cup sliced)

2 bunches watercress, stems intact (about 2 quarts loosely packed)

Tempura Batter (page 363)

Kosher salt

Freshly ground white pepper

Chile-Lime Dressing (see Notebook, page 29)

2 tablespoons coarsely chopped roasted, salted peanuts

½ cup pickled red onion slices (see page 100 for pickling guidance)

Start the salad so that it's ready to be finished when the calamari is freshly fried: Put the shallot, chives, and mint in a large bowl.

▸ To fry the calamari and watercress: Pour canola oil into a deep fryer or a wide, deep, heavy pot, at least 12 inches high, filling it 6 inches deep. Heat over high heat to 350°F. Line a large plate or platter with paper towels and set it aside.

▸ Add the calamari and watercress to a bowl with the batter, gently toss, then lift and allow any excess batter to drip off. Carefully add the calamari and watercress to the hot oil. Fry until the batter coating is golden and crispy, turning with tongs or a slotted spoon as necessary, about 3 minutes. Transfer to the prepared plate and season immediately with salt and pepper.

▸ Add the watercress and calamari to the bowl with the salad. Drizzle the dressing over the salad and toss well. To serve, divide the salad among 4 plates and garnish with a scattering of peanuts and pickled red onions.

Chile-Citrus Combinations

Chiles and citrus are often an ideal combination because the acidity of the citrus balances the heat of the chiles. For the same reason, low-alcohol, highly acidic white wines get along great with spicy foods such as Thai. Here's my recipe for Chile-Lime Dressing, and a handful of other dressings based on similar combinations.

CHILE-LIME DRESSING

MAKES 1 CUP

In addition to the calamari and watercress salad, use this dressing over thin slices of raw sushi-grade fish to make ceviche, allowing the acid in the dressing to "cook" the fish by refrigerating the dressed fish for at least 30 minutes or up to 2 hours before serving.

½ cup plus 1 tablespoon freshly squeezed lime juice

2 Thai red chiles, stems removed and discarded, coarsely chopped

1 garlic clove

3 tablespoons palm sugar or turbinado sugar such as Sugar in the Raw

¼ cup fish sauce

¼ cup canola oil

Put the lime juice, chiles, garlic, sugar, and fish sauce in a blender and blend until a paste is formed. While continuing to blend, slowly drizzle in the oil in a thin stream to make an emulsified dressing. Transfer to an airtight container until ready to use. The dressing may be refrigerated for up to 3 days. Allow it to come to room temperature before using.

YUZU-SHISO DRESSING

MAKES 1 CUP

Use this thick and creamy sauce featuring three popular Japanese ingredients to dress slices of raw tuna, yellowtail, or fluke.

¼ cup yuzu juice

½ cup blended oil or neutral oil such as canola

1 tablespoon white soy sauce

1 shishito pepper, seeded and minced

2 shiso leaves (also sold as perilla), thinly sliced

1 tablespoon minced shallot

Whisk the yuzu juice, oil, soy sauce, shishito pepper, shiso leaves, and shallot together in a medium bowl until combined. Use the dressing right away, as the shiso will oxidize and turn brown.

CHARRED JALAPEÑO– LIME AIOLI

MAKES 1 CUP

Serve this as a dip for deep- and pan-fried fish and shellfish such as battered fried cod, crab cakes, and fried clams and oysters.

3 jalapeño peppers

1 egg yolk

1 tablespoon finely grated lime zest

2 tablespoons freshly squeezed lime juice

Kosher salt

Freshly ground white pepper

½ cup blended oil or neutral oil such as canola

Heat a grill over high heat, or heat a grill pan over high heat for 5 minutes. (See pages 274–75 for grilling guidelines.) Add the jalapeños and grill, turning, until charred on all sides, about 4 minutes. Remove from the heat, and when cool enough to handle, about 6 minutes, remove and discard the stems and transfer the charred jalapeños to a blender. Add the egg yolk and lime zest and juice, and season with salt and pepper. Blend, slowly adding the oil in a thin stream to form an emulsified aioli.

MEYER LEMON—THYME PASTA

SERVES 4

This dish applies the citrus-chile pairing to a pasta. I like the subtle acidity of Meyer lemons, but regular lemons can be substituted.

Kosher salt

1 box (1 pound) short tubular pasta such as penne or ziti

4 tablespoons (½ stick) unsalted butter

Zest and juice of 1 Meyer lemon (1 tablespoon zest, 3 tablespoons juice)

1 tablespoon fresh thyme leaves

¼ teaspoon crushed red pepper flakes

Freshly ground white pepper

2 tablespoons grated Parmigiano-Reggiano cheese

2 tablespoons thinly sliced flat-leaf parsley leaves (see Note at right)

Fill a large pot two-thirds full with salted water and bring to a boil over high heat. When the water boils, add the pasta and cook until al dente, following the cooking time on the box, usually 6 to 8 minutes. Reserve ½ cup of the cooking water and drain through a colander.

▸ Melt 3 tablespoons of the butter in a large sauté pan over medium-high heat. When the butter foams, stir in the lemon zest, thyme, and pepper flakes. Cook until the zest and thyme stop sizzling, about 1 minute. Season with salt and white pepper and stir in the reserved pasta water. Bring to a boil and continue to boil until reduced by half, about 3 minutes. Stir in the remaining 1 tablespoon butter and the lemon juice. Add the cooked pasta, cheese, and parsley and toss to coat.

(For a surprising spin on this dish, make a topping of bread crumbs, adding a teaspoon or two of finely grated Meyer lemon zest to the Toasted Bread Crumbs recipe on page 145. For a more assertive flavor, you can also add minced garlic if desired. Taste and add more zest and/or crushed red pepper flakes to accentuate their respective flavors.)

NOTE: *Slicing rather than chopping delicate herbs such as parsley preserves their freshness and flavor, and also looks nicer on the finished dish. Slice each leaf once or twice, or stack them and slice several at once.*

Crispy Rock Shrimp Salad

with Mizuna, Piquillo Peppers, and Mushroom Soy–Cayenne Dressing

This salad is a symphony of spice with peppery mizuna lettuce and cayenne in its dressing. It's based on a salad I first discovered on a trip to Madrid in my late teens, where it was served atop a portion of paella.

¼ cup freshly squeezed lemon juice

3 tablespoons cayenne

¼ cup mushroom soy sauce

½ cup blended oil or neutral oil such as canola

Kosher salt

Freshly ground white pepper

Canola oil or other neutral oil, for frying

1 cup all-purpose flour

½ cup cornmeal

1 tablespoon ground paprika

Freshly ground black pepper

2 cups (1 pound) rock shrimp (see Notebook, page 32)

2½ cups (loosely packed, about 4 ounces) baby mizuna (other peppery greens such as arugula, peppercress, or baby mustard may be substituted)

1 red onion, thinly sliced

1 cup piquillo peppers, seeded and thinly sliced

¼ cup (loosely packed) flat-leaf parsley

To make the dressing: Put the lemon juice, 2 tablespoons of the cayenne, and the mushroom soy in a medium bowl. Slowly drizzle in the blended oil, whisking to blend. Season with salt and white pepper and set aside.

▶ To fry the shrimp: Pour the canola oil into a large, heavy pot at least 12 inches high, filling it to a depth of 6 inches. Heat over high heat to a temperature of 350°F. Line a large plate or platter with paper towels, and set it aside.

▶ Put the flour, cornmeal, paprika, and remaining 1 tablespoon cayenne in a bowl, season with salt and black pepper, and whisk together. Dredge the shrimp in the flour mixture, gently shake off any excess, and add to the hot oil. Fry until crispy and golden brown, about 2 minutes, using tongs or a slotted spoon to gently stir them periodically as they fry. Transfer the shrimp to the prepared plate to drain, and season immediately with salt and white pepper.

▶ Put the shrimp, mizuna, onion, piquillo peppers, and parsley in a large serving bowl. Season with salt and white pepper and toss to incorporate. Drizzle the dressing over the salad, toss to coat, and serve family-style.

Shrimp

Most home cooks refer to these crustaceans as simply "shrimp" or "prawns," despite the fact that there *are* actually a number of varieties out there, most of which are well suited to specific culinary treatments. Here are a few of my favorite types of shrimp and the best way to use each.

PINK MAINE SHRIMP (AKA SWEET MAINE SHRIMP): The unique sweetness of these shrimp makes them well worth seeking out. They contain an enzyme that causes them to break down immediately upon cooking, so are really only good for a quick grilling or sauté but can be quite delicious.

SPOT PRAWNS: These large shrimp are usually sold alive. Prepare them as you would a live lobster: Slice them between the eyes with a paring knife to kill them, then halve them lengthwise, devein, and remove the flesh from the shell. I love them raw, marinated with olive oil and citrus juice, or with the Yuzu-Shiso Dressing on page 29.

SOUTHERN ROYAL REDS: Available in the southern United States, these shrimp are made to be peeled and eaten because their thick shells contain a lot of flavor. Cook them in boiling water seasoned with Old Bay seasoning until firm and pink, drain them, and serve with drawn butter. (Note that they are always sold frozen, and available only in the South, near the Gulf of Mexico.)

ALL-PURPOSE SHRIMP: Some varieties of shrimp can be used somewhat interchangeably because they all have a meaty texture. White shrimp, rock shrimp, Mayan prawns, and blue tiger prawns are reliable, all-purpose shrimp that work well grilled, sautéed, in pastas, stir-fried, poached and chilled for shrimp cocktail, deep-fried, and even wrapped in prosciutto and grilled.

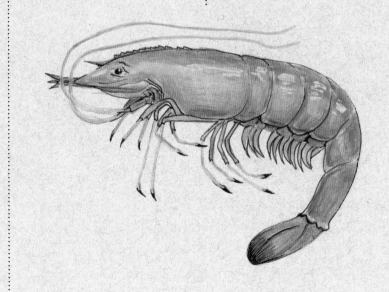

Warm Crab Salad

with Roti, Daikon Purée, and Celery Leaves

This dish was inspired by a classic from Gramercy Tavern, where the original chef, my friend Tom Colicchio, served a crab and sea urchin ragù dressed with a *beurre blanc* (butter sauce) atop a potato purée. My version replaces the potato with velvety daikon purée and pairs the dish with roti—a buttery, puffy flatbread; it's the perfect antidote to a cold night.

2 shallots, thinly sliced

2 cups dry white wine

1 cup (2 sticks) unsalted butter, at room temperature, cut into small pieces

Kosher salt

Freshly ground white pepper

1 tablespoon blended oil or neutral oil such as canola

3 garlic cloves, thinly sliced

1 cup peeled, diced daikon radish

1 cup whole milk

¼ cup chicken stock, preferably homemade (page 366)

1 cup (8 ounces) picked peekytoe or blue crabmeat

1 tablespoon minced chives

¼ cup celery leaves

16 roti (see Notebook, page 35)

To make the beurre blanc: Put half the shallots and all of the wine in a small saucepan over medium-high heat. When the wine simmers, lower the heat and continue to simmer, stirring occasionally, until the liquid is reduced to 1 tablespoon, 10 to 12 minutes. Whisk in the butter, a few pieces at a time, and season with salt and pepper. Strain the beurre blanc through a fine-mesh strainer set over a medium bowl and set aside, covered, to keep it warm.

▸ To make the daikon purée: Heat the oil in a large saucepan over medium heat. When the oil is shimmering, add the remaining shallots and the garlic. Cook, stirring, until the shallots and garlic are softened but not browned, about 1 minute. Add the daikon and season with salt and pepper. Pour in the milk and chicken stock and bring just to a boil. Lower the heat so the liquid is simmering, and continue to simmer until

the daikon is very soft to a knife tip, about 15 minutes. Transfer the contents of the pan to a blender and blend to a smooth purée. Strain through a fine-mesh strainer or chinois into a medium bowl, pressing down with a rubber spatula or the bottom of a ladle to extract as much purée as possible, and season with salt and pepper. Set aside, covered, to keep warm.

▸ To assemble the dish: Heat a small, heavy saucepan over medium heat. Add the beurre blanc and crabmeat and cook, stirring, until the crabmeat is warmed through, about 2 minutes. (Stir the crabmeat as little as possible to avoid breaking it up.) Season with salt and pepper and stir in the chives. Spoon about ¼ cup daikon purée into the bottom of each of 4 serving bowls. Top with the crabmeat mixture and scatter celery leaves over each serving. Top each serving with 4 roti.

Roti

India, Thailand, and Malaysia all have their own versions of roti; this recipe produces an Indian-style roti that puffs up like paratha, but with a buttery, crispy texture, almost like a croissant. It functions as a cross between a bread and a side dish and is the perfect vehicle for soaking up sauces and broths, and for some of the less conventional possibilities listed below.

MAKES 16 ROTI

3 tablespoons all-purpose flour

¼ teaspoon kosher salt

¾ tablespoon margarine, melted, plus more for coating

2 tablespoons whole milk, warmed

1 tablespoon canola oil

Place a fine-mesh strainer over a large bowl and sift through the flour and salt. Add the margarine to the sifted flour and salt and use a spatula or wooden spoon to stir until the mixture is crumbly. Slowly pour in the warmed milk, mixing until just incorporated. Use your hands to knead the dough until it pulls away from the sides of the bowl and forms a soft ball, about 2 minutes. Continue kneading until the dough is slightly sticky, about 10 minutes more.

▶ Roll the dough into a smooth ball. Use the palm of your hand to flatten the ball slightly and massage it with margarine to coat it. Transfer the flattened ball to a baking sheet lined with parchment paper (or use a nonstick sheet) and cover with a damp kitchen towel. Set aside to rest for 30 minutes; the dough should be round and smooth.

▶ Use your hands to lightly coat a rolling pin and work surface with margarine. Roll the dough into a paper-thin circle, about 9 inches in diameter. Use a ½-inch ring cutter to cut it into 16 small disks.

▶ Line a baking sheet with paper towels. Heat the oil in a large saucepan over medium heat. When the oil is shimmering, add the roti rounds in a single layer and fry until the bottoms are golden brown and speckled and the roti are puffy, about 1 minute. (You may have to do this in 2 batches, depending on the size of your pan.) Turn and cook on the other side for 1 minute. Transfer the roti to the prepared baking sheet and repeat until all the roti are fried.

ROTI SANDWICH: Use the roti as an alternative to sandwich bread, shaping it like a taco or wrap. (Cut larger roti for this use.) My favorite roti sandwich is with curried chicken and golden raisins.

ROTI POTPIE: For a spin on chicken potpie, use the roti dough as a covering. Or, next time you have leftover stew, put it in a casserole or individual ovenproof serving dishes, top with roti dough, and bake for a quick potpie effect.

SWEET ROTI: Bake sliced bananas or chocolate chips into the dough (adding them when the dough begins to soften, as you would when adding to a pancake) and serve as a dessert. If you like, top with a dusting of 10-X sugar or a drizzle of sweetened condensed milk or sweetened coconut milk right after removing from the pan.

ROTI COBBLER: Instead of a biscuit topping, stretch raw roti dough over prepared fruit and bake.

Beef Carpaccio
with Arugula, Parmesan Tuiles, and Preserved Lemon–Caper Berry Dressing

SERVES 4

This dish is a 2.0 version of a traditional beef carpaccio, with a dressing that substitutes preserved lemon for lemon juice and borrows the capers from another raw beef dish, tartare. (It also augments the traditional grated Parmesan with a Parmesan tuile.) You either love raw beef, or you hate it. Personally, I love it, and I make my carpaccio with relatively lean beef eye of round or filet because I think they have a pleasing mouthfeel. Incidentally, this is the first dish I ever put on the menu at The Harrison, when I was the sous chef to my good friend Joey Campanaro, who has gone on to open the Little Owl and other restaurants. He showed me the technique of using a resealable plastic bag to roll the meat for an impressive presentation. Note that you will need five large resealable plastic bags for preparing this dish.

½ cup freshly squeezed lemon juice

1 tablespoon minced preserved lemon (see Notebook, page 40)

1 tablespoon Dijon mustard

4 caper berries

1 tablespoon caper berry brine

½ cup blended oil or neutral oil such as canola

4 pieces beef eye of round or filet, 2 ounces each

1 tablespoon extra-virgin olive oil

Kosher salt

Freshly ground black pepper

2 cups (loosely packed) baby arugula

1 shallot, minced

1 tablespoon minced flat-leaf parsley

2 tablespoons finely grated Parmigiano-Reggiano cheese

4 Parmesan Tuiles (page 39)

To make the caper berry dressing: Put the lemon juice, preserved lemon, mustard, caper berries, and brine in a blender and blend to a paste, about 20 seconds. While continuing to blend, slowly add the blended oil in a thin stream to make an emulsified dressing. Strain through a fine-mesh strainer into a small bowl, pressing down on the solids with a rubber spatula or the bottom of a ladle to extract as much dressing as possible. (The dressing may be refrigerated in an airtight container for up to 2 days. Allow it to come to room temperature before serving.)

▶ See photos on page 38 for the following steps: Working with one piece at a time, use a meat mallet or the bottom of a heavy pan to pound the meat between two 1-gallon resealable plastic bags until paper thin, being careful not to shred or pound holes in the meat. Rub the upward-facing side of the beef with extra-virgin olive oil and season generously with salt and pepper. Reuse the top bag for all 4 pieces of meat, and line up the pounded-out pieces, with the bottom bag intact, on a work surface.

continued

▸ Put the arugula, shallot, parsley, and Parmigiano-Reggiano in a large bowl, drizzle with all but 2 tablespoons of the dressing, and toss. Working with one piece of meat at a time, place some salad on top of the meat and pull the bag from under the meat over it, encasing the salad. Rest the back of a chef's knife against the opening. Pull the bottom edge of the bag out from under the knife, and the carpaccio will form a roll around the salad. Repeat with the remaining carpaccios.

▸ Set 1 rolled carpaccio in the center of each of 4 salad plates. Drizzle some of the remaining dressing over each, garnish with a Parmesan tuile, and serve.

NOTE: Purchase beef you plan to serve raw from the best butcher you know; ask him or her if it's of a quality that can be served raw. Signs you can look for yourself: it should be a vibrant red, with no brown from oxidation. When you get it home, keep it well wrapped and chilled in the refrigerator until you are ready use it, and serve it as soon as possible after preparing it.

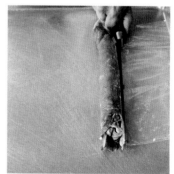

Parmesan Tuiles

MAKES ABOUT 12 TUILES, DEPENDING ON SIZE AND SHAPE

1 Idaho potato, peeled, boiled, and riced

½ cup egg whites (about 4 large egg whites)

¼ cup grated Parmigiano-Reggiano cheese

1 tablespoon minced chives

Kosher salt

Freshly ground black pepper

Nonstick cooking spray

Preheat the oven to 275°F.

▶ Put the potato, egg whites, Parmigiano-Reggiano, and chives in a medium bowl and season with salt and pepper. Whisk together until well incorporated.

▶ Line a baking sheet with parchment paper and spray with nonstick cooking spray. Pour the batter into shapes using a round, square, or rectangular cookie cutter or mold and spreading and smoothing the batter in each mold with a small rubber spatula.

▶ Gently remove the molds and bake the tuiles until golden-brown, about 1 hour. Remove the sheet from the oven and let the tuiles cool for 15 minutes. Use as soon as possible the same day you bake them.

Preserved Lemon

Preserved lemons are most closely associated with Moroccan and Middle Eastern cuisine, and they are one of those ingredients that chefs gravitate toward because they bring a lot of action to the plate, adding color, texture, and flavor in one fell swoop. I love them for their intensely briny, sweet-and-sour character. My method differs from most in that I cook the lemons. Usually preserving lemons requires you to wait a few weeks for them to be ready; cooking them accelerates the flavoring process so they're good to go as soon as you've chilled them.

If you don't want to make your own preserved lemons, many high-quality ones are readily available these days from specialty markets and well-stocked gourmet supermarkets.

MAKES 2 PRESERVED LEMONS

2 lemons

¼ cup sugar

½ cup kosher salt

1 tablespoon whole
    black peppercorns

1 star anise

2 teaspoons coriander seed

2 teaspoons fennel seed

Pierce both lemons all over with a chef's knife, just enough to penetrate the skin without cutting through to the flesh of the fruit.

▸ Put all the ingredients in a pot and add enough cold water to cover. Bring to a simmer over medium heat, then lower the heat and continue to simmer until the lemons are soft, about 30 minutes. Remove the pot from the heat and allow to cool completely. Use right away or refrigerate the lemons in their liquid in an airtight container for up to 2 weeks.

DIRTY CITRUS MARTINI: Because the preserving liquid has some salt in it, it's also a cool stand-in for the olive brine in a dirty martini, creating a "dirty citrus" martini.

PRESERVED LEMON SAUCE: Serve the sauce featured in the dish on page 36 with simply grilled fish and shellfish.

READY-TO-GO ACCOMPANIMENT: The complex flavor and toothsome texture of preserved lemon makes it an accompaniment that's complete on its own. Serve whole or chopped pieces of it alongside assertively flavored foods such as salmon, swordfish, tuna, and grilled lamb.

CANDIED PRESERVED LEMON PEEL: Cut preserved lemon peel into strips, pat dry with paper towels, and candy it by adapting the directions for candied ginger on page 116. Use it to garnish cocktails such as Lemon Drops or desserts featuring any kind of lemon.

Lamb Prosciutto

with Roasted Beets, Baby Arugula, and Goat Cheese Fondue

When I first started cooking professionally in 1998, it seemed like every restaurant in New York City served a salad that featured beets and goat cheese. They're a great combination, the tangy cheese a perfect foil for the sweet beets. The pairing stayed with me, and I still turn to it once in a while for a surefire salad. Here the goat cheese is included in a quick fondue that makes it easier to integrate with the other ingredients, and the salad is built out with pine nuts and slices of lamb prosciutto, which make this a more substantial dish that can be served on its own for a light lunch. The shallot vinaigrette is a wonderful everyday salad dressing to have in your repertoire.

1 cup kosher salt, plus more for seasoning

2 large red beets

1 cup dry white wine, such as sauvignon blanc

1 cup whole milk

8 ounces soft, fresh goat cheese, at room temperature, crumbled

Freshly ground black pepper

1 tablespoon pine nuts, toasted

3 tablespoons extra-virgin olive oil

2 cups (loosely packed) baby arugula

¾ cup Shallot Vinaigrette (recipe follows)

16 thin slices lamb prosciutto (about 8 ounces) or another cured meat such as prosciutto di Parma or capicolla

Preheat the oven to 400°F.

▸ Spread the salt out over the center of a small baking sheet and set the beets on top of the salt. Roast the beets until tender (a sharp, thin-bladed knife will pierce easily to the center), about 1 hour. When the beets are done, remove them from the oven and allow to cool on the baking sheet. When cool enough to handle, peel them and cut them into medium dice.

▸ Meanwhile, to make the goat cheese fondue, heat the wine and milk in a medium saucepan over medium-high heat, stirring them together. When they just begin to simmer, whisk in the goat cheese, a few pieces at a time, until it has melted and the sauce is creamy. Cook,

whisking occasionally, until reduced to a fondue-like consistency, about 20 minutes. Strain the fondue through a fine-mesh strainer into a heatproof bowl, pressing down with a rubber spatula or the bottom of a ladle to obtain as much fondue as possible. Season generously with salt and pepper, cover, and keep warm.

▸ Meanwhile, toss the pine nuts with 1 tablespoon of the extra-virgin olive oil and spread them out in a single layer on a separate baking sheet. Roast until golden brown, shaking the sheet periodically to ensure even cooking and prevent scorching, about 5 minutes. Remove the sheet from the oven and set aside to cool.

continued

▸ To serve, reheat the fondue in a small, heavy pot over medium heat. Put the arugula, beets, pine nuts, and vinaigrette in a large bowl, season generously with salt and pepper, and toss. Spoon 2 tablespoons of fondue onto the center of each of 4 salad plates. (This recipe produces a generous amount of fondue; for a richer dish, use more.) Top with salad and drape slices of prosciutto over the salad. Drizzle the prosciutto with the remaining 2 tablespoons extra-virgin olive oil.

Shallot Vinaigrette

MAKES ABOUT ¾ CUP

1 tablespoon blended oil or neutral oil such as canola

3 shallots, thinly sliced

1 tablespoon sugar

½ tablespoon thyme leaves

¼ cup sherry vinegar

¼ cup extra-virgin olive oil

Kosher salt

Freshly ground white pepper

Heat the oil in a wide, deep sauté pan over medium-high heat. When the oil is shimmering, add the shallots and cook until softened but not browned, about 2 minutes. Stir in the sugar and thyme, and cook, stirring, until the sugar starts to slightly caramelize, about 3 more minutes. Add the vinegar and cook for 1 minute, stirring to loosen any flavorful bits from the bottom of the pan. Transfer the contents of the pan to a blender and blend, slowly adding the extra-virgin olive oil in a thin stream to form an emulsified vinaigrette. Season to taste with salt and pepper and refrigerate in an airtight container until well chilled, at least 1 hour or up to 2 days.

Goat Cheese

Goat cheese gets along well with a lot of other foods because of its soft texture and gentle tang, which are desirable additions to many plates. I prefer young, fresh goat cheeses such as those produced by Montrachet and the Old Chatham Sheepherding Company.

HERB-CRUSTED GOAT CHEESE: Roll disks or small balls of goat cheese in chopped herbs, cracked pepper, and/or dried bread crumbs to create a versatile salad component that can be tossed in or set among other ingredients in a composed salad. Play around with different combinations; my personal favorite coating is rosemary.

MOLTEN GOAT CHEESE: Get a small baking sheet very hot in an oven preheated to 400°F. Remove the sheet from the oven, add a tablespoon or so of olive oil, and set a disk of goat cheese on top. Return the sheet to the oven and cook for 2 minutes. Use a metal spatula to transfer the softened, warm goat cheese to a salad, topping the greens. (Or, for a more decadent but slightly more labor-intensive variation, coat a ball of goat cheese with bread crumbs and deep-fry it following the instructions on page 144, substituting slices of a log of goat cheese for the eggs; be sure the cheese is cold before coating and frying.)

GRATED GOAT CHEESE: For a surprising grating cheese to finish pastas and other dishes, set a log of goat cheese on an oiled baking sheet in an oven preheated to 150°F until dried out, about 12 hours. Allow to cool, then grate over dishes with a microplane or box grater. It is especially good over pastas featuring black olives, tomatoes or tomato sauces, and basil.

QUICK PASTA SAUCE: For a quick sauce for short pasta such as penne, farfalle, or orecchiette, reserve a cup or so of the pasta's cooking water before straining the pasta. Strain the pasta and return it to its cooking pot. For 4 portions, add a few tablespoons of the reserved water and about 8 ounces crumbled goat cheese. Toss and continue to add water and more cheese, if necessary, until the pasta is coated with emulsified goat cheese. Finish with a coarse grating of black pepper. I like to build out the dish with baby arugula, basil, and/or halved cherry tomatoes.

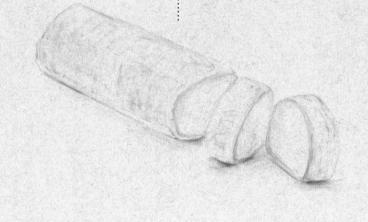

HD Caesar Salad

SERVES 4

This is my version of a Caesar salad, which is my favorite salad to eat for its crunch and the powerful flavors of anchovy, Parmigiano, and cracked black pepper. I prefer oil-packed anchovy fillets to salt-packed for this dish because you can replace a portion of the oil in the dressing with the anchovy oil to up the flavor.

2 large egg yolks

1 tablespoon freshly squeezed lemon juice

2 anchovy fillets, preferably packed in oil

1 tablespoon Worcestershire sauce

½ tablespoon freshly cracked black pepper, plus more for seasoning

½ tablespoon Dijon mustard

1 small garlic clove, peeled and coarsely chopped

½ cup blended oil or neutral oil such as canola

4 cups (loosely packed) chopped romaine lettuce (from about 1 head)

⅓ cup finely grated Parmigiano-Reggiano cheese

1 cup croutons (see page 363)

Kosher salt

To make the dressing: Put the egg yolks, lemon juice, anchovy fillets, Worcestershire, pepper, mustard, and garlic in a blender and blend until smooth. While continuing to blend, slowly add the blended oil in a thin stream to form an emulsified dressing.

▶ To make the salad: Put the romaine, Parmigiano, and croutons in a large bowl. Drizzle the dressing over the salad and season with salt and pepper. Toss to dress the salad, and serve family-style or divide among 4 salad plates.

Caesar Variations

The combination of anchovy, garlic, and lemon juice has many applications beyond salads; in some cases, incorporating the romaine lettuce in different ways yields surprising results as well.

EGGLESS CAESAR DRESSING: For an eggless Caesar dressing, simply omit the egg from the dressing in the preceding recipe (page 45).

CAESAR-STYLE GRILLED ROMAINE: Make a pan dressing by warming 2 tablespoons extra-virgin olive oil in a sauté pan, adding 1 thinly sliced garlic clove and 2 chopped anchovy fillets, and cooking gently until the garlic is softened and the anchovy can be dissolved with a wooden spoon. Off the heat, stir in 1 tablespoon freshly squeezed lemon juice, a pinch of crushed red pepper flakes, and 1 tablespoon whole flat-leaf parsley leaves. Season generously with black pepper, and toss with grilled quarters of a romaine lettuce head in a large heatproof bowl. Serve, topped with finely grated Parmigiano-Reggiano, as a starter or as a side dish to grilled meats.

FRIED LETTUCE WITH CAESAR AIOLI: Toss lettuce in Tempura Batter (page 363), then fry it in a fryer or in a pot of oil heated to 350°F, drain on paper towels, season immediately with salt, and serve with the dressing from the salad.

CAESAR SAUCE: Make a unique sauce by heating 2 tablespoons extra-virgin olive oil in a medium saucepan over medium-high heat. When the oil is shimmering, add 2 minced garlic cloves, 1 sliced shallot, and 2 anchovy fillets and cook, stirring, until the anchovies can be dissolved with a wooden spoon, about 2 minutes. Season generously with black pepper. Add 2 cups (loosely packed) coarsely chopped romaine lettuce to the pan for the last minute of cooking, just to wilt it. Purée the contents of the pan in a blender, adding 1 tablespoon freshly squeezed lemon juice. Pour the sauce through a fine-mesh strainer into a medium bowl set over a larger bowl filled halfway with ice water to cool it down quickly. Press down on the solids in the strainer with a rubber spatula or the bottom of a ladle to extract as much sauce as possible. Serve under oily, strong-flavored fish such as branzino or dorade.

Gem Lettuce Salad
with Honeydew, Shaved Button Mushrooms, Pomelo Cracklings, and Green Peppercorn Vinaigrette

If you've never had gem lettuce, this salad is worth the price of admission just for discovering that green, which is like a cross between romaine and Bibb lettuce, sweet with a nice crunch. Paired here with honeydew melon, pomelo cracklings, and a creamy, pungent vinaigrette, this dish hits many of the same flavor and textural buttons as an iceberg, bacon, and blue cheese salad but in a decidedly different way.

2 tablespoons pickled green peppercorns

¼ cup young (white) coconut meat

2 tablespoons rice vinegar

2 tablespoons soft tofu

Kosher salt

Freshly ground white pepper

¼ cup blended oil or neutral oil such as canola

4 heads gem lettuce, core cut off and discarded, leaves separated

1 shallot, minced

1 cup diced ripe honeydew melon

½ cup thinly sliced button mushrooms

1 tablespoon thinly sliced flat-leaf parsley leaves

1 tablespoon minced chives

Pomelo Cracklings (see Notebook, page 50)

To make the vinaigrette: Put the peppercorns, coconut, vinegar, and tofu in a blender. Season with salt and pepper and blend, slowly adding the oil in a thin stream to make an emulsified vinaigrette. Transfer to a measuring cup or bowl, cover with plastic wrap, and chill well in the refrigerator for at least 30 minutes and up to 4 hours.

▸ To make the salad: Put the gem lettuce, shallot, melon, mushrooms, parsley, and chives in a large bowl.

Season with salt and pepper and drizzle with the green peppercorn vinaigrette.

▸ To serve, use tongs or your hands to remove the lettuce leaves from the bowl and arrange them on 4 salad plates. Top with the rest of the salad and sprinkle with the cracklings.

Cracklings

Cracklings bring a vibrant and crunchy addition to any plate and are one of those elements that are much easier to make than the end result would indicate. This recipe is made with pomelo, but can be easily adapted for just about any type of citrus, such as grapefruit, oranges, or lemons. You can also make it with ginger, juicing some of it and using the ginger's flesh as the "zest." Some of my favorite ways to use cracklings are over salads, yogurt, or cottage cheese, and to garnish canapés, especially those featuring fish tartare.

NOTE: *The pomelo produces ¼ cup zest and 1 cup juice; use these amounts as a guideline for making cracklings with other fruits and ginger.*

Zest and juice of 1 pomelo (ruby red grapefruit can be substituted)

¼ cup plus 2 tablespoons cornstarch

Canola oil or corn oil, for frying

Preheat the oven to 225°F. Scatter the pomelo zest in an even layer on a baking sheet and bake until the zest is dried out and crispy, about 25 minutes. Set aside to cool completely, about 5 minutes, then put the zest in a spice or coffee grinder and grind to a fine powder.

▸ Put the pomelo juice and cornstarch in a medium bowl and whisk together into a smooth, thick mixture (slurry).

▸ Pour the canola oil into a deep fryer, or wide, deep, heavy pot, to a depth of 6 inches. Heat the oil to 300°F. Line a plate with paper towels. Whisk the slurry into the oil and fry until golden brown, about 4 minutes. Use a slotted spoon to transfer the cracklings to the prepared plate, and season with salt and pepper. Toss the cracklings with the pomelo dust. The cracklings can be stored in an airtight container at room temperature for up to 1 week.

Crispy Broccoli Salad

with Chinese Sausage, Plum Chutney, and Basil

This unusual hot salad combines the snap of fried broccoli and sausage with homemade plum chutney and the fragrance of basil. A hodgepodge of Asian staples adds sweet and pungent effects for a roller coaster of flavor and texture.

2½ plums, halved and pitted

1 tablespoon blended oil or neutral oil such as canola

2½ shallots, ½ sliced, 2 minced

2 garlic cloves, sliced

2 tablespoons palm sugar or turbinado sugar such as Sugar in the Raw

1 tablespoon fish sauce

1 tablespoon freshly squeezed lime juice

1 tablespoon fermented yellow bean sauce

2 tablespoons basil chiffonade (see page 362), plus ¼ cup hand-torn basil leaves

Fried broccoli (see Notebook, page 53)

1 cup sliced Chinese sausage

Kosher salt

Freshly ground white pepper

2 tablespoons rice vinegar

2 tablespoons plum vinegar

To make the plum chutney: Char the plums for about 5 minutes on a hot grill or on a grill pan or cast-iron pan that has been heated over high heat for 5 minutes, turning to char the halves all over. Transfer them to a heat-proof bowl and set aside. Heat the blended oil in a deep sauté pan over medium heat. When the oil is shimmering, add the sliced shallot, garlic, and plums, and sauté until the vegetables are softened but not browned, 2 to 3 minutes. Stir in the palm sugar and cook, stirring, until melted and incorporated, about 2 minutes. Transfer the mixture to a food processor fitted with a steel blade. Add the fish sauce, lime juice, and yellow bean sauce and pulse to a salsa-like consistency. Transfer to a bowl, fold in the basil chiffonade, and set aside.

▸ Line a plate with paper towels and set aside. Batter and fry the broccoli, following the directions in the Notebook. Add the sausage to the fryer during the last 30 seconds of frying. Remove the broccoli and sausage from the fryer with a slotted spoon and drain on the prepared plate. Season immediately with salt and pepper. Transfer to a bowl and add the minced shallots, torn basil, and rice and plum vinegars.

▸ To serve, smear plum chutney on each of 4 salad plates and top with salad.

Fried Vegetables

Frying vegetables in a quick tempura batter combines virtue (eating your veggies) with indulgence (fried food). I love the yin-yang effect of biting through a crispy batter into the vegetable contained within. You can use this technique with almost any vegetable; my favorites are cauliflower, Brussels sprouts, string beans, and kale (the amounts to use are in the recipe below). Scatter fried vegetables over hot or cold salads for a cool garnish; toss them into the salads to wilt the greens, if that's a desired effect; or scatter them over seafood dishes. For two good examples of this technique in other contexts, see pages 27 and 61.

NOTE: *To adapt this recipe for other vegetables, replace the broccoli with 2 heads cauliflower, 3 cups Brussels sprouts, 3 cups string beans, or 4 cups (loosely packed) torn kale leaves with the ribs removed.*

Canola oil or corn oil, for frying

2 heads broccoli, stems trimmed, separated into florets, or other vegetables (see above)

Tempura Batter (page 363)

Kosher salt

Freshly ground black pepper

Pour canola oil into a deep fryer, or wide, deep, heavy pot, to a depth of 4 inches. Heat the oil to 350°F. Line a large plate with paper towels and set aside.

▶ Working with one floret at a time, dip the broccoli into the batter to coat it on both sides, allowing any excess to drip off. Carefully lower the floret into the hot oil, coating and adding another piece or two as quickly as possible so they all fry at the same rate, and fry until golden brown, about 2 minutes.

▶ Remove the broccoli with a slotted spoon and drain on the prepared plate. Season immediately with salt and pepper. Repeat with the remaining florets and batter, allowing the oil to return to 350°F between batches.

2

Starters

Grilled King Oyster Mushrooms

with Garbanzo Beans, Baby Turnips, and Sour Yellow Curry

One of the things that made me fall in love with Thai cooking was the combination of vibrant, high-impact flavors in clean, clear dishes that are largely free of butter. Thai cuisine's intensity satisfies so much that vegetarian dishes can sneak by the palate of even the most devout carnivore. This longtime vegetarian offering from my Greenwich Village restaurant Kin Shop is a straightforward coming together of beans and turnips with fragrant Thai basil and grilled mushrooms perched on top, offering a substantial, meat-like garnish.

Kosher salt

1 cup peeled, quartered baby white turnips (about 6 turnips)

4 king oyster mushrooms, halved and scored (peeled portobello mushrooms, ribs removed, may be substituted)

Freshly ground white pepper

2 tablespoons blended oil or neutral oil such as canola

1 quart Sour Yellow Curry (see Notebook, page 57)

½ cup fresh garbanzo beans, shucked (dried garbanzo beans, soaked overnight, drained, and blanched, may be substituted)

8 Thai basil leaves (regular basil may be substituted), hand-torn into bite-size pieces

Fill a large bowl halfway with ice water. Bring a large pot of salted water to a boil. Line a large plate with paper towels and set it aside.

▶ Add the baby turnips to the boiling water and cook until tender to a knife tip, about 3 minutes. Drain in a colander and transfer to the ice water to stop the cooking and preserve their color, about 1 minute. Drain again, and transfer the turnips to the prepared plate to drain.

▶ Season the mushrooms generously with salt and pepper and drizzle with the oil. Heat a grill pan or cast-iron pan over high heat for 5 minutes. Add the mushrooms and cook until very slightly softened and

grill marks form (if using a cast-iron pan, brown the mushrooms slightly before turning), about 3 minutes on each side, being sure the mushrooms do not char.

▶ Meanwhile, heat the turnips, curry, garbanzo beans, and basil in a large pot over medium-high heat. Cook, stirring with a wooden spoon, until the mixture is warmed through, about 5 minutes.

▶ Divide the curry and vegetables among 4 serving bowls, making sure to get a good mix of vegetables in each serving. Top each serving with 2 mushroom halves and serve.

curry

Curries are one of the pillars of Thai cuisine, made by grinding a paste out of a multitude of ingredients that usually includes a base of aromatics. From there, different additional ingredients are added to create different curries, each with its own ideal application. I use curries a bit differently than they are used in Thailand, where one cooks proteins or vegetables in the curry itself; I prefer to cook the dish's primary ingredient independently and sauce it with curry. Here are a number of my favorite curries, many of which are used throughout the book.

SOUR YELLOW CURRY

MAKES 1 QUART

I've adapted the classic sour yellow curry here, using mushroom soy sauce instead of the traditional fish sauce, because I use it in vegetarian dishes such as the preceding mushroom recipe. If you like, you can replace the soy sauce with fish sauce for seafood dishes.

½ tablespoon seeded chopped Thai red chile (about 1 chile), soaked for 15 minutes in 1 cup lukewarm water (soaking liquid reserved)

1 tablespoon thinly sliced shallot

1 tablespoon minced lemongrass (see page 362)

1 tablespoon peeled, minced fresh ginger

2 teaspoons minced garlic

1 teaspoon coriander seeds

1 teaspoon cardamom seeds

2 tablespoons peeled, minced fresh turmeric

1 teaspoon mace

1 teaspoon cumin seeds

1 cilantro stem, leaves removed

½ cinnamon stick

Kosher salt

2 tablespoons blended oil or neutral oil such as canola

2 cups coconut milk

½ cup tamarind concentrate

¼ cup mushroom soy sauce

¼ cup palm sugar or turbinado sugar such as Sugar in the Raw

2 kaffir lime leaves

¼ cup freshly squeezed lime juice

Put the chile, shallot, lemongrass, ginger, garlic, coriander, cardamom, turmeric, mace, cumin, cilantro, cinnamon, and salt in a blender and blend until a smooth purée forms, about 30 seconds, adding some of the chile-soaking water as needed to help the blender's blade catch.

▶ Heat the oil in a large saucepan over high heat. When the oil is shimmering, add the curry paste and cook, stirring, until fragrant, about 2 minutes. Add the coconut milk, tamarind, mushroom soy sauce, palm sugar, and lime leaves. Bring to a simmer, lower the heat, and allow to simmer gently for 30 minutes to mingle the flavors. Stir in the lime juice and simmer for 5 minutes more. Remove from the heat and discard the lime leaves. Use right away or refrigerate in an airtight container for up to 1 week.

MASSAMAN CURRY

MAKES 1 QUART

This heavily spiced—but not spicy—curry (defined by the inclusion of potato and pineapple) gets along great with fatty meats such as beef, lamb, and goat.

2 tablespoons roasted peanuts

1 tablespoon seeded chopped Thai red chile (about 2 chiles), soaked for 15 minutes in 1 cup lukewarm water (soaking liquid reserved)

1 tablespoon thinly sliced shallot

1 tablespoon peeled, minced galangal (fresh ginger may be substituted)

1 tablespoon minced lemongrass (see page 362)

2 cilantro stems, leaves removed

2 teaspoons minced garlic

2 teaspoons coriander seeds

2 teaspoons freshly grated nutmeg

1 teaspoon cumin seeds

1 teaspoon mace

5 whole cloves

3 cardamom pods

1 tablespoon kosher salt

2 tablespoons blended oil or
neutral oil such as canola

2 cups coconut milk

¼ cup tamarind concentrate

¼ cup fish sauce

¼ cup palm sugar or turbinado
sugar such as Sugar in the Raw

1 kaffir lime leaf

½ cup fresh pineapple juice

Put the peanuts, red chile, shallot, galangal, lemongrass, cilantro, garlic, coriander, nutmeg, cumin, mace, cloves, cardamom, and salt in a blender and blend until a smooth purée forms, about 30 seconds, adding some of the chile-soaking water as needed to help the blender's blade catch.

▸ Heat the oil in a large saucepan over high heat. When the oil is shimmering, add the curry paste and cook, stirring with a wooden spoon, until fragrant, about 2 minutes. Add the coconut milk, tamarind, fish sauce, palm sugar, and lime leaf and bring to a simmer. Lower the heat and

continue to simmer gently for 25 minutes to mingle the flavors. Stir in the pineapple juice and simmer for 5 minutes more. Remove the lime leaf. Use right away or refrigerate in an airtight container for up to 1 week.

RED CURRY

MAKES 1 QUART

Most red curries are coconut-based, but I use a blend of duck stock and green mango, as well as a lot of white pepper and sumac, for a potent result. I like to serve this curry with duck.

1 teaspoon shrimp paste

1 tablespoon seeded chopped
Thai red chile (about 2 chiles),
soaked for 15 minutes in
1 cup lukewarm water
(soaking liquid reserved)

1 tablespoon thinly sliced shallot

1 tablespoon thinly sliced garlic

1 tablespoon peeled, minced
galangal

1 tablespoon minced lemongrass
(see page 362)

1 tablespoon whole white
peppercorns

2 teaspoons sumac

1 teaspoon dried shrimp

1 teaspoon coriander seeds

1 cilantro stem, leaves removed

1 tablespoon kosher salt

1 tablespoon blended oil or
neutral oil such as canola

2 cups chicken stock, preferably
homemade (page 366)

½ cup tamarind concentrate

¼ cup fish sauce

1 tablespoon palm sugar or turbinado sugar such as Sugar in
the Raw

½ cup peeled and sliced fresh
green mango

Preheat the oven to 250°F. Put the shrimp paste on a small piece of aluminum foil, wrap loosely, and roast until dried, about 20 minutes. Remove from the oven and set aside.

▸ Put the chile, shallot, garlic, galangal, lemongrass, white peppercorns, sumac, roasted shrimp paste, dried shrimp, coriander, cilantro stem, and salt in a blender and blend until a smooth purée forms, about 30 seconds, adding some of the chile-soaking water as needed to help the blender's blade catch.

▸ Heat the oil in a large saucepan over high heat. When the oil is shimmering, add the curry paste and cook, stirring, until fragrant, about 1 minute. Stir in the chicken stock, tamarind, fish sauce, and palm sugar and bring to a simmer. Lower the heat and continue to simmer for 25 minutes to mingle the flavors. Add the green mango and simmer for 2 minutes more. Transfer to a blender and purée until smooth. Use right away or refrigerate in an airtight container for up to 1 week.

PENANG CURRY

MAKES 1 QUART

Named for the Malaysian city, this curry is encountered on Thailand's southern border with that country. Though not part of the traditional recipe, adding torn basil at the end (as you would to a pasta sauce) provides a nice herbaceous lift. I serve this curry with rich meats such as braised short ribs, pork shank, or veal shank (osso buco).

2 tablespoons roasted peanuts

½ tablespoon seeded chopped Thai red chile (about 1 chile), soaked for 15 minutes in 1 cup lukewarm water (soaking liquid reserved)

1 tablespoon thinly sliced shallot

1 tablespoon thinly sliced garlic

2 teaspoons peeled, sliced galangal (fresh ginger may be substituted)

2 teaspoons thinly sliced lemongrass (see page 362)

1 teaspoon mace, toasted (see page 362) (all spices for this recipe may be toasted together)

1 teaspoon coriander seeds, toasted (see page 362)

1 teaspoon whole cloves, toasted (see page 362)

2 tablespoons freshly grated nutmeg, toasted (see page 362)

1 tablespoon whole cardamom seeds, toasted (see page 362)

2 kaffir lime leaves

2 cilantro stems, leaves removed

1 tablespoon kosher salt

1 tablespoon blended oil or neutral oil such as canola

2 cups coconut milk

½ cup fish sauce

½ cup tamarind concentrate

½ cup palm sugar or turbinado sugar such as Sugar in the Raw

¼ cup thinly sliced Thai basil

Put the peanuts, red chile, shallot, garlic, galangal, lemongrass, mace, coriander, cloves, nutmeg, cardamom, lime leaves, cilantro stems, and salt in a blender and blend until a smooth purée forms, about 30 seconds, adding some of the chile-soaking water as needed to help the blender's blade catch.

▶ Heat the oil in a large saucepan over high heat. When the oil is shimmering, add the curry paste and cook, stirring, until fragrant, about 1 minute. Stir in the coconut milk, fish sauce, tamarind, and palm sugar and bring to a simmer. Lower the heat and continue to simmer for 30 minutes to mingle the flavors. Use right away or refrigerate in an airtight container for up to 1 week. Add the basil just before serving.

SIAMESE GREEN CURRY

MAKES 1 QUART

This medium-spicy curry, made green by the water spinach (aka Siamese watercress), is very herbaceous, making it ideal over fish and shellfish or with white meats such as chicken and lean pork cuts such as the chop or loin.

1 tablespoon seeded chopped Thai green chile (about 2 chiles), soaked for 15 minutes in 1 cup lukewarm water (soaking liquid reserved)

1 tablespoon thinly sliced shallot

1 tablespoon thinly sliced garlic

1 tablespoon peeled, chopped galangal

2 teaspoons thinly sliced lemongrass (see page 362)

2 kaffir lime leaves

1 teaspoon coriander seeds

1 teaspoon cardamom seeds

1 cilantro stem, leaves removed

1 cup (loosely packed) water spinach

1 tablespoon kosher salt

1 tablespoon blended oil or neutral oil such as canola

2 cups coconut milk

¼ cup fish sauce

¼ cup tamarind concentrate

¼ cup palm sugar or turbinado sugar such as Sugar in the Raw

1 kaffir lime leaf

Put the chile, shallot, garlic, galangal, lemongrass, lime leaves, coriander, cardamom, cilantro stem, water spinach, and salt in a blender and blend until a smooth purée forms, about 30 seconds, adding some of the chile-soaking water as needed to help the blender's blade catch.

▸ Heat the oil in a large saucepan over high heat. When the oil is shimmering, add the curry paste and cook, stirring, until fragrant, about 1 minute. Add the coconut milk, fish sauce, tamarind, palm sugar, and lime leaf and bring to a simmer. Lower the heat and continue to simmer for 30 minutes to mingle the flavors; remove and discard the lime leaves. Use right away or refrigerate in an airtight container for up to 1 week.

JUNGLE CURRY

MAKES 1 QUART

This shellfish-based blend is the spiciest of the curries and is traditionally very adaptable. Sort of a "scavenger" curry, it can be made with whatever can be foraged on the day of cooking, even omitting the shellfish elements or adding pickled green peppercorns. Serve with steamed fish or steamed vegetables.

1 teaspoon shrimp paste

½ cup crab paste or roe

3 dried Thai chiles, soaked for 15 minutes in 1 cup lukewarm water, soaking liquid reserved

1 tablespoon thinly sliced garlic

1 tablespoon peeled, sliced galangal (fresh ginger may be substituted)

1 tablespoon thinly sliced lemongrass (see page 362)

1 tablespoon sawtooth herb (cilantro may be substituted)

2 kaffir lime leaves

2 teaspoons thinly sliced shallot

1 teaspoon coriander seeds

1 tablespoon kosher salt

1 tablespoon blended oil or neutral oil such as canola

1 quart shellfish stock, preferably homemade (page 367)

¼ cup fish sauce

¼ cup tamarind concentrate

¼ cup palm sugar or turbinado sugar such as Sugar in the Raw

Preheat the oven to 250°F. Put the shrimp paste on a small piece of aluminum foil, wrap loosely, and roast until dried, about 20 minutes. Remove from the oven and set aside.

▸ Put the crab paste, chiles, garlic, galangal, lemongrass, sawtooth herb, lime leaves, shallot, roasted shrimp paste, coriander, and salt in a blender and blend until a smooth purée forms, about 30 seconds, adding some of the chile-soaking water as needed to help the blender's blade catch.

▸ Heat the oil in a large saucepan over high heat. When the oil is shimmering, add the curry paste and cook, stirring, until fragrant, about 1 minute. Add the shellfish stock, fish sauce, tamarind, and palm sugar and bring to a simmer. Lower the heat and continue to simmer for 30 minutes to mingle the flavors. Use right away or refrigerate in an airtight container for up to 1 week.

Ricotta Cheese

with Acorn Squash Tempura, Truffle Honey, and Toasted Bread

SERVES 4

I grew up eating a lot of baked pasta dishes, and many of them, such as manicotti, lasagna, baked ziti, and cannelloni, featured or were topped with ricotta cheese. I always loved that soft, smooth cheese and became something of a ricotta fiend. I'd raid the refrigerator, taking a spoon to the plastic tubs of supermarket brands like Polly-O or Sorrento that we always had on hand. In time, I began to experiment with it, garnishing bowls of ricotta with fruit from our garden and drizzling honey over it for breakfast.

Today I make my own ricotta, which is actually very easy, and I have developed a number of ways to serve it. This dish is one of my favorites: the honey really activates the taste buds, the sunflower seeds add texture, and the tempura squash offers substance and a surprising, subtle sweetness. It is presented as an appetizer but can also be a small meal, especially if you pair it with a quick salad of frisée dressed with lemon juice and olive oil.

Canola oil or corn oil, for frying

8 (¼-inch-thick) slices sourdough bread

1 acorn squash (butternut or Hubbard squash may be substituted), peeled, halved, seeded, and cut crosswise into sixteen ¼-inch-thick slices

Tempura Batter (page 363)

Kosher salt

Freshly ground white pepper

¼ cup extra-virgin olive oil

About 1 cup ricotta cheese, preferably homemade (see Notebook, page 64)

Freshly ground black pepper

2 tablespoons truffle honey (other honeys, such as clover or elderflower, may be substituted)

3 tablespoons sunflower seeds, toasted (see page 362)

Position one rack in the lower third of the oven and one in the upper third, and preheat the oven to 400°F. Line a large plate with paper towels and set aside.

▸ Pour canola oil into a deep fryer, or wide, deep, heavy pot to a depth of 4 inches. Heat the oil to 350°F.

▸ Meanwhile, to toast the bread, set the bread slices directly on the uppermost rack of the oven and toast until golden brown and crispy, about 5 minutes. Trans-

fer the toast to a baking sheet, lower the heat to 200°F, prop the oven door open slightly (a natural wine cork works perfectly), and keep the toast warm on the lower rack while you continue cooking.

▸ When the oil reaches 350°F, working with one squash slice at a time, dip the squash into the batter to coat it on both sides, allowing any excess batter to drip off. Carefully lower the squash into the oil, coating and adding another

continued

slice or two as quickly as possible so they all fry at the same rate, and fry until golden brown, about 2 minutes.

▶ Use tongs or a slotted spoon to transfer the squash slices to the prepared plate, and season immediately with salt and white pepper. Transfer to a baking sheet and keep warm on the center rack in the oven. Repeat with the remaining squash slices and batter, allowing the oil to return to 350°F between batches.

▶ To serve, put 2 slices of toast on each of 4 salad plates. Drizzle each slice with olive oil, spread ricotta cheese on each one, sprinkle black pepper over the ricotta, drizzle with honey, and scatter sunflower seeds over the top. Set a piece of tempura squash on top of each slice and serve.

Homemade Ricotta cheese

There are different schools of ricotta making that break down according to the source of acid in the cheese, which is essential to causing the curds to separate from the whey. Some recipes use milk, or milk and cream, with a little lemon juice added. Others use buttermilk to provide the acid. Personally, I prefer buttermilk because its acidity is subtler and its fat makes the cheese more flavorful and creamy.

MAKES ABOUT 2 CUPS

2 quarts whole milk

2 cups buttermilk

1 cup heavy cream

Kosher salt

Freshly ground white pepper

Clip a kitchen thermometer onto the side of a heavy, stainless steel pot. Pour the milk, buttermilk, and heavy cream into the pot and set over medium-high heat. Cook, whisking constantly, until cheese curds begin to form, about 10 minutes. Stop whisking but continue to cook until the temperature reaches 170°F, about 5 minutes more. It's essential that you stop cooking as soon as the temperature reaches 170°F.

▶ Remove the pot from the heat and set it aside to rest until the curds cool to room temperature, about 20 minutes. Suspend a fine-mesh strainer over a large bowl and use a slotted spoon to transfer the ricotta curds to the strainer. Allow to strain until well drained but still moist, about 30 minutes. (Take care not to let all the moisture strain out; otherwise, the cheese will be too dry.) Transfer the curds to a bowl, season generously with salt and pepper, and stir gently and briefly with a rubber spatula.

▶ Serve the ricotta cheese right away or refrigerate in an airtight container for up to 3 days. Allow to come to room temperature and stir to reincorporate any liquid before serving.

RAVIOLI FILLING: In a mixing bowl, combine 2 cups fresh ricotta cheese, 1 cup grated pecorino Romano cheese, 1 egg, and 1 tablespoon finely grated lemon zest. Use to fill ravioli made with store-bought pasta or homemade pasta following the recipe on page 364.

TOPPING FOR PASTA WITH RED SAUCE: Top a serving of your favorite pasta with 1 tablespoon fresh ricotta, 1 teaspoon grated pecorino Romano cheese, 1 teaspoon extra-virgin olive oil, and a few grinds of black pepper. (For a good all-purpose red sauce, see page 147.) As the ricotta and sauce meld, a lasagna-like effect takes hold. Where I grew up, different families used different grating cheeses. Ours was a pecorino home, so I use pecorino Romano, but you could also use Parmigiano-Reggiano here.

CANNOLI FILLING: Here's my family's recipe for cannoli filling: Put 2 cups ricotta cheese in the bowl of a food processor fit with a steel blade. Add ¾ cup confectioners' sugar, 2 tablespoons pure vanilla extract, and a pinch of ground cinnamon. Pulse just to combine. If desired, fold in 1 tablespoon chopped, dried fruit or small chocolate chips. Spoon or pipe the filling into store-bought cannoli shells.

"BREAKFAST OF CHAMPIONS": This one comes straight from my childhood. If you have ricotta cheese on hand, it always feels a little harmlessly indulgent to call on it for breakfast: Put ½ cup ricotta cheese in a bowl and top with 1 cup of your favorite fresh seasonal fruit and ¼ cup granola. Drizzle with 1 tablespoon honey or maple syrup.

Raw Oysters
with *Tom Yum* Granita

Growing up as I did in Long Island, New York, I've had a lifelong love of coastal cuisine, but it wasn't until I did my culinary school externship at the Island Mermaid restaurant at Ocean Beach, Fire Island, that I came to love oysters on the half shell. This is a Thai version of oysters that's not nearly as avant-garde as it seems: In Japan, eating Kumamoto oysters with a ponzu granita is actually commonplace. Here I simply adapt that combination for a granita made from *tom yum*, or Thai hot-and-sour soup, which pairs very well with the brininess of the raw oysters, with kaffir lime adding a fresh, spicy finish. Though this dish grew out of my East Coast memories, I actually prefer the sweeter, creamier West Coast oysters, such as Kumamoto, Barron Point, Effingham, or Hog Island, for it because they get along better with the granita.

1 tablespoon blended oil or neutral oil such as canola

1 shallot, thinly sliced

2 garlic cloves, thinly sliced

1 tablespoon peeled, minced fresh ginger

1 tablespoon minced lemongrass (see page 362)

1 Thai red chile, thinly sliced

2 kaffir lime leaves

1 pint shellfish stock, preferably homemade (page 367)

2 tablespoons fish sauce

2 tablespoons freshly squeezed lime juice

2 quarts shaved ice

24 oysters, preferably Kumamoto or another West Coast variety

4 lime wedges

Heat the oil in a medium saucepan over medium heat. When the oil is shimmering, add the shallot, garlic, ginger, lemongrass, chile, and lime leaves and cook, stirring, until the vegetables are softened but not browned, about 4 minutes. Stir in the shellfish stock and fish sauce and bring to a simmer. Lower the heat and simmer for 15 minutes to mingle the flavors, then stir in the lime juice. Strain through a fine-mesh strainer into a large, shallow, temperature-proof vessel, and season to taste, if necessary (the mixture should be salty, sour, and hot). Allow to cool, then freeze, uncovered, until the mixture hardens, about 4 hours, scraping with a fork every 30 minutes or so to form crystals.

▸ To serve, arrange the shaved ice over a large serving dish or platter. Shuck the oysters (see Notebook, page 67) and arrange them over the ice on the half shell. Top each oyster with about 1 teaspoon of the granita. Serve immediately with lime wedges alongside.

Oysters

Oysters are one of nature's great gifts to passionate eaters, requiring little more than a mignonette (a condiment of red wine vinegar, chopped shallot, and cracked black pepper) or hot sauce to bring out their best. There are actually only a handful of different species; the specific names of individual types of oysters usually refer to the body of water they were harvested from, which is responsible for each type's distinct flavor. Very generally speaking, American-harvested oysters break down by coast: the West Coast is separated into Pacific oysters and Kumamoto, and then there are East Coast, or Atlantic, oysters. (I also love belon, or European flats.) I suggest Pacific or Kumamoto oysters as "starter" oysters for new eaters because they are creamier and sweeter than their briny, potently flavored East Coast cousins, which are also more unpredictable, with a greater variance in flavor profile from type to type.

To shuck an oyster: Using a towel to protect your hand, grasp the oyster in one hand. Force an oyster knife into the oyster and turn it repeatedly, then prying, until the shell pops open. To separate the oyster from the shell: Cut the oyster where the muscle meets the shell. Refrigerate oysters in their liquid in an airtight container for up to 2 hours.

Following are some of my favorite ways to enjoy oysters.

FRIED OYSTERS WITH CELERY SEED AIOLI: As prized as fresh oysters are, they are also terrific fried; biting through a crunchy coating and reaching that briny inside is a killer effect. To fry oysters, dip shucked oysters into tempura batter (page 363) and fry following the instructions on page 27. Serve with a celery seed aioli (page 180), replacing the coriander seed with the same amount of celery seed and leaving out the cilantro) alongside for dipping.

GRILLED OYSTERS WITH MAÎTRE D'HÔTEL BUTTER: Make a compound butter by folding together 8 tablespoons (1 stick) softened, room-temperature, unsalted butter, 1 tablespoon minced garlic, 1 tablespoon lemon zest, and 1 teaspoon minced chives. Shuck oysters, set them on the half shell, top each with 1 teaspoon of the butter mixture, put the tops back on, and grill until hot and the butter is melted. To check for doneness, lift the top shell to ensure the oyster is plump and opaque—the top shell should not be hot. Serve on a bed of seaweed, salt, or dried beans, with lemon wedges alongside.

SHAVED FROZEN OYSTERS: Shuck oysters, removing them from the shell, and freeze them until hard, at least 2 hours or up to 24 hours. Use a mandoline to shave them and scatter them over congee (page 262) or plain or seafood risotto.

Sicilian Shellfish Salad
with Prawns, Sea Scallops, Crab, and Pomelo-Basil Dressing

SERVES 4

I first had a version of this dish on a vacation in Sicily. At the Tonnara di Scopello, near a tuna cannery, my wife and I had lunch at a restaurant situated on a high ridge overlooking the pristine water. (The view was beautiful, but the restaurant was swarming with bees. We were forced to put our starter of prosciutto and summer melon on the empty table next to us to draw them away.) The incredible shellfish served there was fantastic, but the thing that really stayed with me was the blood orange dressing, made with fragrant, local fruit. I've toyed with it a bit, but the flavor still brings me back to that trip.

1 tablespoon kosher salt, plus more for seasoning

1 Dungeness crab

1 pomelo or ruby red grapefruit

1 cup extra-virgin olive oil

1 garlic clove, smashed with the side of a chef's knife

2 shallots, 1 sliced, 1 minced

6 whole black peppercorns

4 large shell-on prawns, about 1 ounce each

4 sea scallops, thinly sliced horizontally

½ cup (loosely packed) frisée

¼ cup shaved fennel, plus 4 pieces fennel fronds

8 Sicilian green olives, pitted and quartered

8 basil leaves, torn by hand into bite-size pieces

Freshly ground black pepper

To cook the crab: Fill a large bowl halfway with ice water and set it aside. Fill a large pot with water to a depth of 1 inch. Season the water generously with salt, set a steamer rack inside the pot, and bring the water to a boil over high heat. Using tongs, pick up the crab and place it, back side up, on the steamer rack. Cover the pot and return the water to a full boil. Lower the heat to medium-high and steam until the crab is cooked through and bright red, about 15 minutes. Using tongs, transfer the crab to the ice water to stop the cooking. Once the crab is chilled, about 8 minutes, remove and discard the shell and pick out the meat. Set aside.

▸ To make the prawn confit: Peel and separate the pomelo into segments, reserving 3 thin strips of the peel and discarding the remainder. Peel the membrane from the individual segments, then gather and squeeze the membranes over a small bowl to yield about 2 tablespoons of juice. Set aside.

▸ Heat the olive oil in a large saucepan over medium-high heat. When the oil is shimmering, add the pomelo peel, garlic, sliced shallot, 1 tablespoon salt, and the whole peppercorns and bring to a simmer. Remove the pan from the heat and add the prawns. Cook the prawns in the warm oil (without returning to the heat)

continued

until cooked through, about 5 minutes. Remove the prawns from the pan, transfer them to a plate, and refrigerate them until chilled, at least 4 minutes. Meanwhile, strain the oil through a fine-mesh strainer set over a medium bowl and reserve ¼ cup of the oil, discarding the remainder. Peel and devein the chilled prawns, then split them lengthwise into two pieces.

▸ To assemble the dish: Put the crabmeat, prawns, raw scallops, pomelo segments, minced shallot, frisée, shaved fennel, olives, and basil in a large bowl. Season generously with salt and pepper and stir to combine. Drizzle with the strained confit oil and the reserved pomelo juice. Arrange the salad on a serving platter, being sure all the ingredients are distributed evenly. Garnish with the fennel fronds and serve.

Crab

Crabbing was a major pastime when I was a kid on Long Island, and it was the gateway to my love for eating the crabs themselves. It became a focal point of our family planning: when we ate out near home, my parents always made me order from the kids' menu, but when we were on vacation, they'd pick restaurants based on which ones had crab on the menu and let me order to my heart's content. To this day, there are few foods that make me happier than these sweet, salty crustaceans, and I'm endlessly fascinated by how those qualities vary slightly but significantly from type to type. Here are my favorite varieties of crab and the way I most like to use each one:

BLUE CRAB AND PEEKYTOE CRAB: If there are all-purpose crabs, these are the ones. They are fine go-to crabs for everything from crab tomato sauce to crab boils (in water seasoned with Old Bay) to baked crab. (Two notes: soft-shell crabs are not a type of crab but, rather, blue crabs that are caught within hours of molting, or shedding their outer shells, in the spring and summer; and peekytoe crabs are named for the shape of the legs, from which almost all of their meat is harvested.)

STONE CRABS: These highly seasonal, exquisitely sweet crabs come only from Florida. The claws are the only part we eat because the law mandates that one claw be removed; then the crab is rereleased into the water. Stone crab claws are generally boiled and served chilled with cold mustard sauce.

KING AND SNOW CRABS: Steam the cluster and legs and serve them hot with clarified butter or chilled with mustard sauce for dipping.

DUNGENESS CRABS: These meaty crabs take well to Asian preparations, especially stir-fries served with noodles.

Crispy Soft-Shell Crab
with Ramp Kimchi and Spicy Passion Fruit Sauce

Soft-shell crabs and ramps (wild leeks) both come into season in the spring, and they get along great: when pan-fried, the crispy crabs, with their sweet, succulent meat, are a match made in heaven with the leeks' gentle onion flavor. This particular combination of ramps and soft-shells was inspired by a meal I ate in a Korean restaurant in spring 2008; with seasonal ingredients top of mind, the pungent accompaniment of kimchi gave me the idea to make a ramp kimchi. The passion fruit sauce is also delicious with raw fatty fish such as yellowtail and salmon. Note that the kimchi must be made at least three days in advance.

---

1 cup passion fruit purée

1 passion fruit, split in half, pulp removed with a tablespoon

1 garlic clove

2 tablespoons palm sugar or turbinado sugar such as Sugar in the Raw

2 tablespoons fish sauce

2 teaspoons chopped Thai red chile

2 tablespoons freshly squeezed lime juice

1 quart whole milk

4 jumbo soft-shell crabs, about 5 ounces each, cleaned

2 cups all-purpose flour

1 tablespoon kosher salt, plus more for seasoning

1 tablespoon freshly ground white pepper, plus more for seasoning

1 cup blended oil or neutral oil such as canola

1 cup Ramp Kimchi (see Notebook, page 75)

To make the spicy passion fruit sauce: Heat ¼ cup of the passion fruit purée and the passion fruit pulp in a medium saucepan over medium-high heat, stirring them together with a wooden spoon. Bring to a simmer, then lower the heat and continue to simmer until the seeds turn dark black, about 5 minutes. Transfer the contents of the pan to a medium heatproof bowl and set aside.

▶ Return the saucepan to the stovetop over medium heat and add the remaining ¾ cup passion fruit purée. When the purée simmers, stir in the garlic, palm sugar, fish sauce, chile, and lime juice; immediately remove the pan from the heat. Purée the mixture in a blender or in the pan with an immersion blender, then strain it through a fine-mesh strainer into the bowl with the passion fruit pulp and purée. Stir the ingredients together. The sauce should be sweet, salty, sour, and spicy. Cover the bowl with plastic wrap and refrigerate until well chilled, at least 1 hour or up to 2 days.

▶ To pan-fry the crabs: Pour the milk into a wide, deep bowl. Add the crabs, being sure they are completely submerged in the milk, and soak for 30 minutes.

▶ Meanwhile, combine the flour, 1 tablespoon salt, and 1 tablespoon pepper in a wide, shallow vessel.

continued

▸ Position a rack in the center of the oven and preheat the oven to 425°F. Line a large plate or platter with paper towels and set it aside.

▸ Heat the oil in a wide, deep, ovenproof sauté pan over high heat. When the oil is shimmering, remove the crabs from the milk, dredge them in the seasoned flour, and carefully add them to the pan without crowding. Cook until golden brown and crispy on the bottom, about 2 minutes. Carefully turn them with tongs or a slotted spoon and cook until golden brown and crispy on the other side, about 2 more minutes.

▸ Remove the pan from the heat, gently pour off the oil, and transfer to the oven to cook for 2 minutes to warm the crabs through. Remove the pan from the oven and transfer the crabs to the prepared plate to drain. Immediately season the tops with salt and pepper.

▸ To serve, spoon the passion fruit sauce into the bottom of each of 4 small plates. Top with ramp kimchi and finish each dish by topping the kimchi with 1 crab.

NOTE: Soft-shell crabs are blue crabs that are caught within hours of molting, or shedding their tough outer shell. Your fishmonger will be happy to clean your soft-shell crabs for you, but if you'd like to do it yourself, it's pretty easy: Lift the top shell, remove the gills underneath, then turn the crab over and lift and cut off the apron. Next, snip off the mouth and eyes with scissors or kitchen shears. To keep the legs from "exploding" when heated, it's also a good idea to pierce them with a safety pin before cooking; these small holes will let heat escape.

kimchi

The way that vegetables and pungent, fermented sauce come together in the Korean side dish kimchi has always been fascinating to me, and I began playing with it several years ago, making it with a variety of vegetables. This idea isn't radical—most of us think of kimchi as cabbage-based, but it's made with all kinds of vegetables in Korea as well. Here's my recipe for ramp kimchi, as well as several variations and pairing suggestions. Make all variations by replacing the ramps with 1 pound of the ingredient noted:

RAMP KIMCHI

MAKES ABOUT 1 QUART

2 cups kosher salt

1 head Napa cabbage, core removed and discarded, leaves coarsely chopped

1 pound ramps, stems removed, cleaned

5 garlic cloves

2 tablespoons peeled, sliced fresh ginger

½ cup rice vinegar

2 tablespoons sugar

¼ cup fish sauce

¼ cup sambal

Put the salt and 1 gallon of hot water in a large heatproof bowl and stir to dissolve the salt. Add the Napa cabbage, cover the bowl tightly with plastic wrap, and steep at room temperature for 3 hours. Use tongs to transfer the cabbage from the bowl to a separate wide bowl, discarding the water. Add the ramps to the cabbage.
▸ Put the garlic, ginger, vinegar, sugar, fish sauce, sambal, and ¼ cup cold water in a blender and blend until smooth, about 30 seconds. Pour the blended mixture over the ramps and cabbage and stir well with a wooden spoon to coat all the vegetables with sauce. Transfer to a storage container and cover with an airtight lid. Allow to ferment at room temperature in a cool dark place for at least 3 days or up to 1 week. Remove the ramps and cabbage from the sauce, transfer to a smaller airtight container, and refrigerate for up to 2 weeks. Discard the sauce.

ASPARAGUS: Serve with sautéed or grilled shellfish such as scallops. (Use any size asparagus, breaking off the woody end of the stalks before making the kimchi.)

SCALLION: Serve with grilled beef. (Trim the ends off the scallions before making the kimchi.)

ESCAROLE: Serve with strong-flavored fish such as mackerel, salmon, and sturgeon. (Coarsely chop the greens before making the kimchi.)

APPLE (PREFERABLY HONEYCRISP OR ANOTHER SWEET VARIETY): Serve with various cuts of pork—it's especially delicious with a grilled pork chop. (Core and thinly slice the apples before making the kimchi. Serve this variation within 3 days instead of 2 weeks; after 3 days, the sugar in the apples will cause the mixture to overferment.)

Peekytoe Crab and Sea Urchin Parfait
with Avocado Mousse and Toasted Rice Pearls

SERVES 4

This is probably the most "cheffy" recipe in the book, featuring sea urchin and calling for a CO_2 canister (see Sources, page 370) to aerate and pipe the sauce around the crab. It evolved from a dish of crab and avocado salad from my opening menu at Perilla. Do not to use a pastry bag in place of the CO_2 canister, as it won't produce the same fluffy, airy result.

1 quart lobster stock, preferably homemade (page 366)

1 cup heavy cream

Kosher salt

Freshly ground white pepper

160 grams (about 4 ounces) uni, preferably Santa Barbara (see Sources, page 370)

3 tablespoons peeled, minced fresh ginger

1 tablespoon fish sauce

1½ tablespoons freshly squeezed lime juice

4½ tablespoons blended oil or neutral oil such as canola

8 ounces peekytoe crabmeat

1 teaspoon minced shallot

1 teaspoon minced chives

¼ cup Avocado Mousse (see Notebook, page 78)

2 teaspoons American caviar

1 tablespoon plus 1 teaspoon toasted rice pearls

To make the uni mousse: Fill a large bowl halfway with ice water; set another, smaller bowl on top, and allow to chill for a few minutes until cold to the touch.

▸ Bring the lobster stock to a simmer in a large pot over medium heat. Simmer until the liquid has reduced by half, about 20 minutes. Then stir in the heavy cream and continue to simmer until the liquid is reduced by half again, about 5 minutes. Season generously with salt and pepper and stir in one-quarter (about 1 ounce) of the uni. Blend the mixture in the pot with an immersion blender or transfer to a blender and blend. Strain through a fine-mesh strainer set over the chilled bowl, pressing down on the solids with a rubber spatula to extract as much sauce as possible. Use the rubber spatula to stir the sauce until the temperature reaches 60°F on a digital thermometer. Transfer the mixture to a CO_2 canister fitted with 2 CO_2 charges and set it aside.

▸ To make the ginger dressing: Put the ginger, fish sauce, and lime juice in a blender and blend until smooth, about 30 seconds. While continuing to blend, slowly drizzle in the oil. Season with salt and pepper.

▸ In a large mixing bowl, stir together the crabmeat, shallot, chives, and ginger dressing and season generously with salt and pepper.

▸ Divide the avocado mousse among 4 bowls. Top with the crab mixture, then divide the remaining three-quarters (about 3 ounces) of uni and the caviar in the center of each. Pipe uni mousse around the uni and caviar, taking care not to cover them. Scatter toasted rice pearls over each dish and serve.

Avocado Mousse

This recipe produces a versatile, rich, and creamy mousse with a yogurt-like texture and beautiful light-green color.

MAKES ABOUT ¾ CUP

2 cups (loosely packed) spinach, cleaned

1 avocado, halved, pitted, and peeled

Zest and juice of 1 lime

1 tablespoon cilantro leaves

Kosher salt

Freshly ground white pepper

Fill a large bowl halfway with ice water and set it aside. Fill a large pot two-thirds full with salted water and bring to a boil over high heat. When the water boils, add the spinach and blanch until bright green and tender, about 45 seconds. Drain the spinach in a colander, then transfer it to the ice water to stop the cooking and preserve its color. Squeeze the spinach in a clean kitchen towel to remove the excess water, then transfer to a blender along with the avocado, lime zest and juice, and cilantro. Season with salt and pepper. Purée until smooth, then strain through a fine-mesh strainer, pressing down on the solids with a rubber spatula or the bottom of a ladle to extract as much mousse as possible. Cover and refrigerate until ready to use, up to 6 hours.

Following are some uses for Avocado Mousse:

GUACAMOLE: Add minced red onion, sliced cilantro leaves, diced seeded tomato, and hot sauce or minced seeded jalapeño (all according to taste) to the mousse to make guacamole. Serve with soft corn tortillas or chips.

CHILLED AVOCADO SOUP: Thin the mousse by folding in Greek yogurt, ladle into bowls, and, if desired, garnish with crab salad, a drizzle of olive oil, grilled corn kernels, toasted slivered almonds, or crostini spread with ricotta cheese (page 64).

SHELLFISH ACCOMPANIMENT: Serve the mousse alongside spicy shellfish (seasoned with cayenne or other spicy seasonings), where it will offer a cooling effect.

AVOCADO ICE CREAM: Avocado ice cream is an unexpected savory preparation to add to your repertoire. Serve it on its own or set in bowls to which gazpacho or other chilled soups will be added.

(The core ingredients differ somewhat from those in the mousse, but I wanted you to have this recipe because it's such a cool thing to make.) Put 6 ounces avocado meat (from about 3 avocados), 2 teaspoons freshly squeezed lime juice, ¾ cup milk, and ¼ cup granulated sugar in a blender and purée. Transfer to a bowl and whisk in ½ cup heavy cream. Cover and chill in the refrigerator for 4 to 6 hours. (It should reach a temperature of 40°F.) Process the mixture in an ice cream maker according to the manufacturer's directions; note that the ice cream might take only 5 to 10 minutes to set because of the avocado. If desired, freeze for 3 to 4 hours to harden it. If you serve the ice cream on its own, consider topping it with toasted coconut.

Skillet-Braised Cuttlefish

with *Guanciale*, Water Chestnuts, and Garlic Bread

I'm a big fan of La Quercia, a meat purveyor that turns out an impressive roster of pork products from their base in Norwalk, Iowa. In fact, I'm such a fan that I arranged a dinner for them at one of my restaurants, featuring a different pork product in every course. (This included dessert, for which we served a lardo financier with candied bacon and bourbon ice cream.) This cuttlefish dish was the appetizer from that evening; it combines Italian and Asian elements in a riff on a scampi sauce.

½ cup diced *guanciale*
(see Notebook, page 81)

1 tablespoon blended oil or neutral oil such as canola

8 ounces cuttlefish, cleaned

Kosher salt

Freshly ground white pepper

1 shallot, thinly sliced

2 garlic cloves, thinly sliced

2 tablespoons XO sauce

1 cup dry white wine

1 cup shellfish stock, preferably homemade (page 367)

8 tablespoons (1 stick) unsalted butter

¼ cup halved grape tomatoes

¼ cup diced water chestnuts

2 tablespoons basil chiffonade (see page 362)

Garlic Bread (page 133)

Heat the *guanciale* in a medium saucepan over medium heat, stirring occasionally, until it renders its fat and turns crispy, about 6 minutes. Remove the pan from the heat and set it aside.

▹ Heat the oil in a large sauté pan over high heat. When the oil is shimmering, add the cuttlefish, season with salt and pepper, and cook for 1 minute. Add the shallot, garlic, *guanciale*, and XO sauce and cook for

1 minute. Pour in the wine and stock, stirring to loosen any flavorful bits from the bottom of the pan. Stir in the butter, melting it, and simmer until the liquid is reduced by half, about 5 minutes. Stir in the tomatoes, water chestnuts, and basil and remove the pan from the heat.

▹ Set 1 slice of garlic bread in each of 4 wide, shallow bowls. Spoon the *guanciale* mixture over the bread in each bowl and serve.

Guanciale

Guanciale, or cured pork jowl, has a flavor similar to pancetta but, because it comes from the cheek, has a meatier texture. Though still not a common ingredient in American home kitchens, it is gaining in popularity and is increasingly easy to obtain (see Sources, page 370). It's used the same way slab bacon or sausage is, usually rendered in the pan before being incorporated with or added to other ingredients; cured with salt, sugar, and spices such as black pepper, it brings a huge hit of flavor to any dish. In addition to the uses below, it is one of the defining ingredients in pasta sauces and preparations such as *amatriciana*, a slightly spicy tomato sauce that's usually tossed with tubular pasta such as bucatini, and carbonara, which combines the *guanciale* with shallots, slightly scrambled eggs, pecorino Romano cheese, and black pepper.

GUANCIALE AND EGGS: Cut *guanciale* into small dice or strips and toss into your scrambled eggs for breakfast. For even more flavor, instead of butter or olive oil, render some fat from the *guanciale* in the pan and use it as the cooking medium for the eggs.

GUANCIALE CHIPS: Arrange thin slices of *guanciale* on a nonstick pan and crisp slowly in an oven preheated to 200°F for about 12 hours. They will turn crispy and crunchy and can be used to garnish everything from salads to soups to sandwiches.

BRAISED, GRILLED GUANCIALE: Braise *guanciale* (for guidance, see the instructions for braising pork belly on page 96), and then grill it. It's delicious in a sandwich—with sautéed broccoli rabe and melted provolone—or in a variation of the Vietnamese sandwich *banh mi*, served on a baguette with sriracha sauce, cilantro, and jalapeño slices.

GLT: For an amped-up version of a BLT, crisp slices of *guanciale* in a pan, drain on paper towels, and use in your sandwich.

Seared Sea Scallops

with Blood Orange–Hearts of Palm Salad, Parsnip Purée, and Pumpkin Seed Praline

A variety of textures—voluptuous sea scallops, crunchy praline, and al dente hearts of palm—create a compelling effect in this starter, as do the sweet praline and tart blood orange. Credit for it goes to Perilla chef de cuisine–partner Garett McMahan, who is a bit of a praline fiend and loves using it wherever he can.

The pumpkin seed praline is also delicious over salads, especially those featuring autumn vegetables.

---

4 tablespoons blended oil or neutral oil such as canola

1 garlic clove, thinly sliced

2 shallots, 1 thinly sliced, 1 minced

1 cup peeled, sliced parsnip

Kosher salt

Freshly ground white pepper

½ cup heavy cream

½ cup chicken stock, preferably homemade (page 366)

1 blood orange (a navel orange can be substituted)

¾ cup sliced fresh hearts of palm (see Notebook, page 84)

¾ cup (loosely packed) mizuna (baby arugula or peppercress can be substituted)

1 tablespoon minced chives

1 tablespoon minced flat-leaf parsley

2 tablespoons extra-virgin olive oil

8 sea scallops (about 4 ounces)

1 tablespoon unsalted butter

Pumpkin Seed Praline (recipe follows)

To make the parsnip purée: Heat 2 tablespoons of the blended oil a large saucepan over medium heat. When the oil is shimmering, add the garlic and sliced shallot and cook, stirring, until softened but not browned, about 2 minutes. Stir in the parsnip and season generously with salt and pepper. Cook for 2 minutes, then pour in the cream and stock. Bring to a simmer, lower the heat, and continue to simmer until the parsnips are soft to a knife tip, about 15 minutes. Transfer the contents of the pan to a blender and blend to a smooth purée, about 1 minute. Strain the purée through a fine-mesh strainer into a medium bowl, pressing down with a rubber spatula to extract as much purée as possible, taste, and adjust the seasoning with salt and pepper,

if necessary. The purée can be kept covered and warm for up to an hour after preparing it.

▸ To make the hearts of palm salad: Peel the blood orange and separate it into segments. Peel the webby membrane from the segments, then gather and squeeze the membranes over a small bowl to yield about 2 tablespoons of juice. Put the hearts of palm, mizuna, blood orange segments, minced shallot, chives, and parsley in a large bowl. Toss, drizzle with the olive oil and blood orange juice, season with salt and pepper, and toss again. Set the salad aside.

▸ To prepare the scallops: Heat the remaining 2 tablespoons blended oil in a wide, heavy saucepan over medium-high heat. When the oil is shimmering, season the scallops generously with salt and pepper and add them to the pan without crowding. Sear the scallops until golden brown, about 2 minutes. Add the butter to the pan and use a tablespoon to baste the scallops with the butter as it melts and foams, about 2 minutes more.

▸ To serve, reheat the parsnip purée, if necessary. Spread a few tablespoons of purée in the center of each of 4 plates. Top with the hearts of palm salad and arrange 2 scallops alongside the salad on each plate. Scatter praline over each dish and serve.

Pumpkin Seed Praline

MAKES ABOUT 1½ CUPS

1½ cups sugar

1 cup pumpkin seeds

¾ cup finely ground coffee beans

1 tablespoon Maldon or coarse sea salt

Line a baking sheet with parchment paper and set it aside. Put ¾ cup of the sugar and 1 tablespoon water in a large heavy saucepan, and stir to wet the sugar. Set the pan over medium-high heat, bring to a simmer, and once the sugar bubbles and thickens and has just begun to caramelize, about 1 minute, add the pumpkin seeds. Cook, stirring, allowing the sugar to continue to caramelize, about 5 minutes more. Use a rubber spatula to transfer the pumpkin seed–sugar mixture to the prepared baking sheet and spread it out to cool.

▸ Once the seeds have cooled, put the remaining ¾ cup sugar and 1 tablespoon water in the same saucepan. Set over medium-high heat and cook, stirring, until the sugar begins to caramelize and turn light brown, about 5 minutes. Return the pumpkin seeds to the pan. Cook, stirring, until the sugar is golden brown, about 4 minutes more. Stir in the coffee beans and sea salt.

▸ Line the baking sheet with a fresh piece of parchment paper and pour the seeds onto the paper, using the rubber spatula to spread them out. Set aside to cool completely. Once the praline is cool, break it apart before serving. Store in an airtight container at room temperature for up to 3 days.

Hearts of Palm

I love the fresh, watery crunch and clean flavor of hearts of palm—but they have to be fresh hearts of palm, because the brine that canned varieties are stored in ruins their flavor. The layers of this vegetable make it fun to cook with, and the texture and flavor vary a bit between the firmer exterior and luscious interior. If you can get them, massive Hawaiian hearts of palm are the ultimate.

HEARTS OF PALM CARPACCIO: If you can obtain large Hawaiian hearts of palm (about the same diameter as a half dollar), slice them on a mandoline, arrange the slices on a plate, and dress with olive oil and sea salt. You can adapt the preceding sea scallop recipe (page 82) to make the hearts of palm the center of attention, omitting them from the salad and topping the carpaccio with the salad instead.

HEARTS OF PALM CROQUETTES: Halve the hearts of palm lengthwise and hollow them out by removing the inner layers. Fill them with soybean purée, risotto, or any other soft prepared food. Bread them by dipping them into a succession of flour, beaten eggs, and bread crumbs, then deep-fry them.

HEARTS OF PALM "MARROW": Split the hearts of palm lengthwise and hollow them out by removing the inner layers. Fill them with fish or meat preparations such as tuna tartare, braised oxtail, or warm Duck Meat Mix (page 95). Serve as a canapé.

PICKLED HEARTS OF PALM: Pickle hearts of palm (see page 100 for pickling guidance), julienne them, and toss them into salads or use them to garnish fish and shellfish dishes.

Raw Yellowtail

with Avocado-Cucumber Salad, Cilantro, and Ponzu

SERVES 4

This summery starter, which appeared on the Perilla menu when we first opened the restaurant, refreshes with the fresh, green flavors of the avocado, cucumber, and cilantro and an in-your-face blast of acidity from the tomatoes and ponzu. Yellowtail, my favorite fish to eat raw because of its clean flavor and high fat content, provides an anchor for the light flavors and textures that surround it and is also a stunning presence in the bowl.

6 plum tomatoes

1 tablespoon kosher salt, plus more for seasoning

1 tablespoon yuzu juice

1 tablespoon shiro dashi

1 avocado, pitted, peeled, and diced

1 small cucumber, such as Kirby, peeled, seeded, and diced

1 tablespoon rice vinegar

2 tablespoons extra-virgin olive oil

1 teaspoon minced chives

Freshly ground white pepper

6 ounces sushi-grade yellowtail (*hamachi*), thinly sliced

1 teaspoon Maldon sea salt

2 teaspoons sliced cilantro

To make the tomato water: Put the tomatoes and 1 tablespoon kosher salt in a blender and purée. Suspend a fine-mesh strainer over a medium bowl and line with cheesecloth so that the cloth hangs over the edges. Pour the purée into the lined strainer, cover the strainer with plastic wrap, and allow to strain, refrigerated, for at least 12 hours or up to 24 hours. Discard the solids in the cheesecloth.

▶ In a medium bowl, whisk together the tomato water, yuzu juice, and shiro dashi.

▶ Put the avocado, cucumber, vinegar, 1 tablespoon of the olive oil, and the chives in a separate large bowl and gently toss together. Season with kosher salt and pepper.

▶ To serve, divide the yellowtail among 4 chilled bowls, artfully arranging or overlapping the slices in the center. Drizzle with the remaining 1 tablespoon olive oil and season with sea salt. Top with salad and spoon broth around the yellowtail and salad. Scatter the cilantro over the broth and serve.

Cilantro

If an herb can be polarizing, then cilantro is the one. Those who love it find its singular fragrance and flavor to be the perfect complement to some of the most often called-on Asian ingredients, such as lime juice, fish sauce, lemongrass, and roasted peanuts. Detractors feel that it tastes of soap, which we cilantro lovers simply can't understand.

In addition to scattering cilantro in its raw form over just about any type of Thai, Vietnamese, or Mexican dish you can think of, you can transform this herb in the following ways:

CILANTRO OIL AND PURÉE: To make cilantro oil, blend 2 parts cilantro with 1 part canola oil, then strain and drizzle the oil over salads, soups, and seafood dishes. Or make a purée by blending the same quantities of cilantro and oil, and *not* straining it. Toss with pasta salads or use as a condiment for fish or shellfish.

DEEP-FRIED CILANTRO: Cilantro can be quickly deep-fried and scattered over fish. Or, if you aren't comfortable frying, lay cilantro on a Silpat, brush it with simple syrup (page 363), cover with another Silpat to keep the leaves flat, and bake it until crispy, about 25 minutes at 250°F, for a similar effect.

Pan-Roasted Sardines
with Cauliflower, Snap Peas, and Chili Dressing

Back when I was the sous chef of The Harrison in New York's Tribeca neighborhood, I wasn't technically supposed to put any Asian-influenced dishes on the menu, but I snuck one in every once in a while. This dish was one of my stealth efforts that got a pass because it worked. Years later, I still love the chili dressing with its balance of acid, sweet, and sour elements. And caramelized cauliflower and snap peas are two of my favorite things to eat together.

¼ cup freshly squeezed lime juice

1 tablespoon sambal

1 teaspoon sugar

2 tablespoons extra-virgin olive oil

Kosher salt

Freshly ground white pepper

5 tablespoons blended oil or neutral oil such as canola

½ Spanish onion, minced

½ head cauliflower, stems removed, florets thinly sliced about ⅛ inch thick

1 cup snap peas, cleaned and halved crosswise

1 tablespoon thinly sliced flat-leaf parsley leaves

4 large sardines, about 2 ounces each, filleted (if purchased whole; see Note, page 90)

1½ teaspoons thinly sliced cilantro

To make the chili dressing: Whisk the lime juice, sambal, and sugar together in a large bowl until the sugar dissolves, about 30 seconds. Continuing to whisk, slowly add the olive oil, then season with salt and pepper. Set aside.

▶ To prepare the cauliflower and snap peas: Heat 1 tablespoon of the blended oil in a wide, heavy saucepan over low heat. When the oil is shimmering, add the onion and cook, stirring occasionally, until it caramelizes and turns dark brown, about 30 minutes. Season generously with salt and pepper, transfer the onion to a heatproof bowl, and set aside. Carefully wipe out the pan, add 2 tablespoons of the blended oil to it, and heat over high heat. When the oil is shimmering, add the cauliflower and cook until golden brown and cara-

melized, about 4 minutes. Season generously with salt and pepper and stir in the caramelized onion, cooking until warmed through, about 1 minute. Add the snap peas and cook for 1 minute more. Stir in the parsley, remove the pan from the heat, and set aside, covered with a lid to keep the mixture warm.

▶ To prepare the sardines: Line a plate with paper towels and set it aside. Heat the remaining 2 tablespoons blended oil in a large, heavy saucepan over medium-high heat. When the oil is shimmering, season the sardines generously with salt and pepper and add them to the pan, skin side down. Cook until the skin is crisped, about 2 minutes. Use a fish spatula to turn the sardines over, and cook on the other side for 30 seconds more. Transfer the sardines to the prepared plate to drain.

continued

▸ To serve, divide the cauliflower and snap peas among 4 plates. Whisk the cilantro into the dressing and spoon over the vegetables. Top the vegetables on each plate with 2 sardine fillets and serve immediately.

NOTE: When shopping for sardines, seek out the firmest ones you can find. If filleting them yourself, put them in the freezer first for a few minutes to firm them up, then fillet them immediately or the meat may become mushy. Also note that sardines vary greatly in size; if you can get only small ones, use 8 rather than 4 for this dish.

Cauliflower

Like potatoes, cauliflower is extremely versatile, but with a more complex flavor that's earthy, sweet, and sneakily rich, all at the same time. Also, as with potatoes, you can apply just about any cooking technique to cauliflower to get different results.

CAULIFLOWER-SPINACH PURÉE: Purée sautéed cauliflower and sautéed spinach together for a super-silky side dish to roasted and grilled meats. (For guidance, see the sunchoke recipe on page 289.)

CAULIFLOWER PANNA COTTA: For a savory version of the Italian dessert *panna cotta* (cooked cream), simmer 3 cups heavy cream and 2 cups cauliflower florets in a small pot until the florets are tender to a knife tip, about 15 minutes, depending on the size of the florets. Blend in a blender, then strain into a medium stainless steel bowl. Chill over a larger bowl filled halfway with ice water. While chilling, add 1½ teaspoons powdered gelatin and whisk for 3 minutes. Once fully chilled, about 10 minutes more, pour into 4 ramekins or soufflé cups. Cover with plastic wrap and refrigerate until set, about 4 hours. Serve chilled on their own, or topped with quenelles of caviar.

FRIED CAULIFLOWER: Coat romanesco (a small, beautiful variety of cauliflower) with either breading (see the recipe on page 277 for guidance on using flour, egg, and bread crumbs) or tempura batter (see page 363) and fry. Toss with spicy tomato sauce (page 147) as an appetizer.

MASHED CAULIFLOWER: Caramelize cauliflower as in the sardine recipe (page 88), transfer to a mixing bowl, add 1 tablespoon extra-virgin olive oil, and mash with a potato masher. Season with salt and white pepper and serve as a side to braised meats.

Spicy Duck Meatballs
with Water Spinach, Mint Cavatelli, Parmesan Cheese, and Quail Egg

Pasta and meatballs as you've never had them before: this is a rich and spicy composition that could easily be served on its own as a small lunch. (I also served it on a *Top Chef* reunion show.) The recipe calls for water spinach, a popular vegetable in Southeast Asian cooking that has qualities similar to both spinach and watercress. If you can find it, it's worth adding to your repertoire because there's nothing else quite like it (otherwise, you can use regular spinach). You will need a cavatelli maker to make the mint pasta, or you can use store-bought plain cavatelli and add an extra tablespoon of mint to the sauce.

1 cup all-purpose flour, plus more for dusting

1 tablespoon fresh ricotta cheese, preferably homemade (see Notebook, page 64)

1 large egg

1 tablespoon minced fresh mint

Kosher salt

Duck Meat Mix (see Notebook, page 95)

8 cups duck stock, preferably homemade (page 367)

1 tablespoon extra-virgin olive oil

1 shallot, thinly sliced

1 cup (loosely packed) chopped water spinach (regular spinach may be substituted)

2 tablespoons thinly sliced fresh mint (if using store-bought cavatelli, add an extra tablespoon)

2 tablespoons finely grated Parmigiano-Reggiano cheese

4 raw quail eggs

To make the cavatelli: Put the flour, ricotta, egg, mint, 1 teaspoon salt, and 1 teaspoon room-temperature water in the bowl of a mixer fitted with the paddle attachment, and paddle just to combine. Set aside for 20 minutes at room temperature. Roll out the dough into ½-inch-wide by ¼-inch-thick strips and run the strips through a cavatelli maker.

▶ To make the meatballs: Line a baking sheet with parchment paper and set aside. Position a rack in the center of the oven and preheat the oven to 425°F. Remove the duck mixture from the refrigerator and use your hands to form the meat into 16 (1½- or 2-inch)

balls and place on the prepared baking sheet. Bake until cooked through, 10 to 15 minutes. Carefully pour the grease off the baking sheet by slightly tipping it over a bowl, not letting the meatballs slide off, and set aside.

▶ Bring the duck stock to a simmer in a large, deep pot over high heat. Add the meatballs to the stock and simmer until the stock has reduced and thickened somewhat, about 20 minutes.

▶ Meanwhile, to cook the cavatelli: Fill a large pot two-thirds full with water, salt it, and bring to a boil over high heat. Add the cavatelli and cook until they float to the

continued

surface, about 1 minute. Drain the pasta in a colander and set aside to cool.

▶ To assemble the dish: Heat the olive oil in a large, heavy saucepan over high heat. When the oil is shimmering, add the shallot and water spinach and cook, stirring with a wooden spoon, for 1 minute. Add the meatballs, cooked cavatelli, and 2 cups of the stock. When the stock simmers, stir in the mint. Season to taste with salt and pepper.

▶ To serve, spoon 4 meatballs into each of 4 wide, shallow bowls, along with the broth and cavatelli. Sprinkle with Parmigiano-Reggiano and top each serving with a quail egg. Serve immediately.

NOTE: You can make the cavatelli up to a day in advance. Blanch and drain the noodles, toss in a little olive oil to keep them from sticking, refrigerate in an airtight container, then reheat in the sauce when ready to serve.

Duck Meat Mix

The assertive flavor of duck makes a wonderful alternative protein in a variety of dishes usually made with ground meat. If you don't have a grinder, ask your butcher to grind the meat for you; do *not* use a food processor or chop by hand.

MAKES ABOUT 1 POUND

1 tablespoon extra-virgin olive oil

1 Spanish onion, minced

5 garlic cloves, minced

1 pound ground duck (leg and thigh meat)

2 tablespoons coarsely chopped fresh basil

2 tablespoons chili sauce, such as sriracha or sambal

¼ cup panko bread crumbs

2 large eggs, lightly beaten

Kosher salt

Freshly ground black pepper

Heat the oil in a large, heavy saucepan over medium heat. When the oil is shimmering, add the onion and half of the garlic and cook, stirring, until the onion is softened but not browned, about 5 minutes. Remove the pan from the heat and set aside to allow the onion and garlic to cool. Once they are cool, stir in the remaining garlic, duck, basil, chili sauce, panko, and eggs, and season with salt and pepper. Use right away or cover with plastic wrap and refrigerate for up to 24 hours.

DUCK BURGERS: Fashion burgers out of the meat and cook as you would a regular hamburger. If grilling, be especially careful of flare-ups due to duck's high fat content. At Perilla, we top these burgers with Jack cheese and avocado, and I suggest you do the same at home.

DUCK ENCHILADAS: Replace the ground beef with the duck mix in your favorite enchilada recipe. Top with grated white cheese such as queso blanco.

DUCK MEAT LOAF: Shape the meat mix into a log on a baking sheet and bake at 350°F for about 1 hour. For a finishing touch, stir a little cumin into ketchup (about 1 tablespoon ground cumin to 1 cup of ketchup) and brush over the meat loaf immediately after removing it from the oven.

DUCK TACOS: Make soft tacos with sautéed duck meat. Pickled red onion (page 100), pico di gallo, and Oaxacan cheese make great condiments.

SPICY DUCK BOLOGNESE: Replace the ground meat with the duck mix in a pasta sauce; toss with fettuccine or linguine.

Crispy Braised Pork Belly

with Pea Tendrils, Trumpet Mushrooms, and Banyuls-Vanilla Gastrique

SERVES 4

Pork belly, also known as "fresh bacon," is a rich, fatty cut that meets its match here: the pork is braised; then one side is floured and browned to a crisp before being plated with soft, sautéed mushrooms and the snap of just-wilted pea tendrils. The sweet-and-sour gastrique also offers relief from the intensely flavored but delicious meat.

---

8 ounces (quarter belly) pork belly, preferably Hampshire pork

1 cup kosher salt, plus more to taste

½ cup sugar

1 tablespoon fennel seeds

1 tablespoon coriander seeds

2 quarts plus ¼ cup chicken stock, preferably homemade (page 366)

4 tablespoons blended oil or neutral oil such as canola

½ cup black trumpet mushrooms (shiitake may be substituted)

Freshly ground white pepper

1 garlic clove, minced

2 cups (loosely packed) pea tendrils

1 tablespoon golden raisins

1 tablespoon unsalted butter

Gastrique (see Notebook, page 98), plus 1 split, scraped vanilla bean added with the braising liquid

---

To cure the pork belly: Put the pork belly on a baking sheet. Stir together the salt, sugar, fennel seeds, and coriander seeds in a small bowl to make a cure. Rub the cure all over the pork belly, cover loosely with plastic wrap, and refrigerate for 24 hours.

▶ When ready to proceed, preheat the oven to 300°F. Rinse the pork belly well with water and pat it dry with paper towels. Transfer it to a large Dutch oven or braising dish and pour 2 quarts of the stock over it. If the stock doesn't cover the pork, add just enough additional stock or water to submerge it. Cover loosely with aluminum foil and braise until tender to a knife tip, about 4 hours, periodically checking to ensure that the liquid is barely simmering. If the stock is bubbling too aggressively, lower the oven temperature by 25 degrees; if it's not simmering at all, increase it by 25 degrees. Remove

the pork from the oven and increase the temperature to 425°F. Use a meat fork or tongs to transfer the pork belly to a cutting board. Reserve 1 quart of the braising liquid for the gastrique, straining it through a fine-mesh strainer set over a large bowl; discard the remainder.

▶ When the pork belly is cool enough to handle, about 30 minutes, cut off most of the excess fat, leaving a layer about ¼ inch thick. Slice the pork belly into 4 equal cubes. Heat 2 tablespoons of the oil in a large ovenproof saucepan over medium heat. When the oil is shimmering, add the pork belly to the pan, fat side down, and cook until crisp, 5 to 6 minutes. Transfer the pan to the oven and heat the pork belly until it is warmed through, 3 to 5 minutes.

▶ Meanwhile, heat the remaining 2 tablespoons oil in a large saucepan over medium heat. When the oil is shimmering, add the mushrooms, season with salt and pepper, and cook, stirring with a wooden spoon, until golden brown, about 2 minutes. Stir in the garlic, pea tendrils, and raisins and cook for 1 minute. Stir in the remaining ¼ cup stock and the butter and season generously with salt and pepper. Cook, stirring, until the liquid has evaporated, about 2 minutes.

▶ Divide the mushroom mixture among 4 plates and top each with a pork belly cube. Drizzle with the gastrique and serve.

Gastrique

A gastrique is a sweet-and-sour reduction made by cooking red wine and sugar together. It can be used just like that, or with an addition of stock for a more sauce-like effect. It's a relatively easy way to create an intense finishing element that emphasizes the flavor of the protein being served while also bringing acidity and sweetness to the plate. The recipe below is made with Banyuls vinegar, with the adaptations that follow substituting other vinegars to achieve various effects.

GASTRIQUE

MAKES ABOUT 1 CUP

1 quart veal stock, preferably homemade (page 368), or braising liquid (if braising the meat being served with the gastrique), optional, skimmed of fat

½ cup sugar

1 (250-ml) bottle Banyuls vinegar

If using stock or braising liquid, pour it into a large saucepan and bring to a simmer over medium-high heat. Simmer until reduced by half, about 20 minutes. (If not using stock or braising liquid, the gastrique is simply the sugar-vinegar reduction.)

▸ Cook the sugar and vinegar in a separate large saucepan over medium-high heat, whisking, until the mixture has reduced stock or and is starting to bubble, about 15 minutes. Whisk in the reduced stock or braising liquid, if using, and return to a simmer. Cook until the liquid is reduced by half, about 15 minutes.

FISH SAUCE GASTRIQUE: See the squab recipe on page 284.

CINNAMON-SHERRY GASTRIQUE: Make the gastrique with 1 cup sherry vinegar instead of Banyuls. Add a cinnamon stick, remove from the heat, and set aside for 30 minutes to infuse the gastrique. Just before serving, remove and discard the cinnamon stick and reheat the gastrique. Serve with sautéed foie gras.

RED WINE VINEGAR GASTRIQUE: Use 2 cups red wine vinegar instead of Banyuls. Serve with roasted veal.

RICE VINEGAR–GINGER GASTRIQUE: Instead of Banyuls, use 1 cup rice vinegar, 1 tablespoon ginger juice (page 116), and 1 quart chicken stock (page 366) instead of veal stock. Serve with roasted poultry and fish.

CIDER VINEGAR AND APPLES: Use 1 cup apple cider vinegar instead of Banyuls, and pork stock or chicken stock instead of veal stock. Toss in peeled, diced Honeycrisp apples during the final minute of reduction. Serve with pork.

Beef Brisket Pressé

with Pickled Pearl Onions, Frisée, and Red Cabbage Mostarda

SERVES 4

By braising the fatty meat, then pressing it and cutting it into squares, this recipe makes brisket, usually assumed to be the stuff of main courses and barbecues, ideal for a starter. The beefy flavor is cut by the pickling juice in the salad and the sweet-and-sour red cabbage mostarda. The brisket, pickled onions, and cabbage can all be prepared well ahead of time, making this an ideal recipe for entertaining.

The pickled onions bring flavor bursts to this dish and to any dish you add them to. Slice and toss them into salads, or make a muffuletta mix (see page 169) with them and use it on sandwiches featuring cured and aged meats. Also, the pickling liquid can be used with other ingredients: simply replace the ½ cup pearl onions with the fruit or vegetable you want to pickle. To make larger quantities, multiply the recipe accordingly.

2 pounds beef brisket

Kosher salt

Freshly ground black pepper

5 tablespoons blended oil or neutral oil such as canola

½ cup coarsely chopped Spanish onion

¼ cup peeled, coarsely chopped carrot

¼ cup coarsely chopped celery

1 cup dry white wine

1 quart chicken stock, preferably homemade (page 366), plus more as needed

1 tablespoon fresh thyme leaves

2 tablespoons Wondra flour

1 cup (loosely packed) frisée

½ cup Pickled Pearl Onions (recipe follows), plus 1 tablespoon pickling liquid

¼ cup halved (lengthwise) cornichons

6 large flat-leaf parsley leaves

Freshly ground white pepper

1 tablespoon extra-virgin olive oil

4 teaspoons Red Cabbage Mostarda (see Notebook, page 101)

To prepare the brisket: Position a rack in the center of the oven and preheat the oven to 350°F.

▶ Season the brisket generously with salt and black pepper. Heat 2 tablespoons of the blended oil in a casserole or braising dish over high heat. When the oil is shimmering, add the brisket and sear on all sides, using tongs to turn, until a golden crust forms all over, about 8 minutes total cooking time. Transfer the brisket to a plate and set it aside.

▶ Add the onion, carrot, and celery to the same pan. Cook, stirring with a wooden spoon, until the vegetables are softened but not browned, about 3 minutes. Pour in the wine and cook, stirring with a wooden spoon

continued

to loosen any flavorful bits from the bottom of the pan. Bring to a simmer and continue to simmer until the liquid is reduced by half, about 6 minutes. Pour in the stock and return to a simmer. Return the brisket to the pan, being sure the meat is completely covered in the liquid (if not submerged, add enough additional stock or water to cover). Cover the pan with a lid or aluminum foil, transfer to the oven, and braise in the oven until the meat is fork-tender, about 2 hours, periodically checking to ensure that the liquid is barely simmering. If it is bubbling too aggressively, lower the oven temperature by 25 degrees; if it is not simmering at all, increase it by 25 degrees.

▶ When the meat is done, use the tongs to remove the brisket from the braising liquid and transfer it to a plate to cool completely, about 30 minutes. When it is cool enough to handle, pick the meat apart, removing all the fat and tendons.

▶ Strain the broth through a fine-mesh strainer set over a large bowl. Discard the solids and return the liquid to the pan over medium-high heat. Bring the liquid to a simmer and continue to simmer until reduced to 1 cup, about 15 minutes, periodically skimming any fat from the top with a spoon.

▶ Transfer the picked meat to a bowl, add the reduced liquid and the thyme, and fold together. Taste and adjust the seasoning, if needed.

▶ Line the bottom of a shallow plastic food container, wide and deep enough to hold the brisket in a single layer, with plastic wrap. Set the meat in it, and top with another piece of plastic wrap and a vessel of the same or similar size. Apply pressure to the top vessel to press the meat, adding heavy objects such as canned food to help weight down the meat. Cover loosely with plastic wrap. Refrigerate like so until the meat is very firm, at least 2 hours, or preferably overnight. Once it is firm, remove the brisket from the container and cut it into 4 equal cubes, about 3 inches each.

▶ To serve, preheat the oven to 425°F. Season the beef cubes generously with salt and pepper. Put the flour in a wide, shallow bowl. Dredge one side of each beef cube in the flour. Heat the remaining 3 tablespoons blended oil in a large, ovenproof saucepan over medium heat. When the oil is shimmering, add the beef cubes, floured side down, and cook until golden brown and crispy, about 2 minutes. Transfer the pan to the oven and bake until the beef is heated through, about 7 minutes.

▶ Meanwhile, put the frisée, pickled pearl onions, cornichons, and parsley in a large bowl. Season with salt and white pepper and drizzle with the pickling liquid and olive oil. Toss to dress the salad.

▶ Set 1 beef cube in the center of each of 4 small plates. Top each serving with 1 teaspoon red cabbage mostarda and surround with salad.

Pickled Pearl Onions

MAKES ABOUT ½ CUP

½ cup red pearl onions
1 cup rice vinegar
2 tablespoons sugar
2 tablespoons kosher salt

Put the pearl onions in a medium, heatproof bowl.

▶ Put the vinegar, sugar, and salt in a medium, heavy saucepan and bring to a boil over medium-high heat, stirring to dissolve the sugar and salt. Pour the liquid over the pearl onions and cover the bowl with plastic wrap. Allow to cool to room temperature, then transfer to the refrigerator and chill for at least 2 hours. The onions may be refrigerated in an airtight container for up to 1 week.

Red Cabbage

Most foods are called on for their flavor, but I find that red cabbage, although it has a gently mustardy quality, is most useful for its crunchy texture, and it also brings a vibrant color to many plates.

RED CABBAGE SLAW: Substitute shredded red cabbage for other varieties in your favorite coleslaw recipe.

CURED RED CABBAGE: Use this sweet-and-sour cabbage anywhere you'd use sauerkraut, such as in a Reuben sandwich, alongside sausage, or on a hot dog. See the recipe on page 300.

RED CABBAGE MOSTARDA: To make red cabbage mostarda, a condiment that's delicious alongside boiled and roasted meats, put 2 cups coarsely chopped red cabbage, 2 cups red wine vinegar, ¼ cup honey (preferably clover), and 2 tablespoons yellow mustard seeds in a wide, deep sauté pan, and season with salt and pepper. Bring to a simmer, then lower the heat and cook, stirring occasionally, until the liquid is totally evaporated and the cabbage and mustard seeds become tacky, about 30 minutes. Allow to cool, then refrigerate in an airtight container for at least 1 hour or up to 1 week.

STUFFED RED CABBAGE: Heat 1 tablespoon extra-virgin olive oil in a large sauté pan over medium-high heat. Add ½ cup minced Spanish onion, 2 tablespoons minced garlic, and 2 cups minced or ground pastrami. Cook, stirring, until lightly browned, about 4 minutes. Stir in ½ cup finely diced, blanched (see page 362) Idaho potato, season with salt and black pepper, and remove the pan from the heat. Arrange 16 large blanched, shocked, and drained red cabbage leaves flat on your work surface. Spoon the pastrami mixture into the center of the cabbage leaves, and roll the leaves up into small parcels. Arrange the parcels in a baking dish, seam side down, and cover generously with spicy tomato sauce (jarred, your own recipe, or the one on page 147, finishing with basil). Cover with aluminum foil and bake at 350°F until hot, about 45 minutes. Remove the foil, grate pecorino Romano cheese over the stuffed cabbage leaves, and serve.

3

Soups

Curried Cauliflower Soup
with Roasted Florets, Toasted Pumpkin Seeds, and Golden Raisins

SERVES 4

Cauliflower and curry are a match made in heaven, and this soup brings them together with the complementary sweetness of golden raisins and toasted pumpkin seeds. It's a Thanksgiving favorite in my family and my sneaky way of easing everybody into loving curry, which, though subtly employed here, makes an unmistakable impression.

1 large head cauliflower

2 tablespoons extra-virgin olive oil

Kosher salt

Freshly ground white pepper

2 tablespoons blended oil or neutral oil such as canola

1 shallot, thinly sliced

2 garlic cloves, thinly sliced

3 tablespoons Madras curry powder

1 quart vegetable stock, preferably homemade (page 365)

1 tablespoon unsalted butter

1 teaspoon rice vinegar

2 tablespoons golden raisins

2 tablespoons Toasted Pumpkin Seeds (see Notebook, page 105)

1 tablespoon minced chives

Cut off and discard the cauliflower's stem and remove the core. Separate the cauliflower into florets. Set ½ cup small florets aside for garnish. Reserve the remaining florets (about 2½ cups) separately, cutting the larger florets in half lengthwise.

▶ Warm the olive oil in a large sauté pan over medium heat. When the oil is shimmering, add the ½ cup small cauliflower florets and season with salt and pepper. Cook, stirring, until the cauliflower is golden brown and tender, about 5 minutes. Transfer to a small heatproof bowl and set aside.

▶ Heat the blended oil in a Dutch oven or large soup pot over medium heat. When the oil is shimmering, add the remaining 2½ cups cauliflower florets, the shallot, and the garlic, and cook, stirring, until the cauliflower is glistening but not browned, about 5 minutes. Add the curry powder, season with salt and pepper, stir, and cook until fragrant, about 1 minute. Pour in the stock and bring to a boil. Lower the heat and simmer until the cauliflower is soft to a knife tip, about 10 minutes. Transfer the contents of the pan to a blender and blend, in batches if necessary, adding the butter and vinegar, until a smooth purée forms, about 45 seconds. Strain through a fine-mesh strainer into a large bowl.

▶ To serve, gently stir the reserved sautéed cauliflower florets and golden raisins into the soup. Divide among 4 soup bowls and scatter pumpkin seeds and chives over each.

Toasted Pumpkin seeds

Most of us think of seeds as something to snack on away from the dinner table, and so we are pleasantly surprised when they show up in savory or sweet dishes. Sunflower seeds are probably most familiar, but I find that pumpkin seeds add a gentle sweetness and, when toasted, substantial crunch to a variety of recipes. They also act as wonderful vehicles for salt and pepper, packing a lot of flavor and spice into each bite.

MAKES 2 TABLESPOONS

2 tablespoons pumpkin seeds

1 tablespoon extra-virgin olive oil

Kosher salt

Freshly ground white pepper

Preheat the oven to 400°F. Put the pumpkin seeds and oil in a small bowl and toss to coat with the oil. Season with salt and pepper and spread the seeds out on a baking sheet in a single layer. Bake, shaking the baking sheet occasionally to ensure even cooking and prevent scorching, until the seeds are golden brown, about 5 minutes. Remove the baking sheet from the oven and allow the nuts to cool completely, about 10 minutes, before using or storing in an airtight container at room temperature for up to 1 week.

SNACKING AND SCATTERING: These seeds make a satisfying snack on their own and are a go-to garnish to have in your repertoire for scattering over salads and soups.

PUMPKIN SEED OIL: Use pumpkin seed oil in salad dressings or drizzle it over soups. To make it, heat ½ cup neutral oil such as grapeseed oil in a pot over medium-high heat. When the oil is shimmering, add ½ cup toasted pumpkin seeds, turn off the heat, cover, and allow to steep overnight. Strain and use or store in an airtight container at room temperature for up to 1 month.

PUMPKIN SEED BUTTER: Fold puréed toasted pumpkin seeds into room-temperature butter (use 25 percent as much pumpkin seed by volume as butter) with a rubber spatula. Fold into autumnal risottos and pastas just before serving to melt the butter and transmit its flavor.

PUMPKIN SEED PRALINE: Though the pumpkin seeds are not toasted in this preparation, making a praline of pumpkin seeds (see page 83) creates a cool, crowd-pleasing garnish for salads and soups.

Tomato and Garam Masala Soup
with Yellow Lentils, Basil, and Tofu

SERVES 4

This vegetarian soup is based on a braised chicken dish I had in Chiang Mai, Thailand. I visited the city at the end of a two-week exploration of the country, during which my heat tolerance was put to the test. But the garam masala mix that was at the heart of the dish was different, acting more as a seasoning than as a heat-generating spice, and conjuring a sweet-and-sour effect. Made with tofu instead of meat, this is a very virtuous dish that leaves you satisfied but not uncomfortably full.

1 tablespoon yellow lentils

1 tablespoon blended oil or neutral oil such as canola

10 plum tomatoes, thinly sliced, with their seeds

2 shallots, thinly sliced

4 garlic cloves, thinly sliced

2 tablespoons garam masala (see Sources, page 370)

Kosher salt

Freshly ground white pepper

1 quart vegetable stock, preferably homemade (page 365)

2 tablespoons freshly squeezed lemon juice

1 tablespoon sugar

2 tablespoons diced silken tofu

8 large fresh basil leaves

Put the lentils and enough water to cover in a small, heavy saucepan over medium heat, bring to a simmer, and continue to simmer until the lentils are tender, about 20 minutes. Strain through a fine-mesh strainer and rinse with cold water to wash off the starch. Set aside, covered, to keep the lentils warm.

▸ Heat the oil in a Dutch oven or large soup pot over medium-high heat. When the oil is shimmering, add the tomatoes, shallots, and garlic, and cook, stirring, until softened but not browned, about 4 minutes. Stir in the garam masala and season with salt and pepper. Cook, stirring, until fragrant, about 2 minutes. Pour in the stock. Bring to a simmer, then lower the heat and simmer until the tomatoes are broken down and the flavors have mingled, about 15 minutes. Transfer the contents of the pan to a blender, in batches if necessary, and add the lemon juice and sugar. Blend until smooth, about 30 seconds, then strain through a fine-mesh strainer back into a large bowl, pressing down on the solids with a rubber spatula or the bottom of a ladle to extract as much soup as possible.

▸ To serve, stir the lentils, tofu, and basil into the soup, and divide among 4 soup bowls.

Garam Masala Soups

Garam masala is a very mild spice blend in which the flavors meld into something like a sweet-and-sour soup. The soup on page 106 can be adapted, replacing the tomatoes with different vegetables. In all of the variations, you can vary the thickness of the soup according to your personal taste by blending in ½ to 1 cup additional stock.

AUTUMN SQUASH (BUTTERNUT, KABOCHA, OR HUBBARD): Sauté about 1½ cups peeled, diced squash in a neutral oil such as canola in a wide, deep sauté pan over medium-high heat until very soft, then purée in a blender and substitute for the tomatoes in the preceding soup recipe (page 106), cooking for about 30 minutes. Garnish with toasted squash seeds (adapt the method on page 105) and small cubes of additional roasted, diced squash.

SWEET POTATO: Follow the steps for autumn squash above, replacing the squash with sweet potato. Garnish with candied pecans.

TURNIP: Follow the steps for autumn squash to the left, replacing the squash with turnips. For a Southern twist, garnish with the turnip greens, wilted in a little olive oil, and dressed at the last second with pepper vinegar.

ZUCCHINI: Follow the steps for autumn squash to the left, replacing the squash with zucchini. Garnish with fried zucchini blossoms made using Tempura Batter (page 363).

Heirloom Tomato and Watermelon Gazpacho
with Confit Shrimp and Cucumber

This gazpacho takes advantage of the natural affinity between two summer staples: tomatoes and watermelon. It's a soup that can really be made only in that season, when its primary ingredients are at the peak of ripeness; in fact, the better and fresher your tomatoes and watermelon, the more delicious this gazpacho will be. I incorporate a little Korean pepper paste and cilantro for a subtle Asian inflection that makes this dish just a little more surprising to the palate.

---

2 tomatillos, peeled

1 red onion, halved

1 jalapeño pepper

2 tablespoons blended oil or neutral oil such as canola

2 cups chopped heirloom tomatoes (about 2 tomatoes)

2 cups coarsely chopped seedless watermelon, plus 1 tablespoon diced watermelon

3 tablespoons extra-virgin olive oil

1 tablespoon sherry vinegar

2 tablespoons freshly squeezed lime juice

1 tablespoon Korean pepper paste

Kosher salt

Freshly ground black pepper

2 tablespoons rice vinegar

8 large or jumbo shrimp, about 1 ounce each, peeled

1 tablespoon seeded, diced hothouse cucumber

½ cup halved grape tomatoes

2 teaspoons minced shallot

2 teaspoons roasted slivered almonds

2 teaspoons thinly sliced cilantro

2 teaspoons celery leaves

Preheat a grill or a grill pan over high heat for 5 minutes. (See pages 274–75 for grilling guidelines.)

▶ Put the tomatillos, red onion, jalapeño, and blended oil in a large bowl and toss to coat the vegetables with the oil. Arrange the vegetables in an even layer on the grill and grill until the vegetables are charred and tender, turning them as they char, about 6 minutes for the jalapeño, 10 minutes for the tomatillos, and 18 minutes for the onion. Transfer the grilled vegetables to a blender and add the tomatoes, coarsely chopped watermelon, 2 tablespoons of the olive oil, the sherry vinegar, 1 tablespoon of the lime juice, the pepper paste, and 1 tablespoon water. Purée until smooth, about 1 minute. Season with salt and pepper, if necessary. Strain through a fine-mesh strainer set over a bowl, pressing down on the solids with a rubber spatula or the back of a ladle to extract as much liquid as possible, and refrigerate until chilled, about 1 hour.

▶ To prepare the shrimp: Bring 1 quart water, the rice vinegar, and 1 tablespoon salt to a simmer in a large saucepan set over medium-high heat. Remove the pan from the heat and add the shrimp. Cook until they turn pink and just begin to curl, about 4 minutes. Use a slotted spoon to transfer the shrimp to a plate.

continued

Refrigerate until cooled, then devein and split the shrimp lengthwise.

▸ To serve, put the shrimp, the remaining 1 tablespoon olive oil, the diced cucumber, grape tomatoes, minced watermelon, shallot, almonds, cilantro, and celery leaves in a medium bowl and toss to incorporate. Divide the gazpacho among 4 chilled soup bowls. Top with the cucumber-tomato-watermelon garnish and serve.

Watermelon

As far as I'm concerned, nothing says summer like watermelon. It's fresh, juicy, slightly sweet, and crunchy, all of which makes it fun to eat on its own, *and* to play around with in recipes. Here are a few of my favorite ways to use it in both sweet and savory dishes:

WATERMELON COOLER: Make this cocktail by putting 1½ ounces vodka, 2 Thai basil leaves (cut into chiffonade; see page 362), and 1½ ounces puréed seedless watermelon in a shaker and shaking. Pour into a rocks glass filled with ice. Finish with soda water.

WATERMELON CHIMICHURRI SALAD: My version of the Argentinean green sauce takes an Asian turn and becomes a dressing for watermelon and jicama: Put 1 cup each diced yellow seedless watermelon, diced red seedless watermelon, and peeled and julienned jicama, and 1 tablespoon crumbled feta cheese in a large bowl. To make a dressing, put 2 tablespoons freshly squeezed lime juice, 1 tablespoon sliced perilla (also known as shiso), 2 teaspoons sliced Thai or regular basil, 2 teaspoons pickled green peppercorns, and 2 tablespoons extra-virgin olive oil in a blender and blend until smooth. Season the watermelon-jicama mixture with salt, add 1 cup baby greens to the bowl, drizzle the dressing over it, and toss to coat. Divide among individual plates and serve.

WATERMELON GREEK SALAD: Toss cubes of seedless watermelon into your favorite Greek salad recipe. It provides a surprisingly complementary flavor to salty components such as feta cheese and marinated black olives.

WATERMELON SORBET: Put 1 cup sugar, ½ cup water, and ¼ cup freshly squeezed lemon juice in a medium saucepan over medium-high heat and cook, stirring, until the sugar dissolves, about 5 minutes. Transfer to a temperature-proof vessel and chill in the refrigerator until cold, about 30 minutes. Transfer to the blender, add 3 cups diced seedless watermelon, and purée until all the watermelon breaks down, about 1 minute. Strain through a fine-mesh strainer set over a large bowl, pressing down on the solids with a rubber spatula or the bottom of a ladle to extract as much flavorful liquid as possible. Transfer the mixture to an ice cream machine and freeze according to the manufacturer's instructions.

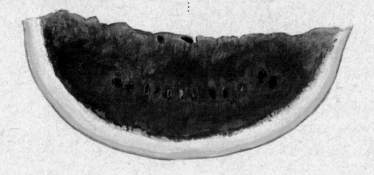

Lobster Bisque
with Snipped Chives and Brandy

For my money, lobster bisque is a perfect soup because of the intensity of lobster flavor and the way it's complemented by brandy (in the stock) and cream; it's a coming together of ingredients that simply seem meant for each other. Though it's based upon a luxury ingredient, it does boast some economy, as making the lobster stock yields just enough meat for the bisque.

Homemade Lobster Stock and reserved lobster meat from stock making (page 366)

¼ cup Wondra flour

1 cup heavy cream

Kosher salt

Freshly ground white pepper

4 tablespoons (½ stick) unsalted butter, cut in pieces

Freshly squeezed lemon juice

1 teaspoon minced chives

Heat the stock in a large pot over medium heat, about 5 minutes. When the stock simmers, whisk in the flour, then the heavy cream. Cook, whisking occasionally, until nicely thickened, about 15 minutes. Season with salt and pepper and whisk in the butter. Strain the soup through a fine-mesh sieve and add lemon juice to taste.

▷ To serve, stir the lobster meat into the soup and heat until warmed through, about 5 minutes. Divide the bisque among 4 bowls and garnish with a scattering of chives.

Bisque

Lobster is the most popular type of bisque, but the soup can be adapted to include almost any shellfish. Here are some of my favorites:

CLAM BISQUE: Steam 2 dozen small clams, such as littlenecks, in a mixture of 1 cup white wine, 1 sliced shallot, and 1 smashed garlic clove. Discard any clams that do not open. From those that do, remove the meat, discard the shells, and substitute for the lobster in the recipe on the facing page. Replace the lobster stock with 2 quarts bottled clam juice.

SHRIMP: Substitute the lobster in the recipe on the facing page with 1 pound peeled, deveined shrimp, preferably white tiger, Mayan, or rock shrimp; replace the lobster stock with 2 quarts shellfish stock (page 367). Allow the shrimp to gently poach in the bisque for the last 2 or 3 minutes of cooking, until firm and pink.

MUSSELS: Substitute the lobster in the recipe on the facing page with 2 pounds mussels (see page 191), preferably Prince Edward Island or Bouchot (cooking them the same way as the clams, at left). Replace the lobster stock with 2 quarts shellfish stock (page 367), adding the mussel cooking liquid to the stock.

OYSTERS: Substitute the lobster in the recipe on the facing page with 1 dozen shucked oysters (see page 67), preferably East Coast or Blue Point, reserving the liquor. Replace the lobster stock with 2 quarts clam broth, stirring in the oyster liquor. Poach the oysters in the bisque until plumped and cooked through.

Steamed Pork Meatball Soup

with Fried Garlic, Bok Choy, and Black Soy

There's a symbiotic relationship between the meatballs and broth in this recipe, each imbuing the other with its flavors. This is a useful soup when you're under the weather, because the spice and salty soy are very invigorating and soothing. The fried garlic is not made at home but rather a high-value garnish available for purchase (see Sources, page 370).

3 tablespoons blended oil or neutral oil such as canola

2 garlic cloves, minced

2 tablespoons peeled, minced fresh ginger

1 pound ground pork (preferably pork shoulder)

½ cup panko bread crumbs

1 large egg

¼ cup sriracha sauce

1 tablespoon thinly sliced Thai basil (regular basil may be substituted)

Kosher salt

Freshly ground white pepper

1 quart chicken stock, preferably homemade (page 366)

1 tablespoon fish sauce

1 tablespoon black sweet soy sauce

2 baby bok choy, quartered through the root

1 tablespoon fried garlic

To make the meatballs: Preheat the oven to 400°F. Line a baking sheet with parchment paper and set aside.

▶ Heat 2 tablespoons of the oil in a large, heavy sauté pan over medium heat. When the oil is shimmering, add the fresh garlic and 1 tablespoon of the ginger and cook until softened but not browned, about 2 minutes. Use a slotted spoon to transfer the garlic and ginger to a medium bowl, leaving the oil behind, and set aside to cool for 6 minutes. Add the pork, bread crumbs, egg, sriracha, and basil to the bowl. Season with salt and pepper and mix by hand just until incorporated.

▶ Roll the meat mixture into 16 balls, each about the size of a golf ball, and place a few inches apart on the prepared baking sheet. Bake until the meatballs are cooked through (a paring knife inserted into the center of a meatball will be warm to the touch when removed;

or test with a meat thermometer, stopping cooking after they register 145°F, being careful not to overcook them because they will be braised in the soup), about 15 minutes. Remove the sheet from the oven and set aside.

▶ To make the soup: Heat the remaining 1 tablespoon oil in a Dutch oven or large soup pot over medium heat. When the oil is shimmering, add the remaining 1 tablespoon ginger and cook until fragrant, about 1 minute. Pour in the stock and bring to a simmer, then stir in the fish sauce and soy sauce. Add the cooked meatballs to the pot. Simmer them in the liquid, adjusting the heat as necessary to prevent the liquid from boiling, about 20 minutes. Stir in the bok choy and cook until tender, about 2 minutes more.

▶ To serve, divide the soup, bok choy, and meatballs equally among 4 bowls. Garnish with fried garlic and serve.

Ginger

Ginger delivers a potent, peppery burst of flavor in whatever form you use it. Most of us probably first had ginger in pickled form, alongside sushi, where it blasts the palate clean between bites of different types of fish. That's just one use for it among many, both savory and sweet.

CANDIED GINGER: To make candied ginger, put peeled, sliced fresh ginger in a small pot and add enough cold water to cover it. Bring to a boil, then strain. Repeat 2 times. While the ginger is still warm, finish with a dusting of sugar, preferably superfine, and toss to coat.

GINGER JUICE: Ginger juice electrifies vinaigrettes (see the recipe on page 323 for an example) and cocktails and brings a little something extra to sauces (whisk it in at the end). To make ginger juice, run cubes of unpeeled fresh ginger through a juicer; alternatively, mince or process it, wrap it in cheesecloth, and wring the ends over a bowl to extract the juice.

GINGER SYRUP: Make a simple syrup by simmering 1 cup sugar and 1 cup water together in a small saucepan over medium-high heat, whisking, until the sugar has dissolved. Add a 1-inch slice of unpeeled fresh ginger to the pot, cover, remove from the heat, and steep for 4 hours. Strain and use in cocktails or in the base for berry sorbets, especially blueberry and blackberry.

GINGER TEA: For a caffeine-free tea that many believe aids digestion, steep slices of fresh ginger in hot water for 5 to 10 minutes and strain.

Squid Ink Soup

with Brisket-Stuffed Squid, Green Beans, and Hot Sesame Oil

SERVES 4

Inspired by a squid-based soup with ground beef that I first tasted on Ko Samui, a Thai island, this variation features squid stuffed with braised brisket for a compelling mix of earth and sea. This recipe calls for shrimp paste in oil; this is not the paste made from the shrimp itself, but rather the lesser-known type made from shells, tomalley, and roe minced together (see Sources, page 370).

---

2 tablespoons blended oil or neutral oil such as canola

3 teaspoons minced lemongrass (see page 362)

3 teaspoons minced shallot

3 teaspoons minced garlic

3 teaspoons peeled, minced fresh ginger

2 tablespoons shrimp paste in oil

1 quart shellfish stock, preferably homemade (page 367)

¼ cup squid ink

1 tablespoon plus 2 teaspoons fish sauce

8 ounces ground beef brisket

1 tablespoon sambal

1 teaspoon freshly ground white pepper

4 squid, heads and tubes separated, cleaned

2 tablespoons chopped green beans

1 tablespoon hot sesame oil

To make the squid ink soup: Heat 1 tablespoon of the blended oil in a Dutch oven or large soup pot over medium heat. When the oil is shimmering, add 2 teaspoons of the lemongrass, 2 teaspoons of the shallot, 2 teaspoons of the garlic, and 2 teaspoons of the ginger and cook, stirring, until softened but not browned, about 2 minutes. Add the shrimp paste and cook, stirring, until fragrant, about 2 minutes. Pour in the stock and bring it to a simmer, then stir in the squid ink and 1 tablespoon of the fish sauce and simmer until the flavors are mingled, about 20 minutes. Check the seasoning and add more fish sauce if necessary. Set aside; cover to keep warm while you make the stuffed squid.

▷ To make the stuffed squid: Warm the remaining 1 tablespoon blended oil in a small sauté pan over medium heat. When the oil is shimmering, add the remaining 1 teaspoon lemongrass, remaining 1 teaspoon shallot, remaining 1 teaspoon garlic, and remaining 1 teaspoon ginger and cook, stirring, until softened but not browned, about 2 minutes. Transfer to a medium heatproof bowl and set aside to cool, about 6 minutes. Once the mixture has cooled, add the beef brisket, sambal, and pepper and stir to incorporate. Use your hands to stuff the brisket mixture inside the squid tubes and set the tubes in a steamer basket.

continued

▶ Set the steamer basket over a medium saucepan with about an inch of simmering water over medium-high heat, and cover. Steam the stuffed squid tubes until the brisket is cooked through, about 5 minutes. Slice the tubes into 1-inch rounds and divide the rounds among 4 soup bowls.

▶ To serve, reheat the soup over medium-high heat until hot, about 2 minutes, and add the squid heads. Cook for 2 minutes, then stir in the green beans. Cook for 1 minute more, then divide the soup among 4 bowls and drizzle with sesame oil just before serving.

NOTE: The hot sesame oil can be replaced by sesame oil gently warmed and infused with Thai chiles, then strained. If you don't like heat, you can just substitute regular sesame oil.

Green Beans

If you're like me, then green beans were a part of your childhood—a ubiquitous vegetable served with things like roasted chicken and meat loaf. They're delicious like that, but green beans also have tremendous potential beyond being steamed or sautéed and served with melted butter. It's important to differentiate between thicker, sturdier string beans and longer, thinner, more delicate beans such as haricots verts or long beans. For a light sauté with melted butter, I like the latter, but for, say, deep-frying, the heartier texture of a string bean is required.

CHILLED GREEN BEAN SALAD: Cook and shock string beans (see page 362), then drain and chill in the refrigerator. Toss with green goddess dressing and sliced red onion. Top with skin-on slivered almonds.

BLISTERED GREEN BEANS: Heat 6 inches of oil in a wide, deep pot over medium-high heat to 350°F. When the oil is shimmering, fry the string beans (with no batter) until golden brown. Drain on paper towels, season immediately with salt and pepper, and dress with *tonnato* sauce (page 240). If desired, top with toasted bread crumbs.

GLAZED GREEN BEANS: Bring a half inch of chicken stock to a simmer in a wide, deep sauté pan over medium-high heat. Add sliced shallots and 1 tablespoon butter, along with haricots verts, and simmer gently until the beans are cooked through and the liquid has reduced to a glaze, about 7 minutes, being sure it does not over-reduce and become syrupy. Serve the beans as a side to grilled or roasted meats or duck.

GREEN BEAN PURÉE: In a wide, deep sauté pan, cook coarsely chopped raw string beans in brown butter with a generous amount of tarragon. Purée, then pass through a strainer and chill in a bowl over ice water. Serve with fish or shellfish.

He-Crab Soup

with Chives, Dill, Sherry, and Homemade Oyster Crackers

This is my variation on a South Carolina she-crab dish, assertively flavored with Old Bay seasoning and sweet sherry. It's called a "he-crab" soup because I don't use female crabs—having grown up on Long Island, I saw the crab population dwindle firsthand, so I don't think a bowl of soup is worth diminishing it further. The intense crab essence comes from frying the crab mustard—the innards.

¼ cup plus 1 tablespoon extra-virgin olive oil

12 male blue crabs, top shell removed, crab mustard reserved (8 ounces crabmeat)

4 garlic cloves, minced

1 Spanish onion, coarsely chopped

1 plum tomato, sliced

½ cup dry white wine

1 teaspoon Old Bay seasoning

1 cup sweet sherry

½ cup heavy cream

1 tablespoon Wondra flour

Kosher salt

Freshly ground white pepper

1 teaspoon minced dill

1 tablespoon minced chives

½ cup Oyster Crackers (see Notebook, page 123)

To make the crab stock: Heat ¼ cup of the oil in a Dutch oven or large, heavy soup pot over medium heat. When the oil is shimmering, add the crabs and fry, stirring constantly, until the shells are bright red, about 5 minutes. Add the garlic, onion, and tomato and cook, stirring, until all the vegetables are softened, about 3 minutes. Pour in the white wine, stirring with a wooden spoon to loosen any flavorful bits from the bottom of the pot. Bring to boil and continue to boil until the liquid has reduced by half, about 2 minutes. Add 3 quarts water and return to a boil. Lower the heat and simmer until reduced by nearly half (you will have about 6 cups), about 45 minutes. Strain through a fine-mesh strainer set over a large bowl. Remove the crabs and pick out the crabmeat. Reserve the meat and liquid separately.

▸ To make the soup: Heat the remaining 1 tablespoon oil in a Dutch oven or large soup pot over medium heat. When the oil is shimmering, add the crab mustard and cook, stirring, for 2 minutes. Sprinkle in the Old Bay and stir to incorporate. Pour in the sherry, stirring to loosen any flavorful bits from the bottom of the pan, and simmer until the liquid has reduced by half, about 6 minutes. Pour in the crab stock and heavy cream and stir to incorporate. Simmer until the crab flavor has intensified, about 15 minutes. Add the flour gradually, whisking vigorously until incorporated. Season with salt and pepper and continue to simmer for 10 minutes.

▸ To serve, fold in the crabmeat and dill and heat until the crabmeat is warmed through. Divide the soup among 4 bowls. Sprinkle with chives and oyster crackers and serve.

Homemade Oyster Crackers

It may surprise you how close these come to your favorite store-bought oyster crackers, even surpassing them with the added enhancement of Old Bay seasoning. The trade-off is that, unlike store-bought crackers, these need to be used shortly after they are made; otherwise, they will deflate.

MAKES ABOUT ½ CUP

1 cup all-purpose flour, plus more for dusting

2 teaspoons Old Bay seasoning

1 teaspoon granulated sugar

1 teaspoon baking powder

Kosher salt

2 tablespoons chilled unsalted butter, cut into small pieces

Put the flour, Old Bay seasoning, sugar, and baking powder in a medium bowl and season with salt. Use your hands to work the butter into the flour mixture until it resembles a coarse meal. Add ⅓ cup water and gently knead together to form a ball, adding more water as necessary to achieve elasticity. Cover the bowl with plastic wrap and set aside to rest at room temperature for 15 minutes.

▶ Preheat the oven to 375°F. Line a baking sheet with parchment paper. Lightly flour a work surface and remove the dough from the bowl. Use a lightly floured rolling pin to roll the dough into a ⅛-inch-thick round. Use a small (about 1-inch) octagonal ring cutter to cut the dough into crackers. (Octagonal is traditional, but any other 1-inch cutter will work.) Transfer the cut dough to the prepared baking sheet, leaving a small amount of space between crackers. Bake until the crackers are just beginning to brown on the bottom, about 15 minutes. Turn the oven off and open the door slightly. (Propping the door open with a natural wine cork is a good trick for keeping it slightly ajar.) Leave the crackers in the oven to cool for 20 minutes, then remove the baking sheet from the oven and season the crackers with salt. Use the same day.

POTPIE TOPPING: Rather than cut your dough into cracker shapes, punch it into circles, set them raw on top of potpies, and bake until the filling is bubbling and the topping is golden brown and slightly crispy.

COBBLER TOPPING: Add ½ cup sugar to the dough, crumble into nuggets, and use as a cobbler topping. For guidance, see the recipe on page 176.

OYSTER CROUTONS: For a variation on croutons, toss the crackers into salads, or scatter them over the top.

HOMEMADE GOLDFISH: For your own version of the popular Pepperidge Farm snack—a treat that kids will love—add ¼ cup grated Cheddar cheese to the dough, cut into fish shapes (with a small mold if you can find one), and bake.

Grilled Vidalia Onion Soup
with Shiro Dashi and Fluke Quenelles

SERVES 4

This dish is a clean, brothy Japanese play on French onion soup in which the onions are strained out at the end, the cheese is omitted, and fluke quenelles take the place of the giant crouton that traditionally caps the crock. Quenelles are the most traditional element here, and one of the first things I learned to make in cooking school. I love how well they get along in this unusual context.

1 tablespoon blended oil or neutral oil such as canola

4 garlic cloves, thinly sliced

Grilled Vidalia Onions (see Notebook, page 126)

1 cup Madeira

6 cups chicken stock, preferably homemade (page 366)

1 bay leaf

10 whole black peppercorns

4 ounces fluke fillet, diced

1 large egg white

1 tablespoon heavy cream

Kosher salt

Freshly ground white pepper

1 teaspoon minced chives

2 tablespoons shiro dashi

2 tablespoons fresh soybeans, shelled, blanched, and shocked (see page 362)

Heat the oil in a Dutch oven or large soup pot over low heat. When the oil is shimmering, add the garlic and onions and cook, stirring, until the onions are very soft and caramelized, about 15 minutes. Stir in the Madeira and cook, stirring, to loosen any flavorful bits from the bottom of the pot. Increase the heat to medium-high, bring to a simmer, and continue to simmer, stirring occasionally, until the liquid has reduced by half, about 6 minutes. Pour in the chicken stock and increase the heat to medium-high. Return to a simmer, then lower the heat. Meanwhile, put the bay leaf and peppercorns in a piece of cheesecloth and knot it or tie it with butcher's twine; add the sachet to the pot and continue to simmer until the flavors mingle, about 45 minutes.

▶ While the soup is simmering, make the fluke quenelles: Put the fluke, egg white, and heavy cream in a food processor fitted with a steel blade. Season with salt and white pepper and purée to a smooth, fluffy consistency. Transfer the mixture to a mixing bowl, using a rubber spatula to scrape out as much as possible, then use the spatula to fold in the chives. Bring a small saucepan of lightly salted water to a simmer over medium-high heat. Use 2 kitchen spoons to form 8 quenelles out of the fluke mixture. Add the quenelles to the water and gently poach until fluffy and opaque, about 3 minutes. Use a slotted spoon to divide the quenelles among 4 wide, shallow bowls.

▸ When the soup is done, use tongs or a slotted spoon to remove and discard the sachet. Stir in the shiro dashi and season with salt and white pepper. Add the soybeans to the soup and heat until warmed through. Ladle the soup around the quenelles in each bowl and serve.

Grilled Vidalia Onions

Vidalia onions have an understated sweetness that is coaxed out by grilling and nicely contrasted by the char that grilling produces.

MAKES ABOUT 1½ CUPS SLICES

2 Vidalia onions, thinly sliced into rounds

2 tablespoons blended oil or neutral oil such as canola

Kosher salt

Freshly ground white pepper

Heat a grill over high heat. (For grilling guidelines, see pages 274–75. You can also use a cast-iron pan or grill pan, preheating it for 5 minutes.) Put the onions and oil in a large bowl and season with salt and pepper. Toss gently to coat, taking care to keep the onion slices intact. Transfer the onions to the grill and grill until charred, about 3 minutes per side, turning once. The cooked, cooled slices can be refrigerated in an airtight container for up to 24 hours.

FINISHING TOUCH: Serve the onions alongside meat dishes; they are especially delicious strewn over meat loaf.

BITTERSWEET ONION PURÉE: Coarsely chop the Vidalia onions and put them in a medium saucepan over medium-high heat along with 1 minced garlic clove and 1 minced shallot. Add ¼ cup water or vegetable stock and simmer until the stock has reduced and the onions and garlic are very soft. Stir in 1 to 2 tablespoons sherry and continue to cook and stir until it has evaporated. Purée the mixture and serve it alongside meaty fish such as salmon or sturgeon, or serve it as an accompaniment to chicken liver mousse on toast.

SHIRO DASHI GRILLED ONIONS: Shake shiro dashi over the grilled onions and use as a condiment for sandwiches or burgers.

DEEP-FRIED GRILLED ONIONS: Toss the onion rounds in all-purpose flour seasoned with salt and white pepper and deep-fry in a few inches of canola oil heated to 350°F just until golden brown, about 1 minute. Remove immediately with a slotted spoon to keep the onion nicely soft, drain on paper towels, and season with salt. Serve over salads and main courses or snack on them.

German-Style Chicken Noodle Soup
with Pretzel Dumplings, Kale, and Mushrooms

SERVES 4

This is a hearty version of chicken noodle soup fashioned after the German style of cooking I grew up with: in place of noodles, there are pretzel dumplings with a dense texture reminiscent of matzo balls; in place of a tender green, there is sturdy kale; and there are beech mushrooms instead of a more innocuous choice such as white button. Make this on a fall or winter night for an antidote to the chilly weather.

2 cups whole milk, plus more if needed

14 ounces (about 2 cups) finely ground pretzels (8 to 10 large pretzels), preferably hard, Amish-style

2 tablespoons all-purpose flour

2 large eggs

4 tablespoons (½ stick) unsalted butter

¼ cup minced cremini mushrooms

1 shallot, minced

Kosher salt

Freshly ground white pepper

3 teaspoons minced marjoram

1 teaspoon minced flat-leaf parsley

¼ teaspoon cayenne

1 teaspoon Colman's mustard powder

1 tablespoon freshly grated nutmeg

3 tablespoons extra-virgin olive oil

1 shallot, minced

1 cup white beech mushrooms (enoki mushrooms can be substituted)

2 cups (loosely packed) coarsely chopped kale (from about ¼ bunch)

6 cups chicken stock, preferably homemade (page 366)

1 cup cooked, shredded chicken meat (if making your own stock, the recipe will produce more than enough meat)

2 tablespoons porcini powder, preferably homemade (see page 363)

1 tablespoon thinly sliced flat-leaf parsley leaves

To make the pretzel dumplings: Put the milk, pretzels, flour, and eggs in a large bowl. Stir together and set aside, uncovered, at room temperature, for 30 minutes. (It will look like matzo meal.)

▸ Melt the butter in a medium sauté pan over medium heat. When the butter foams, add the cremini mushrooms and half the shallot and cook, stirring, until the vegetables are tender, about 3 minutes. Season with salt and pepper and add the mushroom mixture to the pretzel mixture. Add 1 teaspoon of the marjoram,

and the minced parsley, cayenne, mustard powder, and nutmeg, and stir to incorporate, adding additional milk if necessary to achieve a slightly doughy, sticky texture. Season with salt and pepper and roll into about 20 (2 tablespoon–size) balls.

▸ Grease a large glass baking dish with 2 tablespoons of the olive oil. Bring a large pot of salted water to a simmer. Add the balls to the simmering water, in batches if necessary, and poach until firm, about

continued

4 minutes. Use a slotted spoon to transfer the balls to the prepared baking dish and set aside at room temperature for up to 1 hour.

▶ To make the soup: Heat the remaining 1 tablespoon olive oil in a Dutch oven or large soup pot over medium heat. When the oil is shimmering, add the remaining half shallot and cook, stirring, until slightly softened but not browned, about 1 minute. Add the beech mushrooms and continue to cook until they start to brown, about 2 minutes. Add the kale, season with salt and pepper, and cook, stirring, for 1 minute. Add the chicken stock and bring to a simmer. Simmer until the flavors come together, about 30 minutes. Add the chicken, dumplings, porcini powder, remaining 2 teaspoons marjoram, and the sliced parsley and continue to simmer until the dumplings and chicken are hot, about 3 more minutes. Ladle into 4 soup bowls and serve.

Kale

A vegetable that most Americans didn't pay much attention to for the longest time, kale has made up for lost time in recent years. Now it's one of the "hot" vegetables on restaurant menus—a sturdy, nutritious green that can stand up to other assertive flavors and a variety of cooking methods; plus, it's delicious raw. There are several varieties of kale available; I prefer the most common, lacinato kale.

SUNCHOKE-CREAMED KALE: Use kale in place of spinach in the recipe on page 289.

RAW KALE SALAD WITH *GUANCIALE* VINAIGRETTE AND APPLES: Cook diced *guanciale* in a wide, deep sauté pan over medium heat, stirring, until it renders its fat and is crispy. Remove and reserve the *guanciale*. Add red wine vinegar to the pan, stir, and pour it over thinly shaved red apples, thinly sliced shallots, and kale. Add the reserved *guanciale*, season with salt and pepper, toss well, and serve on its own or as a side dish.

KALE CAESAR: Replace the romaine in the HD Caesar Salad (page 45) with kale.

EGGS FLORENTINE 2.0: Replace the spinach in your favorite eggs Florentine recipe with kale.

FRIED KALE: Batter and fry the kale as the watercress is prepared in the dish on page 27; use it to garnish salads and soups or scatter it over grilled and roasted meats and poultry. It gets along especially well with roasted chicken.

Long Island—Style Cioppino

Cioppino is a tomato-rich shellfish stew, originally adapted from Old World soups by Italians who immigrated to San Francisco. This is my version, made with my favorite shellfish from Long Island, including shrimp, mussels, clams, and blue crab. Unlike a Bay Area cioppino, it does not include finfish, but what really makes this stew "Long Island" to me is the inclusion of cubanelles, also known as frying or fryer peppers, which we grew in my backyard when I was a kid. I've also replaced the traditional toasted sourdough that's served alongside with garlic bread.

¼ cup plus 2 tablespoons extra-virgin olive oil

2 shallots, thinly sliced, plus 2 tablespoons minced shallot

12 littleneck clams, scrubbed clean under cold running water

Kosher salt

Freshly ground white pepper

2 cups dry white wine

1 pound mussels, preferably wild Long Island mussels, scrubbed clean under cold running water

2 tablespoons minced garlic

1 cup diced ripe plum tomatoes, with seeds

¼ cup diced, seeded, roasted fryer peppers (see page 362)

1 quart shellfish stock, preferably homemade (page 367)

1 tablespoon thinly sliced oregano leaves

1 tablespoon thyme leaves

1 teaspoon crushed red pepper flakes

12 large shrimp (about 12 ounces), peeled and deveined

1 tablespoon basil chiffonade (see page 362)

1 cup (about 4 ounces) cleaned blue crabmeat

Garlic Bread (see Notebook, page 133)

Heat 1 tablespoon of the oil in a wide, deep sauté pan over high heat. When the oil is shimmering, add half the sliced shallots and cook, stirring, for 1 minute. Add the clams, season with salt and white pepper, then add 1 cup of the wine. Cover the pan and cook until all the clams have opened, about 6 minutes, very gently shaking the pan occasionally. Use tongs or a slotted spoon to discard any clams that have not opened; reserve the clams and cooking liquid separately. Repeat these steps with the mussels, cooking them for only about 4 minutes and again discarding any that have not opened.

Combine the mussel and clam liquids, then strain out and discard the shallots. Reserve 2½ cups of the liquid and discard any extra. When the clams and mussels are cool enough to handle, in about 8 minutes, shell them and discard the shells. Reserve the meat in a small bowl.

▸ Heat the remaining ¼ cup oil in a large soup pot over medium heat. When the oil is shimmering, add the minced shallot and the garlic and cook, stirring, until softened but not browned, about 1 minute. Stir in the tomatoes and fryer peppers, season with salt and white *continued* pepper, and cook, stirring, for 2 minutes. Add the stock, reserved mussel and clam liquid, oregano, thyme, and red pepper flakes. Bring to a simmer, then lower the heat and continue to simmer for 30 minutes to mingle the flavors. Add the shrimp and basil and cook until the shrimp are pink and firm, about 2 minutes. Stir in the crabmeat, clams, and mussels and cook until hot, about 2 minutes more.

▸ Divide the cioppino among 4 wide shallow bowls, being sure to include a good mix of shellfish in each serving. Serve with a slice of garlic bread perched on the side of each bowl, or alongside on a plate.

Garlic Bread

Buttery garlic bread is simple and universally appealing—and it is the ultimate dunking bread for pasta sauces. It's also one of the first things I ever learned to make as a kid, fashioning pizzas out of it with jarred tomato sauce and shredded mozzarella.

MAKES 4 SLICES

2 tablespoons unsalted butter, softened at room temperature

1 garlic clove, minced

Kosher salt

Freshly ground white pepper

4 thick slices Italian bread

Preheat the oven to 400°F. Put the butter and garlic in a medium bowl, season with salt and pepper, and fold the ingredients together with a rubber spatula. Use the spatula to smear each piece of bread with the garlic butter. Transfer the garlic bread to a baking sheet and bake until golden brown and the butter has melted, about 5 minutes.

SANDWICHES: Use the garlic bread in place of regular bread for sandwiches; it's especially good with sandwiches featuring a substantial amount of greens and/or vegetables.

QUICK FLATBREAD PIZZA: Top the garlic bread with tomato sauce, dried oregano, and mozzarella for a quick pizza that can be sliced into small squares and served as a canapé.

GARLIC CROUTONS: After baking, cut the bread into rectangles or squares for a quick crouton; you can also cut it into long croutons that can be served alongside a salad or soup.

SALAD OR SOUP BASE: For a variation on *zuppa di pane* (Italian bread soup), set a piece of garlic bread in the bottom of a soup bowl and ladle vegetable soup or tomato soup over it. For a take on *panzanella* (Italian bread salad), set a slice of garlic bread in the center of a salad plate and top with marinated vegetables or tomatoes.

SAVORY BREAD PUDDING: Whisk together 1 cup heavy cream, 1 large egg, and 1 large egg yolk. Add chopped sautéed broccoli rabe and sautéed sausage and pour over baked, diced garlic bread. Divide among ramekins, bake in a 350°F oven until the mixture is set and the top is golden brown, and serve.

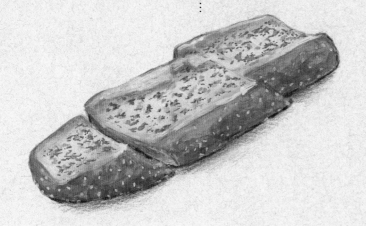

4
Pasta and Risotto

Asparagus Gnudi
with Thyme, Brown Butter, and Parmesan Broth

SERVES 6 AS AN APPETIZER OR 4 AS A MAIN COURSE

The first time I had gnudi—soft, pillowy pasta that literally melt in your mouth—was at the Spotted Pig in New York City. Chef April Bloomfield served such a luscious version that I became fascinated by them and taught myself how to make them. I enjoy contrasting that delicate quality with something rich, saucing the gnudi with Parmesan broth and brown butter, even in the summer. If you find yourself in possession of fresh white truffles, shave some over this dish. Truffle butter (page 220), folded into the pasta just before serving, would also be a terrific finishing touch.

This recipe for asparagus gnudi can be adapted to make gnudi with fiddlehead ferns, wood ear or black trumpet mushrooms, truffles, autumn squash varieties, or even *baccalà* (whipped salt cod). Replace the ½ cup minced asparagus with ½ cup of a cooked, minced substitution.

---

5 tablespoons unsalted butter

1 tablespoon thyme leaves

Kosher salt

Freshly ground white pepper

2 cups Parmesan Broth (see Notebook, page 138)

Asparagus Gnudi (recipe follows)

4 asparagus tips (from the asparagus used to make the gnudi), blanched and shocked (see page 362) and thinly sliced

1 tablespoon sliced flat-leaf parsley leaves

About 1 ounce Parmigiano-Reggiano cheese

Freshly ground black pepper

Cook 4 tablespoons of the butter in a large, shallow saucepan over medium heat, stirring with a wooden spoon. When the butter melts and turns golden brown, about 4 minutes, add the thyme and season with salt and white pepper. Add the Parmesan broth, bring to a simmer, and simmer for 1 minute. Add the gnudi and let simmer in the broth for 3 minutes, being sure the broth does not boil.

▸ Add the remaining 1 tablespoon butter to the pan, allow it to melt, then add the asparagus tips and parsley and cook just until the tips are warmed through, about 2 minutes.

▸ To serve, divide the gnudi and sauce among individual plates or wide, shallow bowls. Top with a grating of pecorino Romano cheese and a few grinds of black pepper.

continued

Asparagus Gnudi

MAKES ABOUT 20 PIECES

4 large asparagus stalks, tips removed,
   wooden ends trimmed, blanched
   and shocked (see page 362)

1 pound fresh ricotta cheese, preferably
   homemade (see Notebook, page 64)

1 large egg

⅓ cup finely grated pecorino Romano cheese

1½ cups all-purpose flour

1 tablespoon finely grated lemon zest
   (from about 2½ lemons)

Kosher salt

Freshly ground white pepper

Extra-virgin olive oil

Mince the blanched and shocked asparagus. If you
have more than ½ cup minced asparagus, discard the
extra. Put the asparagus, ricotta, egg, pecorino, 1 cup of
the flour, and the lemon zest in a bowl and season with
salt and pepper. Mix with a rubber spatula until just
incorporated; do not overmix. To check the seasoning,
blanch a small piece of dough in a small pot of simmering water, remove with a slotted spoon, and taste. Add
more salt and/or pepper to the batch as necessary and
mix briefly with the rubber spatula.

▸ Dust the bottom of a baking sheet with ¼ cup of the
flour. Put the remaining ¼ cup flour in a wide, shallow
bowl. Spread the dough over the flour on the baking
sheet in a layer 1½ inches high. Use a 2-inch ring mold
or vessel with a 2-inch mouth to cut the dough into small
circles, dipping the edge of the mold into the bowl holding the flour between each cut to keep it from sticking.
You should have about 20 gnudi.

▸ The prepared gnudi may be used right away or arranged on a baking sheet, loosely wrapped with plastic
wrap, and refrigerated for up to 24 hours. To freeze
gnudi, arrange them on a baking sheet and freeze until
hard. Transfer the pieces to a freezer bag and freeze for
up to 2 months. Do not defrost before cooking.

▸ To cook the gnudi, fill a large pot two-thirds full with
salted water. Bring to a simmer, gently add the gnudi,
and simmer until they float to the surface, 2 to 3 minutes for fresh, or 4 to 5 minutes for frozen. Use a slotted spoon to transfer the gnudi to a plate and drizzle
with extra-virgin olive oil. Serve.

Frizzled Asparagus Peels

For an easy-to-make garnish for this and other dishes
featuring asparagus, try making frizzled asparagus
peels. Heat a few inches of canola oil or other neutral
oil in a small pot set over medium-high heat. When the
oil reaches 275°F to 300°F, add 1 cup shaved asparagus
to the oil and gently fry until golden brown, about
2 minutes. Use a slotted spoon to transfer to a plate
lined with paper towels to drain, and season immediately with salt.

Parmesan Broth

A lot of cookbooks advise you to save the rinds from Parmigiano-Reggiano cheese, but how often do you actually find a good way to use them? My favorite use for Parmigiano rinds is this broth, which can be used to bring Parmesan flavor to a number of contexts.

For a deeper flavor, make this with stock instead of water—ideally, a stock that reflects the type of dish you will use it for: beef stock for a beef dish, pork stock for a dish featuring pork or sausage, and so on.

MAKES 1 QUART

1 cup Parmigiano-Reggiano cheese rinds

1 cup dry white wine

1 thyme sprig

3 garlic cloves

1 Spanish onion, thinly sliced

Put the rinds, wine, thyme, garlic, onion, and 3 cups cold water, in a medium pot and bring to a simmer. Simmer for 1 hour, stirring often to keep the rinds from sticking to the bottom or sides of the pot.

▶ Strain the broth through a fine-mesh strainer set over a large, heatproof bowl. Discard the solids and save the broth.

▶ The broth can be refrigerated in an airtight container for up to 3 days or frozen for up to 2 months.

COOKING MEDIUM FOR WHITE BEANS: White beans are wonderful flavor absorbers, and many Italian and Italian American dishes featuring white beans are finished with a grating of Parmigiano-Reggiano. So it only makes good sense to cook white beans such as cannellini or butter beans in Parmesan broth rather than chicken or vegetable stock to underscore that flavor.

PARMESAN POLENTA: Add another level of flavor to polenta by using Parmesan broth in place of water or stock in your favorite polenta recipe.

ITALIAN WEDDING SOUP: Make your own version of the classic Italian wedding soup by simmering meatballs in Parmesan broth, adding coarsely chopped escarole, and finishing with a lightly beaten egg, stirring it in with a fork to form ribbons. Top with a fresh grating of Parmigiano-Reggiano and, if desired, toasted bread crumbs (see page 145).

PASTA SAUCE BASE: Use the Parmesan broth as an alternative to chicken stock for any pasta served *in brodo*, an Italian term that simply means "in broth." It's especially good for tortellini or any pasta over which you plan to shave white truffles.

Fiddlehead Fern Ravioli
with Morels, Spring Pea Ragù, and Beurre Fondue

This ravioli is a light, springtime answer to ricotta and spinach ravioli, with the ferns replacing the spinach, and morel butter sauce in place of the more conventional melted butter. I like the crunchy texture of fiddlehead ferns, and the fact that they're available for only a few weeks each spring makes them extra-special. If you can't find them, use pencil asparagus cut into 1-inch pieces.

¾ cup mushroom stock, preferably homemade (page 365) with morels

Kosher salt

Freshly ground white pepper

8 tablespoons (1 stick) unsalted butter, cut into small pieces

½ cup fresh ricotta cheese, preferably homemade (page 64)

2 tablespoons blanched, shocked, drained (see page 362), and chopped fiddlehead fern stems

2 tablespoons grated pecorino Romano cheese

2 large eggs

½ tablespoon finely grated lemon zest

½ tablespoon minced chives

24 (4-inch) fresh pasta rounds, preferably homemade (see page 364)

Spring Pea Ragù (see Notebook, page 140)

To make the mushroom beurre fondue: Bring the mushroom stock to a boil in a medium saucepan over medium-high heat. Lower the heat and season with salt and pepper. Slowly add the butter, a piece at a time, whisking constantly, until the sauce is emulsified. Remove the pan from the heat and set aside; cover to keep the beurre fondue warm.

▸ To make the ravioli filling: Put the ricotta, fiddlehead fern stems, pecorino, 1 of the eggs, lemon zest, and chives in a medium bowl and season with salt and pepper. Mix to incorporate fully.

▸ To make the ravioli: Put the remaining egg in a bowl and whisk until frothy. Use a pastry brush to brush half of the pasta rounds with the egg. Top each round with about ½ tablespoon of the filling and top with a second round. Use a 2-inch ring cutter to cut through the dough, shaping it into a ravioli. Use the tines of a fork to seal its edges.

▸ Bring a large pot of salted water to a gentle boil. Add the ravioli and cook until they rise to the surface, about 3 minutes. Use a slotted spoon to transfer the cooked ravioli to the pan with the beurre fondue and toss gently to coat.

▸ To serve, divide the ravioli among 4 or 6 plates and spoon the spring pea ragù over the top.

spring Pea Ragù

There's no more quintessential spring combination than fresh peas and morel mushrooms, which come together here in a quick, buttery stew, with fiddlehead ferns and minced chives hammering home the seasonal theme. You can add other spring vegetables to this preparation and serve it as a side dish; incorporate sautéed bacon for a smoky undercurrent of flavor; use it as an omelet filling; or toss it with fettuccine and finish it with pecorino Romano cheese for a different pasta treatment.

MAKES 2 CUPS

¾ cup mushroom stock, preferably homemade (page 365)

Kosher salt

Freshly ground white pepper

9 tablespoons (1 stick plus 1 tablespoon) unsalted butter, cut into small pieces

½ cup morels, washed and checked for any small stones

1 tablespoon minced shallot

2 teaspoons thyme leaves

½ cup fresh English peas

½ cup pea greens

¼ cup fiddlehead ferns, blanched, shocked, and drained (see page 362)

1 tablespoon minced chives

To make the mushroom beurre fondue: Bring the mushroom stock to a boil in a medium saucepan over medium-high heat. Lower the heat and season with salt and pepper. Slowly add 8 tablespoons of the butter, a piece at a time, whisking constantly, until the sauce is emulsified. Remove from the heat and set aside, covered to keep warm.

▶ To make the ragù: Melt the remaining 1 tablespoon butter in a medium sauté pan over medium heat. When the butter begins to brown, about 5 minutes, add the morels, shallot, and thyme and cook until the morels begin to soften, about 2 minutes. Stir in the peas and cook until tender, about 1 minute. Stir in the beurre fondue, pea greens, fiddlehead ferns, and chives and remove immediately from the heat. Season with salt and pepper and keep warm until ready to serve.

Black Trumpet and Ricotta Cannelloni
with Melted Leeks, Deep-Fried Egg, and Cauliflower Purée

Traditional cannelloni are made by wrapping the pasta over the filling once. Mine is extra-large, with several layers of pasta, allowing the top to become nice and crispy when baked, without overcooking the filling. It is also decadent, with sensuous textures such as the ricotta filling and oozing egg yolk matching the rich flavors of the Madeira-enhanced black trumpet mushrooms. With a small salad alongside, this dish is a meal in its own right.

1½ teaspoons blended oil or neutral oil such as canola

1 garlic clove, thinly sliced

1½ shallots, thinly sliced, divided into thirds

½ head cauliflower, separated into florets, larger florets halved

Kosher salt

Freshly ground white pepper

1 cup whole milk

½ thyme sprig

2 tablespoons truffle butter (see page 220)

3 tablespoons unsalted butter

1 cup black trumpet mushrooms (wood ear may be substituted)

Freshly ground black pepper

¼ cup Madeira

2 cups fresh ricotta cheese, preferably homemade (see Notebook, page 64)

½ cup finely grated pecorino Romano cheese

2½ tablespoons minced chives

1 (24-inch) sheet Filled-Pasta Dough, freshly cooked (see page 364)

1 cup vegetable stock, preferably homemade (page 365)

2 cups thinly sliced leeks (white parts only), soaked in water to remove any grit, and drained

4 Deep-Fried Eggs (see Notebook, page 144)

To make the truffled cauliflower sauce: Heat the oil in a medium, heavy sauté pan over medium heat. When the oil is shimmering, add the garlic and one-third of the shallots and cook, stirring, for 1 minute. Stir in the cauliflower florets and season with salt and pepper. Cook for 2 minutes without browning, then pour in the milk and add the thyme. Bring to a simmer, then lower the heat and continue to simmer until the cauliflower just begins to soften, about 15 minutes. Transfer the contents of the pan to a blender, in batches if necessary, and purée until smooth, about 1 minute. Season with salt and white pepper. Hold a fine-mesh strainer or chinois over the sauté pan and strain the cauliflower purée back into the pan, pressing on the mixture with a rubber spatula or the back of a ladle to extract as much flavorful liquid as possible. Set over medium heat and stir in the truffle butter to melt it. Remove the pan from the heat and set aside; cover to keep the sauce warm.

▶ To make the filling: Melt 1 tablespoon of the unsalted butter in a medium sauté pan over high heat. When the butter has lightly browned, about 5 minutes, stir in the mushrooms and the remaining shallots and cook, stirring, for 1 minute. Season with salt and black

continued

pepper, pour in the Madeira, and cook, stirring to loosen any flavorful bits from the bottom of the pan, until the liquid has evaporated, about 3 minutes. Spread the mixture out on a baking sheet to cool, about 15 minutes. Once cool, transfer to a large bowl and fold in the ricotta, pecorino, and 2 tablespoons of the chives. Season with salt and black pepper.

▸ To form the cannelloni: Preheat the oven to 400°F. Lay the cooked pasta sheet on a clean work surface, with the short end before you. Spread and shape the black trumpet filling into a cylinder shape about 3 inches from the end nearest you. Roll the pasta tautly over the filling, then continue to roll over and over into a single, tight, multilayered log. Wrap tightly in plastic wrap and, using a small skewer or the tip of a very sharp knife, such as a paring knife, pop any air pockets in the plastic, taking care not to cut into the pasta. Use a serrated knife to slice the log into four 6-inch pieces, keeping them encased in plastic. Place the slices on a rimmed baking sheet without crowding and pour the vegetable stock around the slices. Bake until the cannelloni are heated through, about 10 minutes.

▸ Meanwhile, to make the melted leeks: Melt the remaining 2 tablespoons unsalted butter in a large, heavy sauté pan over low heat. Once the butter is melted, add the leeks and season with salt and white pepper. Cook, stirring, until the leeks are soft, about 3 minutes.

▸ To serve, reheat the cauliflower sauce in its pan over medium-high heat, and stir in the remaining ½ tablespoon chives. Spoon cauliflower sauce over the bottom of each of 4 serving dishes. Remove the plastic from the cannelloni and top the sauce on each plate with 1 cannelloni. Spoon leeks over the cannelloni. Working with one egg at a time, halve the deep-fried eggs lengthwise, season with salt and black pepper, and top each dish with the halves of one egg. Serve immediately.

NOTE: The timing here can be a bit tricky. It's ideal to have a second person in the kitchen to fry the eggs while the cannelloni and leeks are being cooked. Otherwise, have the oil hot and the eggs breaded, and fry them just after the leeks are done.

Deep-Fried Eggs

Deep-fried eggs can be challenging to cook but make a huge impression at the table—a true restaurant flourish of visual drama and a piñata of texture, with the crispy outside giving way to the meltingly soft white and molten yolk. Have a few extra eggs on hand in case one or more break when frying, which happens even to professional cooks. (Two extra eggs have been factored into this recipe.)

MAKES 4 EGGS

8 large eggs

1 cup all-purpose flour

1 cup finely ground panko bread crumbs

Canola oil or other neutral oil, for frying

Maldon sea salt

Fill a large bowl halfway with ice water and set it aside. Bring a large pot of salted water to a boil and add 6 of the eggs. Cook for 5 minutes, then use a slotted spoon to transfer the eggs to the ice water until cool enough to handle, about 5 minutes. Gently peel the shells off the eggs.

▸ Put the flour in a medium bowl. Crack the remaining 2 eggs into a second medium bowl and whisk until frothy. Put the panko in a medium bowl and, working with one at a time, gently dredge the boiled eggs in the flour, then in the beaten eggs, and finally in the panko, gently shaking off any excess.

▸ Pour canola oil into a deep fryer, or wide, deep, heavy pot, to a depth of 4 inches. Heat the oil to 375°F and use a kitchen spoon to carefully lower the eggs into the oil. Deep-fry until the coating is golden brown, about 2 minutes. (If you do not break any eggs, you will have 2 extra.)

▸ In most cases, these are best split down the middle, and the exposed yolk seasoned with Maldon sea salt.

RISOTTO TOPPING: Set a halved deep-fried egg over plain risotto or a risotto made with big, hearty flavors; the rice will drink up the yolk. Do not use with shellfish risottos.

BREAKFAST SHRIMP AND GRITS: Top shrimp and grits with a deep-fried egg for a morning-appropriate version of this dish (and a wonderful hangover meal).

GREENS, EGGS, AND PORK: Top salads made with sturdy greens with one of these eggs. It's especially appropriate for a variation of the classic frisée and lardon salad.

PIZZA BIANCA: These eggs are the ultimate finishing touch for white pizzas topped with cheese and black pepper (and no tomato sauce).

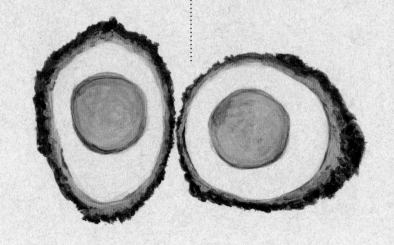

Spaghetti

with Crab Fra Diavolo and Toasted Bread Crumbs

Tomato sauce and seafood were a constant presence when I was growing up in a half-Italian household on coastal Long Island. One of my favorite marriages of the two was this dish my mother used to make, often with crabs that I had caught at popular crabbing locations such as Bergen Point, Captree State Park, and Tanner Park. This dish really shows off the value of a notebook-based approach to cooking: the sauce is adapted from my family's own; the pasta can be purchased fresh or dried or can be homemade from the recipe on page 364; and the bread crumbs are a versatile finishing element you can use on everything from gratins to casseroles to pastas, braised meats, salads, and roasted vegetables.

Kosher salt

4 cups Spicy Tomato Sauce, made with seafood stock (see Notebook, page 147)

1 pound spaghetti, dried, fresh, or homemade (page 364)

8 ounces peekytoe or jumbo lump crabmeat

6 large basil leaves, torn by hand

Toasted Bread Crumbs (below)

Small piece of pecorino Romano cheese, for grating

Bring a large pot of salted water to a boil. Put the sauce in a separate large pot and heat it gently over medium heat while you cook the pasta, allowing the sauce to simmer but not boil.

▸ Add the pasta to the boiling water and cook until al dente, about 2 minutes for fresh or 8 minutes for dried. Meanwhile, stir the crabmeat into the sauce. Drain the pasta in a colander and add to the pot with the sauce. Add the basil and toss.

▸ Divide among 4 to 6 plates or wide, shallow bowls, top each serving with bread crumbs and grated cheese, and serve.

Toasted Bread Crumbs

MAKES ABOUT ¼ CUP

1 tablespoon unsalted butter

¼ cup panko or unseasoned dried bread crumbs

2 teaspoons crushed red pepper flakes

Kosher salt

Freshly ground white pepper

Melt the butter in a wide, heavy sauté pan over medium-high heat. When the butter is melted, add the panko and red pepper flakes. Season generously with salt and white pepper. Cook, tossing or stirring with a wooden spoon, until the bread crumbs are lightly golden, about 5 minutes.

Tomato Sauce

Adapted from my family's recipe, this is a useful, all-purpose tomato sauce to have in your repertoire. Like my family, I make it with canned tomato, garlic, fennel seed, and no tomato paste. Unlike them, I don't cook it all day—just about 30 minutes to keep the flavors fresh and bright.

MAKES ABOUT 5 CUPS

2 tablespoons extra-virgin olive oil

2 tablespoons thinly sliced garlic

½ cup minced Spanish onion

2 teaspoons fennel seeds

1 quart whole canned plum tomatoes, with their juices

2 cups stock, preferably home-made (use seafood stock if planning to add shellfish; vegetable stock or water for all other uses; pages 365–67)

Kosher salt

Freshly ground white pepper

Heat the oil in a large pot over medium-high heat. When the oil is shimmering, add the garlic, onion, and fennel seeds and cook, stirring with a wooden spoon, until softened but not browned, about 3 minutes.

▶ Add the tomatoes and stock, and season with salt and pepper. Bring to a boil over high heat. Lower the heat so the liquid is simmering, and continue to simmer until slightly thickened and intensely flavored, about 30 minutes. Taste, and adjust the seasoning with salt if necessary.

▶ Remove the pot from the heat, and purée the sauce with an immersion blender, in a food processor or blender, or by passing it through a food mill.

▶ The sauce can be refrigerated in an airtight container for up to 3 days or frozen for up to 2 months.

ALL-PURPOSE PASTA SAUCE: This is a reliable, everyday pasta sauce. You can augment it with sautéed ground beef, make it with fresh tomatoes instead of canned, alter the amount of garlic or fennel seeds, or spice it up with crushed red pepper flakes. Experiment and make it your own.

SPICY TOMATO SAUCE: Add 1 tablespoon crushed red pepper flakes along with the garlic, onion, and fennel seeds.

PARMIGIANO SANDWICHES: For a *Parmigiano* sandwich (the name means "topped with cheese," not necessarily Parmesan), top fried eggplant or boneless chicken with the sauce, set it on a split Italian hero or other roll, top it with slices of mozzarella, and melt under the broiler.

SPICY TOMATO AND SHELLFISH SOUP: Turn this sauce into a soup by adding 2 to 3 cups more stock and a total of 8 ounces crabmeat, peeled shrimp, and/or shucked scallops. Add the shrimp and/or scallops for the final 5 minutes of cooking, poaching them in the soup; fold the crabmeat in just before removing the soup from the heat.

SHELLFISH PASTA: This sauce is good with more than just crab. Add 8 ounces poached bay scallops; diced poached sea scallops; poached or sautéed shrimp; chopped cooked lobster meat; or a combination to this sauce and toss with cooked tubular pasta such as bucatini.

Wild Chive Tagliatelle
with Shrimp, Cuttlefish, Shallots, and Sea Urchin Sauce

If you've never seen the value of making your own pasta, consider the tagliatelle here, which is made with chives for a visually arresting, intensely flavored effect that you won't find for sale in any market. The pasta is tossed with an addictive sauce of uni, shellfish stock, and butter. It's based on a pasta I enjoyed at Taverna Paradiso in Trapani, Sicily, way down in the south of Italy, where simply sensational shellfish cookery is a way of life. If you can't find chive blossoms, just use a bunch of chives and simply leave out the blossom garnish.

---

2 cups chive blossoms, greens chopped and blossoms reserved (about 16 blossoms), plus 1 tablespoon minced chives

Kosher salt

3½ cups all-purpose flour, plus more for dusting

4 large egg yolks

Freshly ground white pepper

2 tablespoons extra-virgin olive oil, plus more for tossing the cooked pasta

½ cup thinly sliced shallots

1 cup (4 ounces) uni

½ cup dry white wine

1 cup shellfish stock, preferably homemade (page 367)

2 large or jumbo shrimp (2 ounces total), peeled, deveined, and minced

2 cuttlefish (2 ounces total), minced (squid may be substituted)

2 tablespoons unsalted butter

Coarsely cracked black pepper

To make the chive purée: Fill a medium bowl halfway with ice water. Bring a medium pot of salted water to a boil. Add the chive blossom greens to the boiling water and blanch until bright green, about 1 minute. Transfer to the ice water to stop the cooking. Drain, then transfer the greens to a blender and season with salt. Blend to a smooth purée, about 30 seconds, adding just enough cold water to help the blade catch and working quickly to keep the chives from browning.

▸ Put the purée, 3 cups of the flour, and the egg yolks in a large bowl. Season with white pepper and knead by hand just until a dough forms. Wrap in plastic wrap and refrigerate for 30 minutes. Pass the dough through a pasta machine repeatedly, flouring it as necessary, and lowering the setting each time, until the sheets are as thin as possible (the thinnest or second-thinnest setting). On a lightly floured work surface, using a straightedge to guide you and a sharp knife or pizza cutter, cut the dough into ⅟₁₆-inch ribbons, gather the ribbons in a wide, deep bowl, and dust with the remaining ½ cup flour, gently tossing to coat the ribbons with the flour.

▸ Bring a medium pot of salted water to a boil. Add the pasta ribbons and cook until al dente, about 2 minutes. Drain in a colander, toss with a drizzle of olive oil to prevent sticking, and set aside.

continued

▸ Heat the 2 tablespoons oil in a large saucepan over medium heat. When the oil is shimmering, add the shallots and cook, stirring, until they are softened but not browned, about 2 minutes. Stir in the uni and cook, stirring, for 1 minute. Pour in the wine and cook, stirring to loosen any flavorful bits from the bottom of the pan. Bring to a simmer, and continue to cook until the liquid has reduced by half, about 3 minutes. Add the shellfish stock, shrimp, and cuttlefish and season with salt and white pepper. Cook until the liquid has reduced by half, about 6 minutes, then swirl in the butter to melt it. Toss in the cooked pasta and minced chives and season with salt and white pepper.

▸ To serve, divide the pasta and sauce among 4 to 6 plates. Scatter chive blossoms and freshly cracked black pepper over each serving.

Chives

The color and flavor of chives have been a minor obsession of mine since I was a kid. My mother has never forgotten the time I wandered out into our backyard and ate wild garlic chives, raw, then came home with a big grin on my face and the worst breath in the history of humankind. Today, instead, I just find their color and gentle onion flavor fascinating and turn to the act of cutting them as a meditative exercise that takes me out of my head and relaxes me.

GARNISH: Like parsley, chives are often employed as a default garnish. While they can be scattered over just about anything, I find that they are best as a counterpoint to rich textures and flavors, especially shellfish and poultry dishes—they top the lobster bisque on page 112, finish the sauce for the sea bass on page 228, and are stirred into the creamed corn that accompanies the grilled guinea hen on page 278.

CHIVE OIL: For an elegant finishing touch, make your own chive oil using my technique: Blend 2 parts chives with 1 part neutral oil. Pour the mixture into a small pot and heat over very high heat until the mixture boils and separates, 5 to 6 minutes. Strain through a coffee filter set in a strainer over a bowl for the greenest herb oil you've ever seen. Drizzle it over and around soups, salads, and fish or white poultry dishes.

CHIVE PURÉE: Brown 1 tablespoon unsalted butter in a sauté pan over medium-high heat, allowing it to separate. Stir in 2 cups chopped chives and season with salt and white pepper. Blend the mixture, then pass it through a fine-mesh strainer into a stainless steel bowl, pressing down on the solids with a rubber spatula to extract as much purée as possible. Set the bowl over another bowl filled halfway with ice water and chill the purée. Serve with cooked shellfish.

CHIVE TIES: Use chives to bind stacked canapés such as sliced cured or smoked fish atop black bread; you can also use them to tie the necks of savory parcels such as wontons that will be served as appetizers.

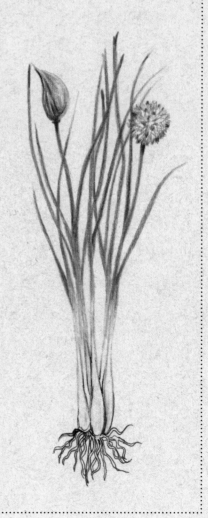

Sautéed Lemon Gnocchi
with Swordfish Confit, Grilled Spring Onions, and Sweet Parsley Sauce

SERVES 6 AS AN APPETIZER OR 4 AS A MAIN COURSE

This pasta dish eats like a main course because the swordfish is presented in large cubes and the gnocchi are made with potatoes. Add the spring onions and you've got the classic protein, starch, and vegetable trio that makes a meal. The interplay between swordfish *confit* (meaning cooked slowly in olive oil) and lemony pasta evokes a powerful seaside vibe, and the charred onions suggest the effect of a grill, making this a perfect summer starter or main course. If you'd rather not make your own lemon gnocchi, purchase ready-made gnocchi and cook it in boiling salted water with the juice of one lemon added to it. But I suggest making your own at least once. You can also use the gnocchi in other dishes, or omit the lemon zest and use it as an all-purpose gnocchi recipe. Gnocchi are also good with tomato sauce (see page 147) or with brown butter and sage. When making gnocchi, take care not to overwork the dough; the less you work it, the more tender and fluffy your gnocchi will be.

---

1 cup (2 sticks) unsalted butter

2 spring onions, plus greens from 1 bunch spring onions, greens coarsely chopped

3 cups (loosely packed) flat-leaf parsley leaves, plus 1 tablespoon thinly sliced parsley leaves

Kosher salt

Freshly ground black pepper

1 tablespoon extra-virgin olive oil

Swordfish Confit (see Notebook, page 156), plus 1 tablespoon confit oil

Lemon Gnocchi (recipe follows), blanched according to recipe

1 tablespoon sliced, pitted green olives such as Castelvetrano

1 tablespoon freshly squeezed lemon juice

1 tablespoon slivered almonds, toasted (see page 362)

Fill a large bowl halfway with ice water. Set another, smaller bowl on top, and let it chill until cold to the touch.

▸ Meanwhile, melt the butter in a wide, heavy saucepan over medium-high heat, stirring with a wooden spoon, until the fats separate and turn brown, about 6 minutes. Add the spring onion greens and cook, stirring, until they start to soften, about 2 minutes. Stir in the 3 cups parsley leaves, season with salt and pepper, and remove the pan from the heat. Immediately

transfer the contents of the pan to a blender, blend to a coarse sauce consistency, and pass through a fine-mesh strainer set over the chilled bowl. Use a rubber spatula to stir the sauce in the bowl, which will help it cool as quickly as possible and keep the sauce from turning brown. Set aside.

▸ Heat a cast-iron pan over high heat for 5 minutes. Meanwhile, put the spring onions in a bowl, toss with

continued

the olive oil, and season with salt and pepper. After the pan has preheated, add the onions to the pan and cook, stirring with a wooden spoon, to char the onions all over, about 5 minutes. Transfer the onions to a cutting board and after about 5 minutes, when they are cool enough to handle, thinly slice them.

▸ Heat the confit oil in a wide, heavy sauté pan over medium-high heat. When the oil is shimmering, add the gnocchi, and cook until golden brown on the bottom, 2 to 3 minutes. Turn over with tongs or a wooden spoon and cook until golden brown on the other side, another 2 to 3 minutes. Add the charred, sliced spring onions and swordfish to the pan and cook, gently tossing, until all the ingredients are warmed through, about 2 minutes. Add the olives and lemon juice, toss, taste, and adjust the seasoning with salt and pepper, if necessary.

▸ Quickly reheat the parsley sauce in a small saucepan.

▸ Spoon parsley sauce into the center of each of 4 to 6 plates. Top with the gnocchi-swordfish mixture, and garnish with the sliced parsley and almonds.

Lemon Gnocchi

MAKES 4 CUPS

Kosher salt

1 pound Idaho potatoes (ideally 2 medium potatoes of the same size and shape)

1¼ cups all-purpose flour

Finely grated zest of 1 lemon

1 large egg, at room temperature, lightly beaten

1 tablespoon minced chives

Freshly ground white pepper

Extra-virgin olive oil

Position a rack in the center of the oven and preheat the oven to 400°F. Coat the center of a baking sheet with kosher salt. Prick the potatoes all over with a fork and set them on the salt. Bake the potatoes until a sharp, thin-bladed knife such as a paring knife pierces easily to their center, about 40 minutes. When the potatoes are cool enough to work with but still warm, peel them and pass them through a food mill or ricer into a large bowl. (You can also use a potato masher, but be sure to mash them thoroughly.)

▸ Add 1 cup of the flour, the lemon zest, egg, and chives to the bowl, season with salt and pepper, and gently knead the ingredients together, taking care not to overwork them. Allow to rest for 30 minutes at room temperature.

▸ Roll the dough into 3 or 4 logs about the diameter of a quarter. Cut into 1½-inch segments and dust with the remaining ¼ cup flour. The prepared gnocchi may be arranged on a baking sheet, loosely wrapped with plastic wrap, and refrigerated for up to 24 hours. To freeze gnocchi, arrange them on a baking sheet and freeze until hard. Transfer the pieces to a freezer bag and freeze for up to 2 months. Do not defrost before cooking.

▸ To cook the gnocchi: Fill a large pot two-thirds full with salted water and bring to a boil. Add the gnocchi and cook until they float to the surface, about 2 minutes for fresh or 3 to 4 minutes for frozen. If not serving the gnocchi immediately, grease a baking sheet with olive oil. Drain the gnocchi and spread them out on the oil-slicked sheet until ready to finish and serve. If serving right away, simply drain the gnocchi, toss gently with sauce or brown butter, and serve.

Swordfish Confit

Gently poaching swordfish in olive oil is a play on the classic French technique of *confit*, or preserving meats in their own fat. The result is similar to that of preserved tuna, rich and versatile. To make more, simply multiply the recipe.

MAKES 4 OUNCES

2 cups extra-virgin olive oil

1 garlic clove, smashed with the side of a chef's knife

1 bay leaf

2 tablespoons finely grated lemon zest

1 thyme sprig

Kosher salt

Freshly ground white pepper

4 ounces swordfish, cut into 1½-inch cubes

Put the oil, garlic, bay leaf, lemon zest, and thyme sprig in a shallow saucepan and season with salt and pepper. Set over low heat and bring to 120°F. Allow to steep for 30 minutes, adjusting the heat as necessary to keep the same temperature, to infuse the oil with the flavor of the lemon and herbs. Add the swordfish cubes and remove the pan from the heat. Gently cook the fish in the heated oil for 5 minutes.

▶ Serve right away by removing the fish from the oil with a slotted spoon, or transfer the fish to an airtight container, strain the poaching oil over the fish, and refrigerate in the oil for up to 1 week.

SWORDFISH SAUCE: For a variation on *tonnato* sauce (page 240), blend the swordfish and its oil with about 1 cup mayonnaise, ½ cup extra-virgin olive oil, 2 tablespoons freshly squeezed lemon juice, 1 jarred anchovy fillet, 2 tablespoons capers, and 2 cornichons. (The sauce is highly adaptable; vary the ingredient amounts according to personal taste.) Use it over cooked and chilled swordfish; over roasted, chilled, thinly sliced veal breast, or as a sandwich condiment; or thin it slightly with warm water and use it as a salad dressing.

SWORDFISH SALAD: Make a variation on tuna salad by pulsing the swordfish in a food processor and stirring in mayonnaise, diced celery, diced red onion, salt, and pepper. Use it as the basis for a salad or a sandwich—it's especially good on a bagel.

SWORDFISH NIÇOISE: Make a variation on a Niçoise salad featuring greens dressed with equal parts lemon juice and olive oil, or olive oil, salt, and pepper; boiled, chilled potato; blanched, chilled green beans; hard-boiled eggs; tomatoes; anchovies or capers; and Niçoise olives.

SICILIAN SWORDFISH SANDWICH: Set the cubes on a roll with sliced pickled onions, citrus segments, lettuce, and ripe tomato slices.

Turducken Lasagna

with Fresh Ricotta Cheese, Tomato Sauce, Basil, and Fennel Seed

SERVES 8 TO 10

I cooked up this crazy-sounding lasagna for Thanksgiving dinner one year, combining the same three meats used in the famous (or notorious, depending on your taste) turducken in a pasta sauce, then making a lasagna with it. The sauce eats like a rich, slightly gamy Bolognese, with the ricotta providing smooth, creamy relief. Although it sounds revolutionary, other than the choice of meats, it's actually a very traditional lasagna; I even use my grandmother's method of "rinsing" the tomato cans into the sauce. This is a terrific dish and conversation piece for entertaining.

2 tablespoons extra-virgin olive oil

8 ounces ground turkey (any parts)

8 ounces ground duck (any parts)

8 ounces ground chicken (any parts)

Kosher salt

Freshly ground black pepper

1 large Spanish onion, minced

10 garlic cloves, minced

2 tablespoons fennel seeds

1 tablespoon crushed red pepper flakes

About 43 ounces (28-ounce can plus 14½- or 15-ounce can) canned crushed tomatoes

About 43 ounces (28-ounce can plus 14½- or 15-ounce can) tomato purée

Leaves from 1 bunch basil

1 pound mozzarella cheese, grated

1 pound provolone cheese, grated

1 cup grated pecorino Romano cheese

3 (1-pound) boxes no-boil lasagna noodles

3 pounds fresh ricotta cheese, preferably homemade (see Notebook, page 64)

To make the sauce: Heat the oil in a large saucepan over high heat. When the oil is shimmering, add the ground turkey, duck, and chicken and season with salt and black pepper. Cook, stirring, until the meat is lightly browned, about 6 minutes. Transfer the meat to a plate. Add the onion, garlic, fennel, and red pepper flakes to the pan and cook, stirring, until the onion is softened but not browned, about 2 minutes. Return the meat to the pan and stir in the crushed tomatoes and tomato purée. Rinse the tomato cans by adding about ¼ cup water to each, swishing it around, and stirring the tomato-tinged water into the sauce. Season with salt and black pepper, bring to a simmer, and continue to simmer for 40 minutes. Remove the pan from the heat and stir in the basil. The sauce can be made ahead of time and refrigerated in an airtight container for up to 2 days.

▸ To make and serve the lasagna: Preheat the oven to 350°F. Put the mozzarella, provolone, and pecorino in a bowl and fold them together. Ladle one-quarter of the sauce into the bottom of a large lasagna pan, roughly

continued

14 by 10 by 6 inches. Top with a layer of noodles, arranging them side by side and cutting them as necessary to fit neatly into the pan. Spread about one-quarter of the ricotta over the noodles, then about one-quarter of the mozzarella mixture. Repeat, starting with the sauce, three more times, and finishing with the mozzarella mixture. Grind black pepper over the lasagna, cover with aluminum foil, and bake until the cheese is melted and bubbly and you can pierce to the center of the lasagna easily with a paring knife, about 45 minutes. Remove the foil and return to the oven to bake until the cheese starts to brown, about 5 more minutes. Remove the lasagna from the oven and set aside to rest for 20 minutes before slicing and serving.

NOTE: If you've never used no-boil lasagna noodles, which go into the pan uncooked, you may be surprised at how well they work; just be sure to generously use all the sauce so there's enough liquid for them to soak up as they bake.

Fennel Seed

Fennel seed boasts an understated anise flavor that's essential in many classic Italian pork recipes and also makes a great addition to sweet and savory dishes. Much as I love it, a little goes a long way, so be sure to use it sparingly unless it's the main flavor in a dish or drink.

FENNEL SUGAR: Make a fennel sugar by adding 1 part ground fennel seeds to 5 parts sugar and stirring together. Use the sugar to dust doughnuts (page 330), or to add a subtle, extra accent to crumble toppings that will top autumn fruits such as pear and quince.

FENNEL TEA: Italian American grandmothers will tell you that fennel tea is the cure for an upset stomach. I don't know if that part is true, but it *can* be a delicious tea that doesn't require a bag: Just steep ½ teaspoon or so of seeds in 1 cup boiling hot water for several minutes, then strain.

FENNEL SIMPLE SYRUP: Make a simple syrup by cooking equal parts water and sugar together over low heat, whisking until the sugar dissolves. Stir in fennel seeds, remove from the heat, and steep to allow the seeds to infuse the syrup with their flavor. Drain and use to sweeten iced tea or in cocktail recipes for which you want a sweet, anise hit of flavor.

FENNEL SEED SALT: Grind equal parts fennel seed and salt together and use the resulting seasoning over poultry and meats; it's especially good for beef that will be grilled.

Farro Risotto

with Artichoke Confit, Parmesan Cheese, and Chili-Grape Salad

SERVES 6 AS AN APPETIZER OR 4 AS A MAIN COURSE

I much prefer farro, a spelt-like grain, to risotto rices such as Arborio because it has a more nuanced, slightly nutty flavor and a more toothsome texture. This dish's creamy, risotto-like preparation is complemented by soft, confit artichokes. Sambal, the Asian chili condiment, brings heat to a salad of grapes that's served on top, like a gremolata, inviting you to mix and match bites of the fresh fruit with the earthy risotto.

Kosher salt

2 cups farro

4 artichokes, turned
   (see page 23)

4 cups extra-virgin olive oil

2 garlic cloves, smashed with
   the side of a chef's knife

Freshly ground white pepper

½ cup thinly sliced seedless
   red grapes

1 tablespoon sambal

2 tablespoons whole flat-leaf
   parsley leaves, plus 2 tablespoons thinly sliced flat-leaf
   parsley leaves

2 cups chicken stock, preferably
   homemade (page 366)

2 tablespoons thyme leaves

4 tablespoons (½ stick) unsalted
   butter, cut into pieces

½ cup finely grated Parmigiano-
   Reggiano cheese

2 tablespoons minced chives

Bring a large pot of salted water to a boil. Put the farro in a large, heatproof bowl and pour the boiling water over it to cover by 2 inches. Allow it to soak until al dente, 30 minutes.

▶ Meanwhile, to make the artichoke confit: Put the artichokes, olive oil, and garlic in a large saucepan and season with salt and white pepper. Set over medium heat and gently cook, taking care not to let the oil simmer, until the artichokes are soft to a knife tip, about 20 minutes. Allow to cool in the oil about 30 minutes. Remove the chokes from the oil with a slotted spoon and cut each one into 6 pieces.

▶ To make the chili-grape salad: Put the grapes, sambal, and whole parsley leaves in a medium bowl and stir to incorporate. Set aside.

▶ Carefully wipe out the large saucepan used for the artichokes, then strain the farro through a fine-mesh strainer into it. Pour in the stock and bring to a simmer over medium-high heat. Cook, stirring often, until the farro is soft, about 8 minutes. Add the thyme, butter, and Parmigiano-Reggiano, stirring vigorously until incorporated. Season with salt and white pepper and fold in the artichokes, thinly sliced parsley, and chives.

▶ Divide the risotto among 4 or 6 bowls, top with the chili-grape salad, and serve.

Farro

Farro has only begun to catch on in the United States in the last few years, but it's been popular in Italy for generations. The nutty, earthy, spelt-like grain can be used just about anywhere you'd use rice. It's also worth getting to know because it's more forgiving to cook than risotto rice, and able to soak up a large quantity of liquid without becoming mushy. Another benefit is that you don't need to add the stock in installments, as you do with traditional risotto recipes, instead pouring it into the farro all at once.

COLD FARRO SALAD: Toss cooked, chilled farro with diced grilled vegetables or fresh vegetables, red wine vinegar, and extra-virgin olive oil for a take on an Italian *panzanella*, or bread salad.

ITALIAN WEDDING SOUP: Stir cooked farro into an Italian wedding soup such as the one described on page 138.

FARRO, FIG, AND PISTACHIO SALAD: Toss blanched, drained farro with dried figs, roasted salted pistachios, sliced shallots, whole flat-leaf parsley leaves, and tahini vinaigrette.

FARRO GRANOLA: Mix cooked farro with granola for breakfast, or scatter it over yogurt or ricotta cheese.

Homemade Farfalle

with Bone Marrow, Baby Leeks, Bread Crumbs, and Littleneck Clam Ragù

Bone marrow and clams come together here for surf and turf, pasta-style. When tossed into hot dishes, bone marrow becomes slick and pleasantly unctuous, which helps it integrate with the clams and bow-tie pasta. The leeks are important here because their snappy texture and onion flavor help cut the richness of the bone marrow, which would otherwise be overwhelming. While you can serve this as a first course, it's really best enjoyed as a main dish because it is a very difficult act to follow.

Basic Pasta Dough (page 364)

Kosher salt

1 tablespoon extra-virgin olive oil, plus more for tossing the cooked pasta

1 shallot, thinly sliced

1 garlic clove, thinly sliced

¼ cup thinly sliced leek whites, soaked in water to remove any grit

1 tablespoon thinly sliced marjoram leaves

¾ cup bottled clam juice

½ cup halved grape tomatoes

2 tablespoons unsalted butter

24 littleneck clams, shucked, with their liquid

½ cup Roasted Bone Marrow (page 295)

1 tablespoon sliced flat-leaf parsley leaves

Freshly ground white pepper

¼ cup Toasted Bread Crumbs (page 145)

To make the farfalle: Use a fluted pasta cutter to slice the pasta sheets into 3 by 3-inch squares. Use your fingers to pinch the middle of each square to form farfalle. Bring a large pot of salted water to a boil. Add the farfalle and cook until tender, about 1 minute. Use a slotted spoon or spider to transfer the farfalle from the water to a large bowl, toss with a drizzle of olive oil to prevent sticking, and set aside.

▶ Heat the olive oil in a large saucepan over medium-high heat. When the oil is shimmering, add the shallot and garlic and cook, stirring, for 1 minute. Stir in the leeks, marjoram, clam juice, and tomatoes and cook for 2 minutes to mingle the flavors. Fold in the butter until melted. Add the clams and bone marrow and stir to incorporate. Add the cooked farfalle and parsley and stir to coat. Season with salt and pepper. Spoon into 4 to 6 serving bowls, sprinkle with bread crumbs, and serve.

NOTE: Because they're so small, shucking littleneck clams can be dangerous for some home cooks, more so than oysters. Ask your fishmonger to do this for you, reserving the liquid.

Clams

Clams are one of the touchstones of summer for me. I love them grilled, as part of a fish fry, and in sandwiches. I also appreciate their versatility; they are equally at home in more formal, plated dishes suited to entertaining. As with so many types of shellfish, different clams have different ideal uses.

▶ **LITTLENECKS** are among the smallest and briniest North Atlantic clams. Top necks are slightly larger but have a similar profile. Both are delicious raw on the half shell or tossed in the shell with olive oil and black pepper, grilled, and served in clam broth with garlic bread (page 133) alongside.

▶ **IPSWICH CLAMS** are the same variety as steamers and are a soft-bellied North Atlantic clam. When the name Ipswich is used, they are generally fried, and I love them that way, usually in a sandwich with lettuce, tomato, and tartar sauce. When referred to as "steamers," they are steamed open and served with a celery-seed broth and drawn butter for dunking. To make the broth, heat 1 cup bottled clam juice in a large saucepan over medium-high heat and stir in 1 tablespoon celery seeds. Add the clams to the pan, cover, and steam to open, about 5 minutes, discarding any that do not open. Transfer the clams to a large bowl with a slotted spoon. Transfer the broth to a medium heatproof bowl, and serve with the steamed clams. Serve the drawn butter in a separate bowl.

▶ **MANILA CLAMS:** These relatively sweet clams are my go-to choice for linguine with clam sauce. I prefer a traditional Italian white sauce: Heat 2 tablespoons extra-virgin olive oil in a large pot over medium-high heat. When the oil is shimmering, add 2 dozen clams and 2 sliced garlic cloves. When the garlic begins to crisp and lightly brown, after about 2 minutes, add a pinch of crushed red pepper flakes and 1 cup dry white wine. Cover and cook until the clams open and the wine reduces slightly, about 6 minutes. Discard any clams that do not open. Finish by stirring in 2 tablespoons unsalted butter and 2 tablespoons sliced flat-leaf parsley leaves. Toss with 1 pound dried linguine, cooked al dente, and serve.

Braised Lamb Cheek Manicotti
with Black Olives, Mint, Pecorino, and Pine Nuts

SERVES 4

If you think manicotti is just cheese-filled pasta with tomato sauce, then this dish may be a revelation to you. It starts almost like an enchilada with braised meat wrapped in a crepe shell, but the surrounding ingredients are unmistakably Mediterranean: briny black olives, earthy pine nuts, and the surprising last-second addition of mint. It is a very complete dish that hits just about every flavor and texture button. I first served it at Perilla, where I used to do a "cheek du jour," drawing on my personal repertoire of braised dishes.

¼ cup blended oil or neutral oil such as canola, plus more for the crepes

4 pounds lamb cheeks (4 lamb shanks may be substituted)

Kosher salt

Freshly ground black pepper

1 Spanish onion, diced

6 garlic cloves, thinly sliced

10 plum tomatoes

2 cups dry white wine

2 quarts chicken stock, preferably homemade (page 366)

1 thyme sprig, plus 1 tablespoon thyme leaves

½ cup thinly sliced black olives

1 tablespoon pine nuts, toasted (see page 362)

2 teaspoons golden raisins

2 teaspoons finely diced feta cheese

2 teaspoons thinly sliced mint

1 tablespoon extra-virgin olive oil

1 teaspoon red wine vinegar

1 cup all-purpose flour

4 large eggs

½ cup whole milk

2 tablespoons unsalted butter, melted

1 cup fresh ricotta cheese, preferably homemade (page 64)

½ cup finely grated pecorino Romano cheese

To braise the lamb cheeks: Preheat the oven to 300°F. Heat the blended oil in a braising dish or Dutch oven over high heat. Season the lamb cheeks generously on both sides with salt and pepper. When the oil is shimmering, add the cheeks to the pan. Sear until the lamb cheeks are golden brown, about 3 minutes per side, then transfer to a large plate or platter. Add the onion, garlic, and tomatoes to the pan and cook, stirring, until softened, about 4 minutes. Pour in the white wine, stirring to loosen any flavorful bits cooked onto the bottom of the pan. Bring to a simmer and continue to simmer until the wine reduces by half, 6 to 8 minutes. Pour in the chicken stock and bring to a simmer. Return the cheeks to the pot and add the thyme sprig. Cover the pot and braise in the oven until fork-tender, about 2 hours, checking periodically to ensure that the liquid is barely simmering. If it is bubbling too aggressively, lower the oven temperature by 25 degrees; if it is not simmering at all, increase it by 25 degrees. Remove the lamb from the oven and transfer the meat to a cutting board to cool. Increase the oven temperature to 425°F.

continued

▸ Meanwhile, to make the olive salad: Put the olives, pine nuts, raisins, feta, mint, olive oil, and vinegar in a medium bowl and toss to incorporate. Season with salt and pepper and set aside.

▸ Once the lamb is cool enough to handle, remove and discard the fat. Chop the meat coarsely and set it aside. (You should have about 1 quart chopped meat.) Run the braising liquid through a food mill, then strain through a fine-mesh strainer set over the pot, pressing down with a rubber spatula or the bottom of a ladle to extract as much flavorful liquid as possible, and set over medium-high heat. Bring to a boil, then lower the heat and simmer until the liquid is thick and reduced by nearly half, about 20 minutes. Reserve 3 cups of the liquid and discard the extra or save it for another use.

▸ To make the crepes: Line a baking sheet with paper towels and set it aside. Put the flour, 2 of the eggs, the milk, butter, and ½ cup water in a medium bowl. Season with salt and pepper and whisk together to incorporate fully. Set aside to rest for 15 minutes.

▸ Set a medium nonstick sauté pan over medium heat and add just enough blended oil to coat the bottom of the pan; tilt the pan to coat it. When the oil is shimmering, add ¼ cup of the crepe mixture and swirl the pan so the batter forms a very thin layer. Cook until golden brown, about 1 minute. Use a rubber spatula to gently flip the crepe and cook on the other side for about 1 minute more. Transfer to the prepared baking sheet and repeat with the remaining batter to make 8 crepes. Use immediately.

▸ To assemble the dish: Put the ricotta, pecorino, and the remaining 2 eggs in a medium bowl and whisk to combine. Fold the chopped lamb meat into the mixture. Lay the crepes on a clean work surface and divide the ricotta filling evenly among the crepes. Roll the crepes around the filling, leaving them open at both ends. Transfer the filled crepes, seam side down, to a 9 by 13-inch baking dish. Pour the reserved braising liquid over them and place in the oven. Bake until the manicotti are heated all the way through, about 15 minutes. Transfer 2 manicotti to each serving plate and top with the olive salad just before serving.

Black Olives

Black olives, like all olives, are so ubiquitous—sliced and sprinkled on pizzas, minced and folded into tuna salads, tossed into cold pasta salads, and so on—that we rarely give them any thought. But they are an incredible and versatile ingredient. Pitted black olives are available in cans, but I prefer marinated fresh olives such as kalamata, which these days can be found at olive bars in many gourmet markets and grocery stores. Olives pack a briny punch that serves as punctuation of a kind; how often we want to experience that punctuation dictates how we cut or blend the olives into a given recipe.

TAPENADE: This finely chopped or blended olive paste (see page 240) has many uses. It can be tossed with pasta for a quick sauce. Spread it on croutons for an hors d'oeuvre or salad accompaniment. (You can also spread goat cheese on the croutons before the tapenade for an extra layer of texture and a wonderful sidecar to braised lamb.) Tapenade can also be whisked with olive oil for a quick salad dressing.

BLACK OLIVE PURÉE: Purée about ¾ cup pitted, marinated black olives with about 1 cup extra-virgin olive oil in a blender and serve with grilled fish.

BLACK OLIVE OIL: Spread marinated kalamata olives on a baking sheet and dry in the oven at 200°F overnight (about 10 hours). Process with extra-virgin olive oil (2 parts oil to 1 part olives); do not strain. Warm the oil and poach a white-fleshed fish such as yellowtail or swordfish in it. The exterior will turn a beautiful black. For a vegetarian option, poach tofu in the oil.

DRIED AND CANDIED BLACK OLIVES: Toss marinated kalamata olives in superfine sugar and dry as for Black Olive Oil, to the left. Scatter over Peruvian-style dishes such as ceviche.

BLACK OLIVE MUFFULETTA SALAD: Coarsely chop olives with celery, red onion, carrots, marinated Italian artichokes, red wine vinegar, and extra-virgin olive oil, and use to garnish Italian cold cut sandwiches.

Braised Rabbit Leg and *Badische Schupfnudeln*

with Nutmeg, Mustard Greens, and Pickled Mustard Seeds

Schupfnudeln is a traditional German potato dumpling that's similar to gnocchi, but rolled into torpedo shapes instead of cut into logs. Here it's cooked with sautéed mustard greens, braised rabbit legs, and pickled mustard seeds for a hearty dish that tastes unmistakably of its home country. Serve it with a Grüner Veltliner.

The pickled mustard seeds can also be scattered over salads or served as part of the accoutrement to a charcuterie platter.

Kosher salt

1 pound (2 to 3) Idaho potatoes

1½ cups all-purpose flour

1 large egg

2 teaspoons freshly grated nutmeg

1 tablespoon minced chives

Freshly ground white pepper

Extra-virgin olive oil

2 tablespoons blended oil or neutral oil such as canola

½ shallot, thinly sliced

½ garlic clove, thinly sliced

2 cups diced mustard greens (about ½ head)

Braised Rabbit (see Notebook, page 173), plus 1½ cups braising liquid

1 tablespoon tarragon leaves

1 tablespoon unsalted butter

1 tablespoon Pickled Mustard Seeds (recipe follows)

To make the *Badische Schupfnudeln*: Preheat the oven to 400°F. Spread enough kosher salt on a rimmed baking sheet to cover it evenly to a depth of 1 inch. Nestle the potatoes in the salt and bake until fork-tender, about 40 minutes. Remove the potatoes from the oven and set aside to cool slightly, about 6 minutes. While the potatoes are still warm, peel them and pass through a food mill or ricer set over a large bowl. Add 1¼ cups of the flour, the egg, nutmeg, and chives, season with salt and pepper, and stir to combine. Set aside to rest at room temperature for 30 minutes.

▸ Drizzle a clean baking sheet with olive oil and set it aside. On a clean work surface, roll the dough into 6 logs, each about ¾ inch in diameter. Use a sharp paring knife to cut the logs into about 40 (1-inch) pieces. Use your hands to roll the pieces into torpedo shapes (*schupfnudeln*). Dust with the remaining ¼ cup flour. To freeze *schupfnudeln*, arrange them on a baking sheet and freeze until hard. Transfer the pieces to a freezer bag and freeze for up to 2 months. Do not defrost before cooking.

▸ Bring a large pot of salted water to a boil. Add the *schupfnudeln* and blanch until they float to the top, about 3 minutes for fresh, or 4 to 5 for frozen. Transfer the cooked *schupfnudeln* to the olive oil–coated baking sheet and allow to cool completely, about 15 minutes.

▸ Meanwhile, to make the braised mustard greens: Heat 1 tablespoon of the blended oil in a Dutch oven

continued

or braising dish over medium heat. When the oil is shimmering, add the shallot and garlic and cook, stirring, until softened but not browned, about 1 minute. Add the mustard greens and season with salt and pepper. Cook until the mustard greens are soft, about 5 minutes more. Transfer to a colander and set in the sink or suspend over a bowl to strain until the greens do not give off any more liquid.

▶ To finish and assemble the dish: Heat the remaining 1 tablespoon blended oil in a sauté pan over medium-high heat. When the oil is shimmering, add the *schupfnudeln* and cook until browned on all sides, about 3 minutes. Add the rabbit, braising liquid, and mustard greens and cook, stirring, until the rabbit is heated through, about 4 minutes more. Stir in the tarragon leaves and butter, melting the butter, then season with salt and pepper. Divide the *schupfnudeln* among 4 plates, garnish each with pickled mustard seeds, and serve.

Pickled Mustard Seeds
MAKES ABOUT 2 TABLESPOONS

2 tablespoons mustard seeds
1 cup rice vinegar
1 tablespoon sugar
2 teaspoons kosher salt

Place the mustard seeds in a medium heatproof bowl. Put the rice vinegar, sugar, and salt in a medium saucepan and bring to a boil over medium-high heat, stirring until the sugar is dissolved. Pour the vinegar over the mustard seeds and set aside to cool completely, at least 45 minutes. The pickled seeds can be refrigerated in an airtight container for up to 1 week.

Braised Rabbit

Even if you've never had rabbit, or have never cooked with it, I think you will enjoy this versatile preparation. Rabbit legs are cooked slowly in a braising liquid made with white wine and chicken stock for a gentle final flavor. As they braise, the rabbit legs become meltingly tender and obscenely delicious. Because it is dark meat cooked in a light braising liquid, the applications for it are almost endless. Use rabbit as the substitute for beef in Bolognese sauce or as a non-barbecue riff on pulled pork, making sandwiches and topping the meat with pickles and coleslaw. You can also coarsely chop the meat and use it in croquettes or reheat the legs in braising liquid and sauce with Sour Yellow Curry (page 57). If possible, use hind legs, which are larger and yield more meat.

MAKES 2 CUPS PICKED MEAT AND 2 CUPS SAUCE

1 tablespoon blended oil or neutral oil such as canola

2 rabbit hind legs, about 8 ounces each (4 forelegs can be substituted)

Kosher salt

Freshly ground white pepper

3 garlic cloves, thinly sliced

1 shallot, thinly sliced

3 plum tomatoes, sliced, with their juices

2 cups dry white wine

1 quart chicken stock, preferably homemade (page 366)

1 thyme sprig

1 cup heavy cream

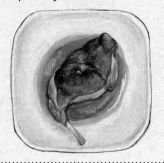

Preheat the oven to 300°F. Heat the oil in a Dutch oven or braising dish over high heat. Season the rabbit legs all over with salt and pepper. When the oil is shimmering, add the rabbit legs and brown on all sides, 5 to 6 minutes total cooking time.

▶ Use a pair of tongs to transfer the rabbit legs to a heatproof bowl and set aside. Add the garlic, shallot, and tomatoes to the pan and cook, stirring, until the garlic has softened, about 3 minutes. Pour in the wine and cook, stirring to loosen any flavorful bits from the bottom of the pan, until the liquid is reduced by half, about 5 minutes. Pour in the stock, add thyme sprig, and bring the liquid to a simmer. When the liquid simmers, add the rabbit legs back to the pan and place in the oven. Braise until fork-tender, about 2 hours, periodically checking to ensure that the liquid is barely simmering. If it is bubbling too aggressively, lower the oven temperature by 25 degrees; if it is not simmering at all, increase it by 25 degrees.

▶ Remove the legs from the pan and transfer them to a plate to cool, about 10 minutes. When cool enough to handle, pick the meat from the legs and discard the bones. Pass the braising liquid through a food mill and return it the pan over medium-high heat. Stir in the heavy cream and bring to a simmer, then lower the heat and cook, stirring occasionally, until the sauce reduces and thickens enough to coat the back of a spoon, about 1¼ hours. Set a fine-mesh strainer over a medium bowl and strain the sauce. The sauce and meat may be used right away or refrigerated together in an airtight container for 2 to 3 days.

Slow-Cooked Egg
with Arugula Risotto, Mustard Crumble, and Mustard Seed Oil

This dish is perfect for the spring and summer, with verdant arugula purée stirred into the risotto, and fresh arugula and a slow-cooked egg on top. The mustard crumble and mustard oil add just enough heat and crunch.

4 or 6 large eggs (depending on number of servings)

2 cups vegetable stock, preferably homemade (page 365)

3 cups (loosely packed) arugula (about 1 bunch), blanched, shocked, and drained (see page 362), plus 1 cup (loosely packed) arugula

1 tablespoon extra-virgin olive oil

1 shallot, minced

1 cup risotto rice, such as Arborio

1 cup dry white wine

½ cup finely grated Parmigiano-Reggiano cheese

4 tablespoons (½ stick) unsalted butter

Kosher salt

Freshly ground white pepper

Mustard Seed Crumble (see Notebook, page 176)

1 tablespoon mustard oil

1 teaspoon Maldon sea salt

To slow-cook the eggs: Pour 1 quart water into a large saucepan and set over medium-high heat. Bring the water to 130°F, then carefully lower the eggs into the water, one at a time, with a kitchen spoon. Lower the heat to medium-low and cook gently for 40 minutes.

▶ Meanwhile, to make the risotto: Bring the stock to a simmer in a medium saucepan over medium-high heat.

▶ While the stock is heating, purée the blanched, shocked, drained arugula in a blender (the purée will be thick). Transfer to a small bowl and set aside.

▶ Heat the olive oil in a medium saucepan over medium heat. When the oil is shimmering, add the shallot and cook, stirring, until softened but not browned, about 1 minute. Stir in the rice and cook, coating the rice with the oil, until the rice turns opaque, about 1 minute (do not brown). Stir in the wine and cook, continuing to stir, until the wine has either evaporated or been absorbed by the rice, 3 to 4 minutes. Pour in 1 cup of the hot stock and cook, stirring, until the stock is almost completely absorbed by the rice, about 6 minutes. Add the remaining 1 cup stock in small increments, stirring constantly until it is absorbed before adding the next small increment. It should take about 10 more minutes to incorporate the remaining stock. When the risotto is done, stir in the cheese, butter, and arugula purée, melting the butter into the risotto. Season generously with kosher salt and pepper and stir vigorously one last time.

▶ To serve, divide the risotto among 4 or 6 bowls. Carefully remove the eggs from the simmering water, peel them, and top each serving with an egg. Scatter arugula around the egg in each bowl. Finish with mustard seed crumble and a drizzle of mustard oil over the egg. Season with sea salt and serve.

Crumbles

Crumbles are one of those restaurant-style flourishes that aren't that difficult to prepare but make a big impression at home because they are so visually arresting and have a "How did the cook do *that*?" impact. They are made by folding the main flavoring ingredient into a simple batter of butter, sugar, flour, and milk; the mixture is then spread out, baked, and crumbled on top of a variety of dishes. I think the best crumbles feature a brightly colored ingredient for maximum impact. The recipe below produces mustard crumble; you can replace the mustard powder and seeds with a total of 2 tablespoons of other ingredients such as ground caraway seeds (good over cassoulet), ground dried berries (delicious over yogurt), ground dried mushrooms (see page 363; a nice finishing touch to mushroom pastas), ground sesame seeds (to accent Asian dishes), and pulverized nuts (equally good over salads and sundaes).

MUSTARD SEED CRUMBLE

MAKES ENOUGH TO GARNISH 4 TO 6 DISHES

Nonstick cooking spray

2 tablespoons unsalted butter

1 tablespoon granulated sugar

1 tablespoon Colman's mustard powder

1 tablespoon yellow mustard seeds

½ cup bread flour

2 teaspoons kosher salt

2 teaspoons whole milk

Preheat the oven to 325°F. Line a baking sheet with parchment paper and spray with nonstick cooking spray.

▶ Put the butter and sugar in a mixing bowl and use a hand mixer or a whisk to beat them together until creamy and fluffy. Fold in the mustard powder with a rubber spatula, then fold in the mustard seeds, bread flour, and salt. Add the milk and fold just until clusters form.

▶ Spread the mixture out on the prepared baking sheet and bake until the crumble is golden brown, about 20 minutes. Remove from the oven and set aside to cool completely. Break up the crumble before serving. The crumble may be stored, crumbled, in an airtight bag at room temperature for up to 3 days.

Arroz Negro

with Grilled Baby Squid, Scallions, and Duck Chorizo

This dish is an eye-popping, crowd-pleasing take on a Portuguese classic that is loaded with boldly favored components. Black rice, made even darker with squid ink (see Notebook, page 179), is the perfect backdrop both for oceanic elements such as shrimp and for earthy, spicy chorizo, made here with the surprising choice of duck. A scattering of scallions provides crucial crunchy relief to the intense flavors.

½ pound ground duck

2 large garlic cloves, 1 minced, 1 thinly sliced

1 tablespoon paprika

2 teaspoons chili powder

2 tablespoons minced epazote (1 tablespoon ground fennel seeds plus 1 teaspoon dried oregano may be substituted)

2 tablespoons sherry vinegar

Kosher salt

Freshly ground black pepper

2 teaspoons blended oil or neutral oil such as canola

1 cup black glutinous rice

3 tablespoons extra-virgin olive oil

1 bunch scallions, whites and greens separated and thinly sliced

1 cup shellfish stock, preferably homemade (page 367)

1 tablespoon squid ink

1 cup baby squid, cleaned and thinly sliced into rounds

1 teaspoon crushed red pepper flakes

¼ cup dry white wine

1 tablespoon unsalted butter

1 tablespoon thinly sliced flat-leaf parsley leaves

1 tablespoon fried garlic (see page 369)

To make the duck chorizo: Put the duck, minced garlic, paprika, chili powder, epazote, and sherry vinegar in a large bowl. Season with salt and black pepper and stir to incorporate. Refrigerate for 4 to 6 hours to develop the flavors.

▸ Heat the blended oil in a large sauté pan over medium-high heat. When the oil is shimmering, add the duck chorizo mixture and cook, stirring, until browned and crispy, about 7 minutes. Transfer to a plate and set aside.

▸ To prepare the rice: Put the rice and 1½ cups water in a medium saucepan and set over medium-high heat. Bring to a simmer, then lower the heat, cover, and con-

tinue to simmer until the liquid has evaporated and the rice is al dente, about 8 minutes. Fluff with a fork and set aside, covered, to keep it warm.

▸ Heat 2 tablespoons of the olive oil in a large sauté pan over medium-high heat. When the oil is shimmering but not smoking, add the sliced garlic and the scallion whites and cook, stirring, until the garlic and scallions are softened but not browned, about 2 minutes. Stir in the rice and season with salt and black pepper. Add the shellfish stock and squid ink, stirring vigorously to activate the starches in the rice and help the grains bind.

continued

▶ Heat the remaining 1 tablespoon olive oil in a separate large sauté pan over high heat. When the oil is shimmering, add the squid, season with salt and black pepper, and cook, stirring, until opaque, about 2 minutes. Stir in the chorizo, red pepper flakes, and wine, and cook until the wine evaporates, about 2 minutes.

Stir in the butter and cook for 1 minute. Season with salt and black pepper and stir in the parsley leaves and scallion greens.

▶ To serve, divide the rice among 4 or 6 wide, shallow bowls and top with the squid-chorizo mixture. Sprinkle with fried garlic and serve.

Squid Ink

Squid ink is, of course, not actually ink, but rather a pigment released to throw off predators. It can be purchased in bottles and small packets from many fishmongers and specialty markets (see Sources, page 370). Squid ink stains everything it touches a stunning, stark black and imbues it with an understated, elegant shellfish flavor.

SQUID INK PASTA: Make a beautiful black fresh pasta by kneading a few tablespoons of squid ink into the dough—and wear latex gloves to keep from staining your hands. (See page 364 for homemade pasta instructions.) It's especially good with spaghetti, linguine, and gnocchi. Toss cooked squid-ink pasta with poached, shelled clams, mussels, and/or squid, or liven it up with spicy tomato sauce (page 147).

SQUID INK RISOTTO: Stir a few table-spoons of squid ink into shellfish risotto after the final addition of stock to underscore the oceanic flavor and create an arresting visual effect.

THICKENING AGENT: Stir a few drops of squid ink into soups that will be finished with shellfish or sauces that will be served over it. Doing so will thicken them and intensify their flavor.

Hen of the Woods Mushroom Paella

with Peas, Sweet Sausage, Shellfish, and Coriander Aioli

SERVES 4

The quintessential Basque rice dish, paella can be expanded to include a number of complementary ingredients. In addition to the shellfish, peas, and sausage we expect, the recipe here also features meaty, roasted hen of the woods mushrooms and a coriander aioli, which adds an herbaceous, cooling condiment that also helps pull the disparate elements together. Be sure to lower the heat as called for in the paella instructions to allow the *socarrat*—the hard crust on the bottom of the pan—to form; breaking it up and snacking on it is one of the great pleasures of paella eating.

1 pound ground pork shoulder

3 garlic cloves, 1 whole, 2 minced and kept separate

2 teaspoons fennel seeds

2 teaspoons kosher salt, plus more for seasoning

1 teaspoon freshly ground white pepper, plus more for seasoning

½ teaspoon dried basil

1½ teaspoons sweet paprika

2 large egg yolks

2 tablespoons freshly squeezed lemon juice

1 oil-packed anchovy fillet

1 tablespoon Dijon mustard

1 tablespoon coriander seeds

1 tablespoon cilantro leaves

1 teaspoon finely ground black pepper, plus more for seasoning

1 cup plus 4 tablespoons blended oil or neutral oil such as canola

½ cup extra-virgin olive oil

1 tablespoon minced shallot

2 cups short-grain white rice

1 tablespoon saffron threads

6 cups chicken stock, preferably homemade (page 366)

8 ounces canned crushed tomatoes, with their juices

1 (6- to 8-ounce) hen of the woods mushroom

½ cup fresh English peas

8 large head-on prawns, about 1 ounce each

12 mussels

12 Manila clams

1 tablespoon thinly sliced flat-leaf parsley leaves

To make the sweet sausage: Put the pork, 1 of the minced garlic cloves, the fennel seeds, salt, white pepper, basil, and ½ teaspoon of the paprika in a large bowl and use clean hands to knead together just to incorporate. Refrigerate in an airtight container for at least 1 hour or up to 24 hours.

▸ To make the coriander aioli: Put the egg yolks, lemon juice, anchovy, mustard, coriander seeds, cilantro, whole garlic clove, and black pepper in a blender and blend, slowly adding 1 cup of the blended oil in a thin stream until emulsified. Transfer to a small bowl and set aside.

continued

To make the paella: Heat the olive oil in a paella pan or wide, deep sauté pan over high heat. When the oil is shimmering, add the sausage and cook, using a spoon to break it into bite-size pieces, until browned all over, about 5 minutes. Add the remaining minced garlic clove, the shallot, and the remaining 1 teaspoon paprika and cook, stirring, for 1 minute. Stir in the rice and saffron and cook, stirring, for 2 minutes. Pour in the stock and tomatoes with their juices, and season with salt and white pepper. Stir to incorporate, and use the back of the spoon to spread the rice evenly in the pan. Lower the heat and cook slowly so the rice forms a hard crust (*socarrat*) on the bottom of the pan, about 20 minutes.

Meanwhile, to roast the mushroom: Preheat the oven to 450°F. Drizzle the mushroom with 1 tablespoon of the blended oil and season generously with salt and black pepper. Heat the remaining 3 tablespoons of blended oil in a large, ovenproof sauté pan over high heat. When the oil is shimmering, set the mushroom in the pan and cook until golden brown and starting to crisp around the edges, about 4 minutes. Transfer the pan to the oven and roast until the mushroom is crispy on the outside and soft in the middle, about 8 minutes.

Stir the peas into the paella, and set the mushroom in the middle of the pan. Arrange the prawns, mussels, and clams around the mushroom and cover the pan with a lid or aluminum foil. Cook over medium heat until the prawns are pink, the mussels and clams have opened, and the rice is cooked but still al dente, about 4 minutes. (Discard any mussels and clams that do not open.) Garnish the paella with parsley, serve family-style with the coriander aioli alongside, and set bowls out for discarding mussel and clam shells.

Saffron

Saffron threads impart a golden hue and distinct, faintly Provençal flavor to soups, seafood stews, or risottos—most famously risotto Milanese. Saffron is expensive, but you rarely need to use more than a pinch at a time, blooming it in hot liquid. To do so, put a pinch of threads in a small bowl and add a few tablespoons of whatever liquid you are cooking with, such as seafood broth if making bouillabaisse. (In the recipe for paella, I do not do this because I prefer it toasted in the pan with the other aromatics for a stronger effect.) If you are adding it to non-broth preparations, bloom the threads in a tablespoon or two of hot water.

AIOLI: Whisk bloomed saffron into homemade garlic mayonnaise; serve on toasted bread as an accompaniment to fish and shellfish soups and stews.

RISOTTO MILANESE: Add saffron to whatever stock you are using in your risotto. Serve with osso buco or other braised meats.

CORN SOUP: Stir bloomed saffron into corn soup (see page 227); if you like, finish with poached shrimp or cooked crabmeat.

BOUILLABAISSE: Add saffron to the recipe on page 131 for a bouillabaisse-like effect.

5

Fish
and Shellfish

Blue Crab Cakes

with Grilled Poblano Remoulade and Jicama Salad

Pardon me for boasting, but if there's one thing I think I make better than anybody, it's crab cakes. I think it's because I have such a fondness for the crab itself (see page 71), so my main crab cake mission is to preserve its texture and flavor. The key to making these, which feature no breading inside, is to be gentle, gentle, gentle. You want to combine the ingredients *just* enough that they hold together. I also apply two cooking techniques, first pan-frying the cakes just to give them the expected, crispy texture and help them hold, then finishing them in the more tender ambient heat of the oven. You will need to be very attentive when shaping, breading, and cooking these, but the result is a luxurious crab cake that may just change the way you think about them. They are paired here with a jicama salad and poblano remoulade, which offer contrasts of temperature and texture. This is my wife Meredith's favorite dish, and she often asks me to make it on vacation; it doesn't take much persuasion because they're among my favorite things to eat as well.

2 tablespoons blended oil or neutral oil such as canola, plus more for frying

½ cup minced Spanish onion

½ cup minced celery

2 tablespoons Old Bay seasoning

2 tablespoons cider vinegar

2 tablespoons extra-virgin olive oil

1 tablespoon sugar

1 cup thinly sliced jicama

2 tablespoons seeded, thinly sliced jalapeño

½ cup thinly sliced radishes

¼ cup thinly sliced red onion

¼ cup thin carrot matchsticks

1 tablespoon thinly sliced cilantro

Kosher salt

Freshly ground white pepper

¾ cup mayonnaise

2 tablespoons Dijon mustard

2 pounds jumbo lump blue crabmeat or peekytoe crabmeat, cleaned

2 cups all-purpose flour

4 large eggs

2 cups panko bread crumbs, crushed by hand into a fine powder

2 cups Poblano Remoulade (see Note, page 187)

To make the crab cakes: Heat the blended oil in a medium sauté pan over medium heat. When the oil is shimmering, add the onion and celery and cook, stirring, until the vegetables are softened but not browned, about 2 minutes. Stir in the Old Bay and remove the pan from the heat. Transfer the mixture to a large temperature-proof mixing bowl and set aside to cool slightly. Refrigerate until chilled, about 15 minutes.

▸ Meanwhile, to make the jicama salad: Put the cider vinegar, olive oil, and sugar in a medium bowl and whisk until the sugar dissolves. Add the jicama, jalapeño, radishes, red onion, carrot matchsticks, and cilantro and toss well. Season with salt and white pepper and toss again. Set aside.

▸ When the onion-celery mixture has chilled, use a rubber spatula to fold in the mayonnaise and mustard, then fold in the crabmeat; the mixture will look like a loose crab salad. Form the crab mixture into 8 balls, each about the size of a baseball. Put the flour in a medium bowl. Put the eggs in a second medium bowl and beat them to blend. Put the bread crumbs in a third medium bowl. Dredge the balls first in the flour, then in the egg, and finally in the panko, generously coating them. While they are in the panko, use your hands to press each ball into a 5-inch cake, about 1 inch thick, and transfer to a large plate or platter.

▸ Position a rack in the center of the oven and preheat the oven to 400°F. Line a baking sheet or platter with paper towels and set it aside. Heat a large, deep sauté pan over medium-high heat and pour in enough blended oil to come 1 inch up the sides of the pan. When the oil is shimmering but not smoking, add the crab cakes in batches, and cook until golden brown on the bottom, about 3 minutes. Gently turn the crab cakes over and cook until golden on the other side, about 3 minutes more. Transfer the crab cakes to the prepared baking sheet or platter and season immediately with salt and white pepper. Transfer to a clean baking sheet without crowding. Once all the cakes have been pan-fried and gathered, bake until they are heated through, about 2 minutes.

▸ To serve, divide the jicama salad among 4 plates. Place 2 crab cakes on the side of each salad, and drizzle the cakes with the remoulade.

NOTE: To make poblano remoulade, add 2 roasted (see page 362), peeled, seeded, and diced poblano peppers to a food processor along with the other ingredients at the beginning of the remoulade recipe in the following Notebook entry.

Remoulade

In my opinion, remoulade is one of those perfect creations that hits our taste buds just right: a mayonnaise-like emulsification of egg yolks, mustard, and oil with salty cornichons and capers, acidity from lemon juice, and heat from cayenne. (If all of this sounds like plain old tartar sauce, it basically is, but remoulade came first and feels a little fancier.) It's the perfect accompaniment to just about any shellfish preparation, and—as you can see below—can be easily flavored for other purposes.

MAKES ABOUT 2 CUPS

2 fresh large egg yolks

2 cornichons, plus 1 tablespoon cornichon brine

1 tablespoon freshly squeezed lemon juice

½ tablespoon Dijon mustard

½ teaspoon capers (preferably brine-packed; do not rinse)

1 teaspoon cayenne

1½ cups blended oil or neutral oil such as canola

Kosher salt

Freshly ground white pepper

Put the egg yolks, cornichons, cornichon brine, lemon juice, mustard, capers, and cayenne in a food processor fitted with a steel blade, and process to a paste. While continuing to blend, slowly drizzle in the oil in a thin stream until emulsified. Season with salt and pepper and serve. The remoulade can be refrigerated in an airtight container for up to 3 days.

OLD BAY REMOULADE: For a perfect condiment for fish and shellfish boils, fold Old Bay seasoning, to taste, into the remoulade.

CHIPOTLE REMOULADE: Stir adobo (the liquid in which canned chipotle peppers are stored) into the remoulade. Serve it under, over, or alongside grilled meats and poultry.

SAFFRON REMOULADE: Heat 3 tablespoons of the blended oil called for in the remoulade recipe in a small, heavy pan over medium heat. After 1 minute, add a pinch of saffron threads, remove the pan from the heat, and let bloom for 5 minutes. Strain out the threads, allow the oil to cool, and use it along with the remaining oil in the remoulade. Use it as a condiment for bouillabaisse or any poached fish dish.

TAPENADE REMOULADE: Make the remoulade, omitting the cornichons and capers, fold in tapenade, and serve it with grilled, meaty fish such as tuna or swordfish.

Steamed Mussels

with Taro *Frites*, Cilantro, Kaffir Lime, and Siamese Green Curry

SERVES 4

This is my Asian-inflected play on the Belgian classic *moule frites*, or mussels and fries. Rather than in a Provençal-like base of white wine, shallots, and garlic, the mussels here are cooked in green curry. Even if you usually prefer straight-up, classic potato French fries, try these shoestring, or haystack, fries, which take advantage of the character of the taro to produce a crispy, crunchy side that gets along great with the Asian flavors here.

1 taro root

Canola oil or corn oil, for frying

Kosher salt

Freshly ground white pepper

1 quart Siamese Green Curry (page 59)

2 pounds mussels, preferably Bouchot (see Notebook, page 191)

2 kaffir lime leaves

¼ cup (loosely packed) cilantro leaves

2 tablespoons hand-torn Thai basil leaves

2 limes, halved

To make the taro *frites*: Peel the taro root and thinly slice it by hand into French fry slices, or on a mandoline with the French fry or julienne attachment. Put the slices in a bowl, cover with cold water, agitate with your fingers for a few seconds to rinse off any starch, and drain. Pour oil into a deep fryer, or wide, deep, heavy pot, to a depth of 4 inches. Heat the oil to 300°F. Line a plate with paper towels. Remove the taro from the water, pat dry with paper towels, and season with salt and pepper. Add to the oil and fry, stirring occasionally with a slotted spoon, until the taro is crispy, about 5 minutes. Use a slotted spoon or spider to transfer the *frites* to the prepared plate and season generously with salt and pepper.

▸ To prepare the mussels: Heat the curry in a large, deep, heavy saucepan over medium-high heat. When the curry simmers, add the mussels and kaffir lime leaves, cover, and steam until the mussels open, about 5 minutes. (Discard any mussels that haven't opened.) Taste and add salt and pepper, if necessary.

▸ Divide the mussels among 4 bowls, and garnish each with cilantro and basil. Serve with taro *frites* alongside and lime halves for squeezing over each dish. Pass extra bowls for discarding mussel shells.

NOTE: The *frites* are fried at a lower temperature than most frying recipes call for because they need to cook longer to achieve the desired crunchy texture. They are not soft on the inside like traditional fries.

Steamed Mussels

Mussels are and forever will be popular because they have a few irresistible qualities: they are relatively inexpensive; they are easy to cook; they have a pleasing texture and take on a variety of flavors well; and most recipes for cooking them follow a similar series of steps, inviting variation and experimentation. My favorite variety of mussels are Bouchot from Maine, but Prince Edward Island (PEI) mussels are also dependable. Both are a bit more expensive than other mussels, but well worth it for their plump size and sweet flavor.

To work with mussels, first clean them under cold, running water, scrubbing the shells clean of any debris and debearding them by pulling off the fibrous tuft protruding from the crevice. Gently pinch any that are open before cooking; if the shells don't close, the mussels are dead and should be discarded.

SCAMPI-STYLE MUSSELS WITH CURED PORK: In a large sauté pan over medium heat, render diced pancetta, *guanciale* (page 81), or slab bacon in a pot until it's crispy and has given off enough fat to coat the bottom of the pan, about 6 minutes. Add 1 sliced garlic clove and a pinch of crushed red pepper flakes, and sauté the garlic for 1 minute. Add the mussels and 2 tablespoons butter, pour in 1 cup white wine, and simmer until reduced by half, about 6 minutes. Cover and steam until the mussels open, about 5 minutes.

MUSSELS FRA DIAVOLO: Steam the mussels open in spicy tomato sauce. Use your own recipe or the one on page 147, omitting the crab.

MUSSELS WITH WHITE WINE AND CREAM: In a large sauté pan, sauté 1 sliced garlic clove and 1 sliced shallot in 2 tablespoons olive oil over medium-high heat. Add the mussels, season with salt and white pepper, pour in 1 cup white wine, and simmer until reduced by half, about 6 minutes. Gently stir in 1 to 2 tablespoons heavy cream, cover, and simmer until the mussels open, about 5 minutes.

BEER-BRAISED MUSSELS: Adapt the recipe for Mussels with White Wine and Cream, to the left, by adding 1 teaspoon celery seeds along with the garlic and shallot, and replacing the wine with a light beer such as a lager, a pilsner, or even Corona. Omit the cream.

Poached Maine Lobster

with Baby Bok Choy, Wood Ear Mushrooms, Crispy Shallots, and Coconut Broth

SERVES 4

The first time I tried to make a version of *tom kha*, or Thai coconut soup, I challenged myself to spin it into a main-course dish. The result? An aromatic coconut broth with many of the most popular Thai flavors, such as lemongrass and kaffir lime. The lobster is separated into parts, some of which are roasted for flavoring the broth, while others are poached and then finished in the coconut broth. Garnished with baby bok choy, wood ear mushrooms, and fried shallots, this dish is a real feast for the senses, relatively light but brimming with big flavors.

4 Maine lobsters, about 1¼ pounds each

2 cups dry white wine

1 (1-inch) piece fresh ginger, peeled and thinly sliced, plus 3 tablespoons peeled, minced fresh ginger

1 lemongrass stalk, coarsely chopped (see page 362), plus 2½ teaspoons minced lemongrass

4 kaffir lime leaves

2 tablespoons blended oil or neutral oil such as canola

3½ teaspoons minced garlic

4 teaspoons minced shallot

2 cups coconut milk

1 tablespoon fish sauce

1 tablespoon palm sugar or turbinado sugar such as Sugar in the Raw

1½ Thai red chiles, the half chile soaked in water for 5 minutes, then drained, seeded, and minced, 1 chile thinly sliced

2 teaspoons tamarind concentrate

1 tablespoon freshly squeezed lime juice

1 cup wood ear mushrooms, ends trimmed (black trumpet may be substituted)

4 baby bok choy, ends trimmed, thinly sliced lengthwise

Kosher salt

Freshly ground white pepper

¾ cup (loosely packed) cilantro leaves

¼ cup (loosely packed) hand-torn Thai basil leaves

¼ cup fried shallots (see page 369)

Preheat the oven to 400°F. Fill a large bowl halfway with ice water.

▸ Kill the lobsters by impaling them just behind the eyes with a large, heavy knife and bringing the knife forward between the eyes like a lever. Remove the tails, claws, and knuckles from the lobsters and set them aside. Place the bodies on a baking sheet. Roast in the oven until bright red, shaking the pan occasionally to ensure even cooking, about 20 minutes. When the lob-

ster bodies have finished roasting, remove the baking sheet from the oven and set it aside.

▸ Meanwhile, put 1 gallon water, the wine, sliced ginger, chopped lemongrass, and 2 of the lime leaves in a large, deep pot and set over high heat. Bring to a boil, then lower the heat so the liquid is simmering; continue to simmer for 15 minutes to develop the flavors. Add the lobster claws and knuckles to the liquid and simmer

continued

for 2 minutes. Add the tails and continue to simmer until bright red, about 6 minutes. Transfer the claws, knuckles, and tails to the bowl of ice water until chilled, about 12 minutes. Remove the lobster meat from the shells and reserve. Return the lobster shells to the poaching liquid and add the lobster bodies and continue to simmer for 1 hour. Strain through a fine-mesh strainer set over a large bowl. Discard the solids and reserve 1 cup of the poaching liquid, discarding the rest.

▸ To make the coconut broth: Heat 1 tablespoon of the blended oil in a large pot over medium heat. When the oil is shimmering, add 2 teaspoons of the minced lemongrass, 2 teaspoons of the minced ginger, 2 teaspoons of the garlic, and 2 teaspoons of the shallot and cook, stirring, until softened but not browned, about 2 minutes. Add the coconut milk, reserved 1 cup lobster poaching liquid, the fish sauce, palm sugar, minced chile, tamarind, and remaining 2 lime leaves and bring to a simmer. Lower the heat so the liquid is simmering; continue to simmer until nicely thickened and the flavors have mingled, about 20 minutes, then stir in the lime juice. Taste and adjust the seasoning if necessary; the sauce should be sweet, salty, sour, and spicy. Strain through a fine-mesh strainer set over a bowl, pressing down on the solids with a spoon or the bottom of a ladle to extract as much flavorful liquid as possible. Discard the solids and set the liquid aside. Keep covered and warm.

▸ Heat the remaining 1 tablespoon blended oil in a large, heavy sauté pan over medium-high heat. When the oil is shimmering, add the remaining ½ teaspoon minced lemongrass, remaining 2 teaspoons shallot, 1 teaspoon of the minced ginger, and remaining 1½ teaspoons garlic and cook, stirring, until the shallot turns translucent, about 1 minute. Add the mushrooms and cook until they soften slightly, about 3 minutes. Add the bok choy, season with salt and white pepper, and cook until al dente, about 1 minute.

▸ Reheat the coconut broth in a large, heavy saucepan over medium heat. As soon as it simmers, add the lobster meat and heat until warmed through, about 3 minutes.

▸ To serve, use a slotted spoon to divide the lobster meat among 4 bowls, and pour the broth over and around it. Top with the stir-fried vegetables, and garnish with cilantro, basil, fried shallots, and chile slices.

Wok Mix

At Kin Shop, we use a mixture of 2 parts minced shallot, 1 part ginger, ½ part minced lemongrass, and 1½ parts minced garlic as the aromatics for stir-frying vegetables. Though not named, the mixture is incorporated into this recipe and the one on page 197. It's a good, all-purpose mix for stir-frying dishes served in an Asian context.

Baby Bok Choy

Bok choy is my favorite cabbage variety, with its pleasing crunch and high water content; it adds a refreshing element to a lot of plates. Baby bok choy cooks quickly, is more tender than regular bok choy, and is very attractive on the plate; it makes your cooking look extra-accomplished without any extra work. If halving or quartering baby bok choy before cooking, do so through the root to preserve its essential shape.

STIR-FRIED BABY BOK CHOY: You don't need a wok to stir-fry baby bok choy. Just get a heavy skillet or pot nice and hot over high heat, briefly heat enough oil to coat the bottom, add the quartered baby bok choy, a few tablespoons of oyster sauce, and some wok mix (see facing page), and cook, stirring constantly, until wilted, about 3 minutes. Serve as a freestanding side dish or plate alongside fish, poultry, or meat.

STEAMED BABY BOK CHOY: Arrange whole baby bok choy in a steamer basket over an inch or so of simmering water in a pot. Serve plain or season lightly with salt. Serve with just about anything—though it's especially good with white-fleshed fish.

GRILLED BABY BOK CHOY AND TOMATOES: Put halved baby bok choy in a large, wide bowl. Add halved plum tomatoes (with their seeds) and olive oil. Season with salt and pepper and toss well. Grill the tomatoes and bok choy over indirect heat until the bok choy is wilted, with nice grill marks on both sides. Serve with grilled beef or poultry.

BUTTER-BRAISED BABY BOK CHOY: Bring about an inch of water or chicken or vegetable stock to a simmer in a sauté pan over medium-high heat and swirl in 1 to 2 tablespoons unsalted butter to melt. Lay halved baby bok choy in a single layer in the simmering liquid, adding more liquid if necessary to just cover the bok choy. Partially cover the pan, and simmer until al dente, about 8 minutes. Serve as a side dish, along with white rice.

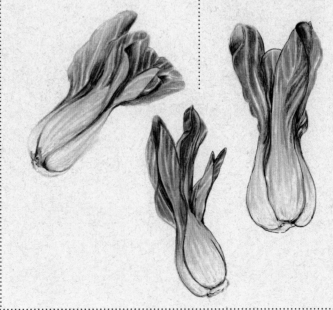

Grilled Shrimp
with Sticky Rice and Phuket-Style Black Pepper Sauce

This is a potently flavored shrimp dish that's put over the top by the spicy black pepper sauce, with the sticky rice providing crucial relief. The preparation on which this shrimp marinade is based is traditionally made only with curry paste, but I add unsweetened coconut milk to lighten it up and allow the flavor of the shrimp to shine through. If you can get them, banana leaves really are the best way to cook and present the rice.

1 hothouse cucumber, seeds removed, flesh sliced into half circles

1 cup rice vinegar

Kosher salt

1 tablespoon sugar

1 teaspoon shrimp paste

1 cup sticky rice, soaked in water overnight and drained

1 cup unsweetened coconut milk

1 tablespoon fish sauce

Banana leaf, optional

1 Thai red chile, seeded and soaked for 5 minutes in warm water, then drained

2 teaspoons thinly sliced shallot

2 teaspoons thinly sliced garlic

2 teaspoons peeled, minced fresh ginger

2 teaspoons chopped lemongrass (see page 362)

½ teaspoon dried shrimp

2 teaspoons freshly ground white pepper, plus more for seasoning

2 teaspoons sumac

1 teaspoon coriander seeds

1 cilantro stem, leaves removed

1 pound large or jumbo shrimp, with the heads on

2 cups Phuket-Style Black Pepper Sauce (see Notebook, page 199)

2 limes, halved

To make the pickled cucumber: Put the cucumber in a medium, heatproof bowl and set it aside. Bring the rice vinegar, 2 teaspoons salt, and the sugar to a simmer in a medium saucepan over medium-high heat, stirring to dissolve the sugar, about 1 minute. When the sugar has dissolved, pour the hot mixture over the cucumber and immediately transfer it to the refrigerator. Refrigerate for at least 1 hour or cover and refrigerate overnight.

▶ Preheat the oven to 250°F. Put the shrimp paste on a small piece of aluminum foil, wrap loosely, and roast until dried, about 20 minutes. Remove from the oven and set aside.

▶ To prepare the rice: Set a medium, heavy saucepan over medium heat and add enough water to come 2 inches up the sides of the pan. Place a steamer basket in the pot and add the soaked rice to the basket. Bring the water to a boil, then lower the heat so the water is simmering, cover the pan, and steam until the rice is tender, about 40 minutes. Transfer the rice to a medium bowl and stir in ½ cup of the coconut milk and the fish sauce. Wrap the rice in a banana leaf or a resealable plastic bag to lock in its moisture.

continued

To make the prawn spread: Put the chile, shallot, garlic, ginger, lemongrass, roasted shrimp paste, dried shrimp, white pepper, sumac, coriander, cilantro stem, and remaining ½ cup coconut milk in a blender and blend until smooth.

Preheat a grill to high, or heat a grill pan over high heat for 5 minutes. (See pages 274–75 for grilling guidelines.) Use a pastry brush to brush one side of each prawn generously with the prawn spread. (You will not use all the spread; leftover spread may be refriger-ated in an airtight container for up to 3 days and used on other fish, meat, and vegetables before grilling.) Season the other side with salt and white pepper. Add the prawns to the grill, spread side down, and grill for 2 minutes. Turn the prawns over and cook until cooked through, about 1 minute more.

To serve, spoon rice into the center of each of 4 plates. Top each serving with 4 prawns, then the black pepper sauce, then the cucumbers. Garnish each plate with a lime half for squeezing.

Phuket-Style Black Pepper Sauce

This sauce never fails to remind me of my first trip to Thailand, during which I visited a marketplace on Phuket, an island off the southern coast, where you picked out your own fresh fish and shellfish at various stalls, and the proprietor would cook it for you. I asked one purveyor if I could pay extra and cook my own food. The woman who owned the stall was reluctant, telling me it was dangerous, but after I showed her my burn-covered arms, the pride and joy of every cook, she figured I could take care of myself. I started making a Phuket sauce based on ones I'd eaten on the trip. She didn't like the direction I was going—she especially didn't appreciate my tossing black peppercorns into her wok—so she began trying to course-correct for me, adding things like coconut milk and hoisin sauce. This recipe is for the sauce we ended up with. I thought it was *delicious*; she didn't.

Serve this sauce over poached or grilled shellfish, white-fleshed fish such as halibut or cod, grilled pork, and grilled chicken dishes or fried chicken.

MAKES ABOUT 1 QUART

2 tablespoons blended oil or neutral oil such as canola

1 tablespoon minced garlic

1 tablespoon peeled, minced fresh ginger

1 tablespoon minced shallot

1 tablespoon minced lemongrass (see page 362)

2 tablespoons coarsely ground black pepper

2 cups unsweetened coconut milk

1 cup hoisin sauce

¼ cup rice vinegar

2 tablespoons fish sauce

Juice of 1 lime

Heat the oil in a large saucepan over medium heat. When the oil is shimmering, add the garlic, ginger, shallot, and lemongrass and cook, stirring, until the vegetables are softened but not browned, about 2 minutes. Add the pepper and cook, stirring, until fragrant, about 2 minutes.

▶ Pour in the coconut milk, hoisin, vinegar, and fish sauce. Stir, bring to a boil, then lower the heat and simmer for 30 minutes to develop the flavor. Stir in the lime juice. The sauce can be refrigerated in an airtight container for up to 3 days.

Sautéed Skate Wing
with Red Onions, Cabbage, Pastrami, and Hot Mustard Sauce

Believe it or not, this skate dish is a loose play on a Reuben sandwich, with pastrami relegated to the background and sautéed with cabbage and other vegetables that reference the sauerkraut. The piquant sauce hits many of the same flavor buttons as Russian dressing.

2 teaspoons Colman's mustard powder

2 teaspoons soy sauce

1 cup plus 1 tablespoon rice vinegar

1 cup dry white wine

2 shallots, thinly sliced

Kosher salt

Freshly ground white pepper

2 tablespoons heavy cream

6 tablespoons unsalted butter, softened at room temperature

1 teaspoon minced chives

4 tablespoons extra-virgin olive oil

½ cup large pastrami matchsticks (see Note on facing page)

2 cups shredded green cabbage

½ cup thin carrot matchsticks

½ cup thinly sliced red onion

1 teaspoon minced flat-leaf parsley

4 skate wings, about 6 ounces each

1 tablespoon all-purpose flour

To make the mustard sauce: Put the mustard powder, soy sauce, and 2 teaspoons water in a small bowl and whisk together. Put 1 cup of the vinegar, the wine, and shallots in a small, heavy saucepan over medium heat. Season with salt and pepper, bring to a simmer, and continue to simmer until the liquid is almost completely evaporated, about 8 minutes. Pour in the heavy cream and cook until reduced by half, about 2 minutes. Whisk in 4 tablespoons (½ stick) of the butter and add the mustard powder mixture. Strain through a fine-mesh strainer set over a bowl and stir in the chives. Remove the pan from the heat, cover to keep warm, and set aside.

▶ To cook the pastrami and cabbage garnish: Heat 2 tablespoons of the oil in a wide, deep sauté pan over medium-high heat. When the oil is shimmering, add the pastrami and cook, stirring occasionally, until crispy, about 2 minutes. Add the cabbage, carrot, and onion to the pan, and season with salt and pepper. Cook, stirring, until the vegetables are just al dente, about 1 minute. Stir in the remaining 1 tablespoon vinegar and cook, stirring, until the liquid has evaporated, about 1 minute. Stir in the parsley. Set aside, covered, to keep the pastrami warm.

▶ To prepare the skate: Season the wings generously with salt and pepper. Put the flour in a medium bowl and dredge the skate, flesh side down, in the flour to conceal the bloodline, shaking off any excess. Heat the remaining 2 tablespoons oil in a large sauté pan over high heat. When the oil is shimmering, add the skate to the pan, floured side down, and cook until golden brown, about 4 minutes. Add the remaining 2 tablespoons butter to the pan, allow it to melt, and use a tablespoon to baste the fish with the melted butter. Use a fish spatula to gently turn the skate over and cook until the fish is golden brown on the other side and cooked through, about 2 minutes more.

▶ To serve, spoon mustard sauce into the center of each of 4 plates. Pile cabbage on top, and finish with a skate wing.

NOTE: Pastrami is made from beef brisket, and if you visit a serious butcher, you should be able to select a lean cut or the fattier part, which comes from the deckle. I prefer the lean portion, sliced super-thin, which really showcases the smoky, peppery quality of the cured meat.

Reuben-Inspired Combinations

The quintet at the center of a Reuben sandwich—rye bread, pastrami, Swiss cheese, cabbage, and Russian dressing—can be adapted in a number of ways. Some use all five ingredients, and some borrow more selectively, as I do in the recipe for the sautéed skate wing on page 200.

REUBEN OMELET: Make an omelet with shaved or diced pastrami, Swiss cheese, and chopped cabbage that's been braised or sautéed with mustard greens. Serve with toasted rye bread alongside.

STUFFED CABBAGE WITH GROUND PASTRAMI, TOMATO SAUCE, AND PECORINO: The stuffed red cabbage recipe on page 101 is based on this flavor profile. Make it with white cabbage instead of red for a Reuben-inspired variation.

EMMENTAL AND PASTRAMI FONDUE: Make a fondue using Emmental cheese, or another alpine variety, and serve it with cubed rye bread, cabbage, and pastrami for dunking. To really drive home the Reuben theme, prepare skewers with cubes of all three ingredients and present a dish of Russian dressing alongside for dipping after the fondue.

RAW CABBAGE AND FRIED PASTRAMI SALAD: Make a mustard-cornichon vinaigrette by stirring together ¼ cup white wine vinegar, ½ cup extra-virgin olive oil, 1 teaspoon Colman's mustard powder, 2 teaspoons minced cornichons, and 1 teaspoon minced shallot. Put shredded cabbage, shredded carrots, and thinly sliced red onion in a mixing bowl. Add slices of hot pastrami, drizzle the vinaigrette over it, and toss well. Serve on its own, alongside roasted white-fleshed fish, or as a taco filling.

Grilled Jerk-Style Black Grouper

with Tostones, Dandelion Greens, Yams, and Black Bean Purée

SERVES 4

Some of the signature flavors of the Caribbean come together in this dish, which was inspired by a trip my wife and I took to St. Barths in 2007. We stayed at the Tom Beach hotel and took our meals at a restaurant with a deck situated right on the beach, where they combined local ingredients with the day's catch. It was a very simple, natural, and delicious way of eating, and I came to love the indigenous ingredients, such as black beans, yams, and plantains. When I got home, with those flavors fresh in my mind, I came up with this slightly more fancified take, turning the beans into the basis of the sauce and dicing the yams before frying them.

- 3 tablespoons blended oil or neutral oil such as canola
- 5 garlic cloves, 3 thinly sliced, 2 minced
- 1 shallot, thinly sliced
- 2 tablespoons cumin seeds
- 1 cup dried black beans, soaked overnight in cold water and drained (2 cups rinsed, drained canned beans can be substituted)

- Kosher salt
- Freshly ground white pepper
- 2 cups chicken stock, preferably homemade (page 366)
- Canola oil or corn oil, for frying
- 1 yellow plantain, peeled and cut into 1-inch disks, soaked in cold water for 5 minutes, and then drained

- 1 cup peeled, diced yams
- 2 cups coarsely chopped dandelion greens
- 4 skinless grouper fillets, about 6 ounces each
- ½ cup Jerk Marinade (see Notebook, page 206)

To make the black bean sauce: Heat 1 tablespoon of the blended oil in a large, heavy saucepan over medium-high heat. When the oil is shimmering, add the sliced garlic cloves, shallot, and cumin and cook for 1 minute. Stir in the beans and season with salt and pepper. Pour in the chicken stock, bring to a simmer, then lower the heat and continue to simmer until the beans are soft, about 30 minutes, or 15 minutes for canned beans. Transfer the contents of the pan to a blender and blend until smooth. Season with salt and pepper and strain through a fine-mesh strainer set over a large bowl, pressing down on the solids with a rubber spatula or the bottom of a ladle.

▸ Pour canola oil into a deep fryer, or wide, deep, heavy pot, to a depth of 4 inches. Heat the oil to 350°F. Line a plate with paper towels and set aside. Pat the plantain disks dry with paper towels, add them to the fryer, and fry until they begin to turn golden brown, about 2 minutes. Use a slotted spoon to transfer the plantains

continued

to a cutting board, and use the back of the spoon to flatten lightly. Return the slices to the fryer and fry until crisp. Transfer to the prepared plate. Add the yams to the fryer and fry until crispy, about 3 minutes. Transfer to the prepared plate with the plantains and season with salt and pepper.

▸ Heat the remaining 2 tablespoons blended oil in a large, deep sauté pan over medium heat. When the oil is shimmering, add the crispy yams and plantains and cook for about 1 minute to warm them through. Add the minced garlic and cook, stirring, until the garlic is golden brown, about 3 minutes. Add the dandelion greens and cook until wilted, about 1 minute. Season with salt and pepper.

▸ Season the grouper fillets with salt and pepper and brush both sides with the jerk marinade. (For a less spicy result, use less marinade, and vice versa.) Heat a grill. (See pages 274–75 for grilling guidelines.) Add the fillets and grill until dark grill marks form and the fish is cooked through, about 4 minutes on each side.

▸ To serve, spoon black bean sauce on the bottom of each of 4 plates. Spoon plantains, yams, and greens over the sauce, and perch a fish fillet on top.

Jerk Marinade

I love jerk spice mixtures for the pungent combination of chiles, pepper, spices, and rum. I'm especially fond of how the sweet rum perfectly balances the heat of the other ingredients. My version of this Jamaican staple was borrowed from the one my friend Jeff Allen makes. Use this on fish, chicken wings, baby back ribs, or portobello mushrooms bound for the grill. Vary the marinating technique and time based on the density of the ingredient being grilled and how concentrated a result is desired. For vegetables and lean cuts such as whitefish, brush on a small amount of jerk seasoning and allow to marinate for 1 hour or less—in the recipe on page 203, the jerk is brushed on immediately before grilling and still makes an impact. For poultry and meat, toss the protein in the seasoning, place in a resealable plastic bag, and marinate in the refrigerator overnight.

MAKES ½ CUP

1 tablespoon minced scallions, white part only

1 tablespoon minced garlic

1 seeded, minced habanero chile

1 tablespoon dark rum

1 tablespoon kosher salt

1 teaspoon dried thyme

1 teaspoon garlic powder

1 teaspoon ground allspice

½ teaspoon freshly ground black pepper

½ teaspoon chili powder

½ teaspoon paprika

¼ teaspoon ground cinnamon

1 tablespoon blended oil or neutral oil such as canola

Put the scallion whites, garlic, habanero, rum, salt, thyme, garlic powder, allspice, black pepper, chili powder, paprika, cinnamon, oil, and 2 tablespoons water in a blender and purée until smooth. The marinade can be refrigerated in an airtight container for up to 3 days.

Steamed Red Snapper

with Brussels Sprouts, Chanterelles, Squash Purée, and Veal-Ginger Jus

I first came up with this dish when I was a sous chef at Della Femina restaurant in New York City. It's a very conservative combination of snapper and vegetables, but what makes it unique is the addition of ginger juice to the veal jus. It was the first time I'd used fresh juice in my cooking and I loved the effect, as well as the impact the ginger made. You can also serve the squash purée with roasted meats and game. It's especially good with duck.

---

1 quart veal stock, preferably home-made (page 368)

Kosher salt

Freshly ground white pepper

3 tablespoons unsalted butter

¼ cup fresh ginger juice (see page 116)

1 tablespoon blended oil or neutral oil such as canola

2 cups (loosely packed) Brussels sprout leaves (from about 8 sprouts)

½ cup chanterelle mushrooms, larger ones halved or quartered

½ shallot, thinly sliced

1 tablespoon plus 2 teaspoons minced chives

2 teaspoons thinly sliced flat-leaf parsley leaves

2 cups dry white wine

1 Spanish onion, sliced

1 (1-inch) piece fresh ginger, peeled and thinly sliced

1 lemongrass stalk, thinly sliced (see page 362)

2 limes

4 skin-on red snapper fillets, about 6 ounces each

1 tablespoon extra-virgin olive oil

1 cup Squash Purée (recipe follows)

To make the veal-ginger jus: Bring the veal stock to a simmer in a small saucepan over medium-high heat and simmer until the stock has reduced to ¾ cup, about 12 minutes. Season with salt and pepper and remove the pan from the heat. Whisk in 2 tablespoons of the butter and the ginger juice. Cover the jus to keep it warm, and set it aside.

▶ To prepare the vegetables: Heat the blended oil and melt the remaining 1 tablespoon butter in a large sauté pan over high heat. Continue to cook, stirring, until the butter begins to brown, about 3 minutes. Add the Brussels sprout leaves and chanterelles and cook, stirring, until the vegetables are golden brown, about 3 minutes.

Add the shallot and cook until tender, about 2 minutes. Stir in 2 teaspoons of the chives and the parsley. Remove the pan from the heat and set aside, covered to keep the vegetables warm.

▶ To prepare the snapper: Put 1 gallon water, the wine, onion, ginger, and lemongrass in a large saucepan and set over high heat. Halve the limes, squeeze the juice into the liquid, then add the lime skins to the liquid as well. Season generously with salt and pepper. When the liquid begins to simmer, suspend a steamer basket over the liquid, lower the heat to medium-high, and allow to simmer for 15 minutes. Season both sides of the snapper with salt and pepper and drizzle the flesh side

continued

of the fish with the olive oil. Add the fish to the basket, skin side up, and steam until opaque, about 5 minutes.

▸ To serve, divide the squash purée among 4 serving plates. Top with a snapper fillet and spoon the Brussels sprout mixture along the surface of the fish. Stir the remaining 1 tablespoon chives into the veal-ginger jus, and spoon the jus around the fish and squash.

Squash Purée

MAKES ABOUT 3 CUPS

1 butternut squash (about 2 pounds), peeled, seeded, and sliced

¼ cup (packed) dark brown sugar

1 tablespoon crushed Szechuan peppercorns

3 tablespoons blended oil or neutral oil such as canola

Kosher salt

Freshly ground white pepper

1 shallot, thinly sliced

2 garlic cloves, thinly sliced

1 cup chicken stock, preferably homemade (page 366)

4 tablespoons (½ stick) unsalted butter, cut into ½-inch pieces

1 tablespoon rice vinegar

Position a rack in the center of the oven and preheat the oven to 375°F. Put the squash, sugar, peppercorns, and 2 tablespoons of the oil in a medium bowl, season with salt and pepper, and toss to coat the squash. Transfer the squash mixture to a baking sheet in an even layer and bake until fork-tender, about 30 minutes. Remove the sheet from the oven and set it aside.

▸ Heat the remaining 1 tablespoon oil in a medium saucepan over medium heat. When the oil is shimmering, add the shallot and garlic and cook, stirring, until softened but not browned, about 2 minutes. Add the squash to the pan and pour the chicken stock over the squash. Season with salt and pepper and bring to a boil. Lower the heat and simmer until the flavors come together, about 15 minutes. Transfer the contents of the pan to a blender, in batches if necessary, and blend until smooth, about 1 minute. While continuing to blend, add the butter, a piece at a time, then the vinegar. Strain through a fine-mesh strainer set over a large bowl, pressing down with a rubber spatula or the bottom of a ladle to extract as much purée as possible. The purée can be refrigerated in an airtight container for up to 3 days.

Brussels Sprouts

Brussels sprouts have a slightly mustardy flavor and a toothsome texture that can be deployed any number of ways: The whole sprouts can be sautéed or fried, either whole or halved or quartered. The leaves can also be separated and used in recipes. Though I do not feature an example below, Brussels sprouts can also be shaved on a mandoline and used raw in salads.

DEEP-FRIED BRUSSELS SPROUTS WITH CHINESE SAUSAGE: Follow the instructions for the crispy broccoli on page 51, replacing the broccoli with Brussels sprouts and omitting the tempura batter. Add 1 cup quartered Chinese sausage during the final minute of frying. Drain, then transfer to a bowl and toss with ¼ cup sweet apple vinegar, 2 thinly sliced shallots, and 2 tablespoons torn Thai basil leaves.

BOILED ARMY-GREEN-STYLE BRUSSELS SPROUTS WITH BACON: This is how my grandmother made Brussels sprouts, and I still love them this way to this day: Sauté diced bacon in a wide, deep sauté pan over medium heat until crispy, about 6 minutes. Add whole, trimmed Brussels sprouts to the pan, raise the heat to high, and stir to coat them with the rendered bacon fat. Add just enough water, chicken stock, or vegetable stock to cover the sprouts, and simmer until soft to a knife tip, about 12 minutes.

BRUSSELS SPROUT LEAVES SALAD: Separate, blanch, and shock Brussels sprout leaves (see page 362). Drain and add to salads. These get along very well with sliced shallots, nuts, and honey-mustard vinaigrette.

BABY BRUSSELS SPROUTS GLAZED WITH CANDIED PECANS: Trim and blanch baby Brussels sprouts, drain them, then sauté them in blended oil over medium-high heat until lightly caramelized. Add enough chicken or vegetable stock to come an inch up the side of the pan, bring to a simmer, and cook until the sprouts are nicely glazed. Toss with candied pecans, transfer to a bowl, and serve. This is a wonderful Thanksgiving side dish.

PERILLA BRUSSELS SPROUTS: Caramelize Brussels sprout leaves in a pan with oil and butter over medium-high heat, allowing the butter to brown. Add shallots and store-bought trail mix, or your own combination of toasted hazelnuts, toasted sunflower seeds, toasted pumpkin seeds, raisins, and dried cranberries. Toss and finish with sliced flat-leaf parsley and minced chives.

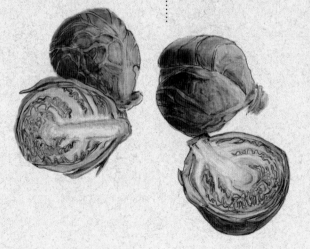

Grilled Bigeye Tuna
with Merguez Sausage, Escarole, and Israeli Couscous Ragù

SERVES 4

Tuna is one of the meatier fish around, which facilitates pairing it with similarly meaty accompaniments, such as the ragù here, which combines slightly spicy Merguez sausage with escarole, garlic, and herbs. Bigeye tuna has a higher fat content than yellowfin and isn't overfished like bluefin. It's available from midsummer to early fall—the perfect time to make and enjoy this dish.

Kosher salt

½ cup Israeli couscous

¼ cup plus 1 tablespoon extra-virgin olive oil

1 pound Merguez sausage, removed from its casing

¼ cup minced garlic

1 tablespoon minced shallot

1 quart coarsely chopped escarole

1 cup shellfish stock, preferably homemade (page 367)

5 tablespoons unsalted butter, cut into cubes

1 tablespoon thinly sliced basil

1 tablespoon thinly sliced flat-leaf parsley leaves

1 tablespoon minced chives

Freshly ground white pepper

¼ cup Dijon mustard

2 tablespoons Colman's mustard powder

2 tablespoons thinly sliced cilantro

4 Bigeye tuna fillets, about 6 ounces each

Maldon sea salt

To make the escarole and couscous ragù: Fill a medium pot halfway with salted water, bring to a boil over high heat, and add the Israeli couscous. Cook until al dente, about 10 minutes. Drain and set aside.

▶ Heat 1 tablespoon of the oil in a large, deep sauté pan over medium heat. When the oil is shimmering, add the sausage and cook, stirring periodically, until it is cooked through and has rendered enough fat to coat the bottom of the pan, about 5 minutes. Add 2 tablespoons of the garlic and the shallot and cook without browning, stirring, for 1 minute. Stir in the escarole and cook until slightly wilted, about 2 minutes. Pour in the stock, stir in the couscous, and cook for 3 minutes. Add

the butter, a few pieces at a time, stirring until incorporated and emulsified. Once all the butter is added, stir in the basil, parsley, and chives and season with salt and pepper. The ragù should be thick enough to coat the back of a spoon; if it is too thin, continue to cook, stirring, until the proper consistency is achieved. Remove the pan from the heat and set aside, covered, to keep the ragù warm.

▶ To prepare the tuna: Heat a grill to high, or heat a grill pan over high heat for 5 minutes. (See pages 274–75 for grilling guidelines.) Put the Dijon mustard, mustard powder, remaining 2 tablespoons garlic, and the

continued

cilantro in a medium bowl and whisk together. Continue whisking, slowly adding the remaining ¼ cup oil in a thin stream to make an emulsified marinade. Season the tuna with salt and pepper and brush the marinade on both sides of the fillets. Grill the tuna until rare, about 2 minutes per side. Transfer to a cutting board, allow it to rest for 2 to 3 minutes, then cut each piece crosswise into 4 slices.

▸ To serve, divide the ragù among 4 serving bowls, top each with 4 tuna slices, and season the tuna with sea salt.

Sausage

My family is half German and half Italian, so sausage plays a big part in the culinary heritages of both sides. It's one of those products that can be enjoyed on its own or can deliver huge flavor to any number of recipes. If you've never made your own sausage, you should try it: it's easy to do, and you don't necessarily have to case it, although it's easier than you might think. The jagerwurst on the facing page is the only one of the recipes that needs to be cased in order to smoke it. (See Sources, page 370, for casing supplies and equipment.) Each of these recipes produces a pound of sausage ready to be cooked and enjoyed. All you need to do is briefly pulse the ingredients together in a food processor, taking care not to overwork them.

ITALIAN HOT SAUSAGE

The quintessential Italian sausage: there are a million uses for it, but my favorites are in a sausage and pepper sandwich, in a Bolognese sauce, or atop a pizza.

1 pound ground pork shoulder

1 tablespoon kosher salt

¼ teaspoon sugar

½ teaspoon minced garlic

¼ teaspoon crushed red pepper flakes

¼ teaspoon fennel seeds

Pinch of ground coriander seed

¼ teaspoon cayenne

¼ teaspoon paprika

Briefly pulse the ingredients together in a food processor, taking care not to overwork them.

BRATWURST

Grill this sausage and make it the basis of a sandwich, or serve it with a green salad for a light meal.

1 pound ground pork shoulder

1 tablespoon kosher salt

Pinch of sugar

¼ teaspoon freshly ground white pepper

Pinch of ground mace

¼ teaspoon caraway seeds

Pinch of ground ginger

¼ teaspoon minced lemon zest

½ teaspoon heavy cream

½ cup ground ice

Briefly pulse the ingredients together in a food processor, taking care not to overwork them.

WEISSWURST

Cook this sausage, then allow it to cool and serve it cold with grainy mustard.

1 pound ground veal (ask your butcher to grind it 3 times for a fine grind)

1 cup ground ice

1 tablespoon plus ½ teaspoon kosher salt

½ teaspoon freshly ground white pepper

¼ teaspoon Colman's mustard powder

Pinch of ground mace

¼ teaspoon minced lemon zest

2 tablespoons heavy cream

Briefly pulse the ingredients together in a food processor, taking care not to overwork them.

CHIANG MAI SAUSAGE

You can cook the sausage as described below, or skewer and grill it. Use it in Thai-style noodle dishes or Thai-style sandwiches.

MAKES ABOUT 1½ POUNDS SAUSAGE

4 garlic cloves

2 tablespoons peeled, finely chopped fresh ginger

2 tablespoons minced lemongrass (see page 362)

1 shallot, thinly sliced

3 Thai red chiles, seeded

4 kaffir lime leaves

2 tablespoons sawtooth herb (cilantro may be substituted)

¼ cup fish sauce

3 tablespoons oyster sauce

1½ pounds ground chicken

Put the garlic, ginger, lemongrass, shallot, chiles, lime leaves, sawtooth herb, fish sauce, and oyster sauce in a blender and blend until smooth, about 1 minute. Transfer to a large bowl and add the chicken, mixing it with clean hands just until incorporated. Set the mixture in plastic wrap and form it into a sausage, wrapping tightly in the plastic. Use a paring knife to poke holes in the plastic to release any air bubbles.

▸ Bring 1 inch of water to a simmer in a pot sized to hold a steaming basket. When the water is simmering, set the steaming basket in the pot, add the sausage to the basket, and cover. Steam until a meat thermometer inserted into the center of the sausage registers 150°F, about 10 minutes. Set aside to cool for 3 minutes, then cut the sausage in half and remove and discard the plastic.

JAGERWURST

Serve this smoked sausage with Dijon mustard or yellow mustard. After mixing and casing the jagerwurst (see Note at right), smoke using wood chips, lighting them with a brûlée torch or stick-style barbecue lighter. (See Note, page 304, for smoking instructions.)

12 ounces ground pork shoulder

4 ounces chopped cured pork

1 tablespoon kosher salt

¼ teaspoon pink curing salt

½ teaspoon freshly ground black pepper

¼ teaspoon minced garlic

½ teaspoon Colman's mustard powder

Pinch of freshly grated nutmeg

Pinch of ground ginger

4 teaspoons heavy cream

Briefly pulse the ingredients together in a food processor, taking care not to overwork them, then stuff into the casings (see Note at right).

NOTE: *You should follow the manufacturer's directions for stuffing sausage casings, but here are some general guidelines: Soak the casings overnight in warm water and rinse them well before using them. Put the sausage mixture into the stuffer. Tie a knot at the end of the casing and slide it onto the stuffing tube. You want to fill the casing amply, but not so much that it bursts. As the sausage fills the casing, make links by twisting at 8-inch intervals, alternating direction—twisting the first link five times to the right, the next to the left, the third to the right, and so on. After the links are formed, use a clean safety pin, cake tester, or needle to carefully pop any air bubbles.*

Braised Salmon and Squid
with Green Peppercorns, Lychee, and Jungle Curry

In Thai cooking, sweet ingredients often show up in what we in the West think of as savory contexts because tropical fruits grow year-round in Thailand. This dish, in which salmon and squid meet pickled green peppercorns and sweet lychee in a spicy curry sauce, is a fascinating example of the possibilities of this dynamic. The salmon, squid, and lychee interact completely differently with the curry; the salmon and squid take on its flavor while the lychee serves as a powerful counterpoint. This is a wonderful late-winter recipe that combats the elements with sweetness and spice.

1 quart Jungle Curry (page 60)

1 pound salmon fillets, cut lengthwise into 16 (1-ounce) slices

8 ounces calamari, cleaned and cut into bite-size pieces

¼ cup pickled green peppercorns, drained

16 peeled, pitted lychees

¾ cup diced bamboo shoots

1 cup water spinach leaves (watercress may be substituted)

Bring the curry to a simmer in a large saucepan over medium heat, then add the salmon and calamari and cook, stirring, until opaque, about 3 minutes. Stir in the peppercorns, lychees, bamboo shoots, and water spinach and cook for 1 minute.

▸ To serve, divide the mixture among 4 bowls, being sure to include a good mix of ingredients in each serving.

Black Truffles

Aromatic truffles don't necessarily take over the flavor of a dish, but they add such a fragrant quality that they make the experience of eating any dish more intense. White truffles are the gold standard, but they are expensive. Black truffles are a more accessible and perfectly delicious option for most home cooks. When purchasing black truffles, choose ones that are firm and neither too dry nor too moist. Be sure there are no peppers or stones in the crevices. If not using them right away, refrigerate the truffles in an airtight container in dry rice or wrapped in a paper towel to absorb any moisture and prevent mold from forming.

SHAVED: Shave black truffles over plain risotto or plain, buttered pasta. The best way to do this is with a truffle slicer, but a microplane zester works as well.

TRUFFLE BUTTER: Fold black truffle trimmings into softened butter and season with fine sea salt. Refrigerate in an airtight container for up to 1 week. Toss it into pastas and risottos, or melt it over steaks, veal, or even lobster for an instant and luxurious sauce.

PÉRIGORD SAUCE: Make a pan sauce by cooking 1 minced shallot in the fat left behind by poultry or beef over medium-high heat. Add 1 to 2 tablespoons Madeira, reduce it, then add about 2 cups veal stock and simmer until reduced to about ½ cup, about 6 minutes. Turn off the heat and swirl in minced black truffles. Serve over chicken or beef.

TRUFFLE SALT: Let truffle trimmings air-dry at room temperature overnight, or spread them out on a parchment paper–lined baking sheet and dry in an oven on low heat until dehydrated (time will vary based on the water content of individual truffles). Grind in a spice grinder or coffee grinder and mix with salt. Toss the truffle salt with fries immediately after frying, add to steak tartare, or use it anywhere you want to add or underscore truffle flavor.

Grilled Branzino and Spicy Cumin Lamb
with Water Chestnuts, Red Onion, and Bitter Lime Sauce

This dish was inspired by the incredible, addictively tasty cumin lamb served at Spicy and Tasty, a Szechuan restaurant in Flushing, Queens, an outer borough of New York City, where lamb and cumin are stir-fried together. Here that combination becomes the accompaniment to branzino, a rich and fatty fish.

3 tablespoons blended oil or neutral oil such as canola

1 shallot, thinly sliced

4 garlic cloves, 3 thinly sliced, 1 minced

1 cup thinly sliced preserved limes (store-bought, or follow the recipe on page 40, substituting limes for lemons)

1 cup chicken stock, preferably homemade (page 366)

2 kaffir lime leaves

Juice of 2 limes

2 tablespoons palm sugar or turbinado sugar such as Sugar in the Raw

1 cup all-purpose flour

2 tablespoons ground cumin

8 ounces lamb top round, cut into 1-inch cubes

Canola oil or corn oil, for frying

Kosher salt

Freshly ground black pepper

1 tablespoon peeled, minced fresh ginger

1 tablespoon ground Szechuan peppercorns

1 tablespoon chili oil

1 red onion, cut into thick rings

¼ cup minced water chestnuts

¼ cup (loosely packed) Thai basil leaves

4 skin-on branzino fillets, about 6 ounces each

Freshly ground white pepper

To make the bitter lime sauce: Heat 1 tablespoon of the blended oil in a medium saucepan over medium-high heat. When the oil is shimmering, add the shallot and sliced garlic and cook, stirring, for 1 minute. Stir in the preserved limes, stock, and lime leaves. Bring to a boil, then reduce the heat and simmer to mingle the flavors for 15 minutes. Transfer the contents of the pan to a blender and blend until a smooth purée forms. Add the lime juice, sugar, and 1 to 2 tablespoons water, if necessary for consistency (the sauce should coat the back of a spoon). Strain the sauce through a fine-mesh strainer into a medium bowl. The sauce should be sour, bitter,

and slightly sweet. Carefully wipe out the saucepan to remove any solids, return the sauce to the pan, and allow to cool.

▶ To fry the lamb: Combine the flour and 1 tablespoon of the cumin in a large bowl and add the lamb. Toss to coat the lamb with the flour mixture. Pour canola oil into a deep fryer, or wide, deep, heavy pot, to a depth of 4 inches. Heat the oil to 350°F. Line a plate with paper towels and set aside. Carefully lower the lamb cubes into the oil and fry until golden brown and crispy, about 3 minutes. Use a slotted spoon to transfer the cubes

continued

to the prepared plate to drain, and season immediately with salt and black pepper.

▸ To make the stir-fry: Heat 1 tablespoon of the blended oil in a large sauté pan over very high heat. When the oil is shimmering but not smoking, add the ginger, minced garlic, remaining 1 tablespoon cumin, and the peppercorns and stir-fry for 1 minute. Add the chili oil, onion, water chestnuts, and 1 tablespoon water and cook just until the onions begin to soften, about 2 minutes. Stir in the fried lamb and basil and season with salt and black pepper.

▸ Preheat the oven to 450°F. Heat a grill pan over high heat for 5 minutes. Season the branzino generously with salt and white pepper. Rub the remaining 1 tablespoon blended oil on the skin side of the fish and add the fish to the grill, skin side down. Grill until grill marks form, about 2 minutes. Use tongs to turn the fish 45 degrees to form crosshatch marks, and cook for 2 minutes more. Transfer the branzino to a baking sheet, flesh side down, and roast until the fish is cooked through and opaque, about 2 minutes.

▸ To serve, gently reheat the bitter lime sauce in its pan over medium heat until hot. Spoon sauce into the center of each plate. Top with a fish fillet, spoon the stir-fry around the fish, and serve.

NOTE: If preparing them in advance of the rest of a dish, always allow sauces made with citrus juice to cool. Reheat them when it's time to serve them. Keeping these sauces warm causes them to lose their fresh flavor. (Although also acidic, sauces made with vinegar can be kept warm without sacrificing flavor.)

Combinations of Lamb and Cumin

It takes a potent spice to make an impression next to the assertively gamy quality of lamb, but cumin is up to the task. When the two come together in this classic Szechuan pairing, the combination of fat and flavor is intense and invites you to up the ante by complementing them with equally big, bold flavors.

CUMIN-LAMB TACOS: Stir cumin into ground lamb as it sautés, then make tacos with the lamb, filling the shells with diced tomatoes, shredded lettuce, and avocado mousse or guacamole (page 78). Serve with lime wedges alongside for squeezing.

GRILLED LAMB AND CUMIN-YOGURT: Stir cumin into Greek yogurt as a condiment for grilled lamb. Cumin-yogurt is also delicious drizzled over roasted root vegetables such as carrots, beets, and parsnips.

CUMIN-MARINATED LAMB CHOPS: Marinate lamb chops in a marinade of cumin, garlic, and blended oil before grilling or roasting them. Serve with orzo tossed with butter and a few drops of lemon juice, and with grilled vegetables—asparagus and yams are especially good accompaniments.

SAUSAGE AND PEPPER SANDWICH: Knead cumin into lamb sausage (if the sausage is in casings, squeeze it out into a bowl before seasoning), then sauté, or form into a patty and grill it. Serve on a hero roll along with roasted peppers and onions for a memorable spin on the Italian American sausage and pepper sandwich.

White Balsamic–Glazed Black Cod
with Melon-Cucumber Salad and Sweet Corn Sauce

This super-light and refreshing coming-together of summery ingredients takes advantage of the natural charms of the melon, cucumber, corn, and fish, enhancing them with minimal intervention: the salad is dressed with a slightly sweet vinaigrette; the corn sauce is a simple reduction that's mounted with butter; and the fish is glazed with a thickened balsamic. It's a terrific dish for spontaneous summertime entertaining or an extra-special everyday meal that doesn't take a lot of work, although you will need one piece of special equipment—a juicer, for the melon and corn.

1 cantaloupe or Crenshaw melon

2 tablespoons extra-virgin olive oil

2 tablespoons rice vinegar

¼ cup plus 1 tablespoon sugar

2 teaspoons kosher salt, plus more for seasoning

Freshly ground white pepper

1 (3-inch) section hothouse cucumber, halved lengthwise, seeded, and thinly cut crosswise

1 ear corn, grilled or charred and kernels sliced from the ear

½ cup (loosely packed) watercress

2 tablespoons hand-torn basil leaves

1 tablespoon minced shallot

1 tablespoon thinly sliced flat-leaf parsley leaves

1 tablespoon minced chives

3 cups fresh corn juice (from about 6 large cobs)

4 tablespoons (½ stick) unsalted butter

Juice of 1 lime

1 cup white balsamic vinegar

1 tablespoon blended oil or neutral oil such as canola

4 skin-on black cod fillets, about 6 ounces each

Dice the melon. Set half of the dice aside and juice the other half to produce ½ cup juice.

▶ To make the salad: Put the melon juice, olive oil, rice vinegar, and 1 tablespoon of the sugar in a large bowl and whisk to dissolve the sugar. Season with salt and pepper and whisk to incorporate. Add the diced melon, cucumber, corn, watercress, basil, shallot, parsley, and chives, and toss gently.

▶ To make the sweet corn sauce: Heat the corn juice in a small, heavy saucepan over low heat, whisking constantly, until the liquid reduces and thickens, about

7 minutes. Whisk in the butter until melted, then stir in the lime juice and season with salt and pepper. Remove the pan from the heat and allow to cool.

▶ To prepare the cod: Bring the balsamic vinegar and remaning ¼ cup sugar to a simmer in a medium saucepan over medium-high heat, whisking to dissolve the sugar. Continue to simmer until reduced to a glaze, 5 to 6 minutes. Remove the pan from the heat and set aside.

▶ Preheat the broiler. Heat the blended oil in a medium, ovenproof sauté pan over medium-high heat.

continued

Season the black cod fillets with salt and pepper. When the oil is shimmering, add the fillets, skin side down, to the pan. Cook until the skin begins to crisp, about 2 minutes. Transfer the pan to the oven and broil until opaque, about 5 minutes. Use a pastry brush to brush half of the glaze over the fish fillets and return to the oven for 1 minute more. Remove the fish from the oven and brush with the remaining glaze.

▶ To serve, gently reheat the corn sauce in its saucepan over medium heat until hot. Spoon ¼ cup of the sauce into the center of each of 4 dinner plates. Top with the salad and finish with a cod fillet. Serve immediately.

Corn

Corn is so casually perfect in its natural state, easy to cook *and* eat on the cob, that its incredible potential is often overlooked. Bicolor corn—a hybrid of yellow and white varieties—is a good, dependable type, as is white Silver Queen corn from the South. The best corn comes from the Midwest; if that's where you live and cook, buy local! These are some of my favorite ways to showcase corn's distinct sweetness.

CORN SOUP: Make a stock by heating 1 tablespoon extra-virgin olive oil in a large pot over medium-high heat. When the oil is shimmering, add 1 sliced shallot and 2 sliced garlic cloves and sauté for 1 minute. Add 8 large corncobs with the kernels removed (reserve the kernels for the soup) and 2 quarts water and simmer for 30 minutes. Strain through a fine-mesh strainer set over a large bowl, discarding the solids. Carefully wipe out the pot; add 1 tablespoon extra-virgin olive oil and heat over medium-high heat. When the oil is shimmering, add 1 sliced shallot and 1 sliced garlic clove and cook, stirring, for 1 minute. Add the reserved corn kernels, season with salt and white pepper, and cook, stirring, for 3 minutes. Add a pinch of saffron and the corn stock, bring to a simmer, then lower the heat and continue to simmer for 20 minutes. Transfer to a blender, add 2 teaspoons rice vinegar and 2 tablespoons butter, and purée until smooth. Taste and add more salt and pepper, if necessary. Ladle into bowls and garnish with chopped chives.

CORN SAUCE: Follow the recipe for Corn Soup to the left, reducing the water to 1½ quarts for a thicker result, and omit the saffron. Serve with scallops and sweet fish such as black sea bass and grouper. This variation is less sweet than the corn sauce on page 225, which is made with corn juice.

CORN PUDDING: Juice the kernels of 2 large corncobs in a juicer to yield 1 cup corn juice. Simmer the juice gently in a medium pot until thickened to a pudding consistency, about 20 minutes. With the pot off the heat, fold in 1 tablespoon unsalted butter, melting it. Season with salt and white pepper. Serve warm alongside duck or venison.

Pan-Roasted Black Sea Bass

with Shiitake Mushrooms, White Turnip Purée, and Toasted Hazelnut Dressing

SERVES 4

This dish brings together earth and sea in a way that seems utterly natural. Take note of the white turnip purée and hazelnut dressing, both of which could have justified entries in my Notebook. The purée can be substituted for mashed potatoes alongside fish or meat, and the dressing used to sauce other white-fleshed fish.

4 tablespoons blended oil or neutral oil such as canola

5 shallots, 1 thinly sliced, 4 peeled and left whole

2 garlic cloves, thinly sliced

3 cups peeled, quartered baby white turnips (about 24 turnips), greens reserved

Kosher salt

Freshly ground white pepper

1 cup chicken stock, preferably homemade (page 366)

¼ cup whole milk

2 tablespoons cold unsalted butter, cut into small pieces, plus 4 tablespoons (½ stick) unsalted butter, at room temperature

1 quart mushroom stock, preferably homemade (page 365)

2 tablespoons hazelnut oil

¼ cup balsamic vinegar

3 tablespoons chopped roasted hazelnuts (see page 362)

2 tablespoons extra-virgin olive oil

1 cup quartered shiitake mushrooms

2 cups (loosely packed, from turnips at left) turnip greens

1 tablespoon minced thyme

1 tablespoon minced oregano

1 tablespoon minced flat-leaf parsley

1 tablespoon minced chervil

1 tablespoon minced tarragon

4 skin-on black sea bass fillets, about 6 ounces each

1 tablespoon minced chives

Heat 1 tablespoon of the blended oil in a medium saucepan over medium heat. When the oil is shimmering, add the sliced shallot and the garlic and cook, stirring, until slightly softened but not browned, about 1 minute. Add 2 cups of the turnips and season with salt and pepper. Pour in the chicken stock and milk and bring to a simmer. Lower the heat and simmer until the turnips are soft to a knife tip, about 20 minutes. Transfer the contents of the pan to a blender and blend, adding the 2 tablespoons cold butter, a few pieces at a time, until a smooth purée forms. Season with salt and pepper and strain through a fine-mesh strainer set over a large bowl, pressing on the purée with a rubber spatula or the bottom of a ladle to extract as much purée as possible. Cover to keep warm and set aside.

▶ To make the hazelnut dressing, first make a shallot purée: Preheat the oven to 425°F. Put the whole shallots and 1 tablespoon of the blended oil in a medium bowl, toss to coat the shallots with the oil, and season with salt and pepper. Wrap the shallots loosely in aluminum foil and place on a baking sheet. Roast until soft

continued

(a paring knife easily pierces through to the center), about 30 minutes. Remove the shallots from the oven and let cool for about 10 minutes. When cool enough to handle, remove the foil, transfer the shallots to a blender, and blend to a smooth purée, about 30 seconds. Season with salt and pepper.

▸ Bring the mushroom stock to a boil in a medium saucepot over high heat, then lower the heat and simmer until the stock has reduced to ½ cup, about 8 minutes. Remove the pot from the heat and set it aside. Heat the hazelnut oil in a separate medium saucepan over medium heat. Add the shallot purée and cook, stirring, until most of the moisture is cooked out, about 3 minutes. Stir in the balsamic vinegar and the mushroom stock. Season with salt and pepper and bring to a simmer. Cook until thick enough to coat the back of a spoon, about 2 minutes, then stir in 2 tablespoons of the hazelnuts and 1 tablespoon of the room-temperature butter. Remove the pot from the heat and set aside, covered to keep the dressing warm.

▸ To prepare the vegetables: Heat ¼ cup water, 2 tablespoons of the room-temperature butter, and the remaining 1 cup turnips in a large sauté pan over medium heat, covering the pan with a parchment paper round, or partially covering with a lid. Simmer until the turnips are tender to a knife tip, about 12 minutes. Season with salt and pepper and use a slotted spoon to transfer the turnips to a bowl and set aside to cool. Discard the liquid, carefully wipe out the pan, then

return it to medium-high heat and add the olive oil. When the oil is shimmering, add the shiitakes and cook, stirring, until golden brown, about 4 minutes. Stir in the turnip greens and season with salt and pepper. Cook until the greens are wilted, about 4 minutes, then add the braised turnips and season with salt and pepper. Remove the pan from the heat and set aside, covered to keep the turnips and greens warm.

▸ To prepare the black sea bass: Put the thyme, oregano, parsley, chervil, and tarragon in a medium bowl and stir to incorporate. Score the sea bass skin with a paring knife, taking care not to cut into the meat. Season the fillets with salt and pepper. Use your hands to press the herb mixture into the flesh side of the fillets. Heat the remaining 2 tablespoons blended oil in a medium sauté pan over medium heat. When the oil is shimmering, add the bass, skin side down, and cook until the skin begins to crisp, about 4 minutes. Use a spatula to gently turn the fish over and add the remaining 1 tablespoon room-temperature butter to the pan. Use a spoon to baste the fish with the butter for 2 minutes.

▸ To serve, divide the vegetables among 4 plates and top each with a sea bass fillet, skin side up. Stir the chives into the hazelnut dressing and spoon the dressing around the dish. Finish with a scattering of the remaining 1 tablespoon hazelnuts and serve.

Shiitake Mushrooms

Of all the mushrooms, the ones that have the most pronounced nutty flavor are shiitakes, especially oak-cultivated shiitakes. Roasting is the best way to bring that quality out in all its glory, but shiitakes can also be grilled or sautéed.

Stem the shiitakes for all the preparations below, saving their stems for use in mushroom stock (see page 365).

ROASTED SHIITAKES: Toss shiitake mushrooms in blended oil, season with salt and black pepper, spread out on a baking sheet, and bake until slightly darkened and crisp at the edges, 7 to 8 minutes per side. Toss with pasta or sautéed vegetables.

GRILLED SHIITAKES: Toss shiitake mushrooms in blended oil, season with salt and black pepper, and grill over indirect heat (see pages 274–75) until light grill marks form and the mushrooms are slightly softened, 5 to 6 minutes per side. Slice and serve over grilled beef.

SHIITAKE FRICASSEE: Make a mushroom stew by roasting 2 cups sliced shiitake mushrooms in 2 tablespoons unsalted butter in a pan, then adding ¼ cup Madeira and stirring until almost completely reduced. Stir in 2 tablespoons heavy cream and 1 tablespoon chopped herbs. If desired, toss in sliced cooked chicken toward the end of the cooking.

SAUTÉED SHIITAKES WITH PASTA: Slice shiitake mushrooms and sauté them in olive oil, seasoning with salt and black pepper, until al dente. Add cooked, drained short or tubular pasta to the pan, along with butter and herbs, and toss for a quick dish. If desired, add other ingredients such as halved grape or cherry tomatoes and a splash of tomato sauce or heavy cream.

Pan-Roasted Wild Striped Bass

with Fried Salami, Tuscan Kale, and Preserved Lemon Sauce

SERVES 4

I came to love wild striped bass as a kid, when I discovered it surf-casting off Sore Thumb, a jetty near Babylon, Long Island. But delicious as it is, the two stars of the show on this plate are the preserved lemon sauce—a sweet-and-sour concoction that keeps you coming back for more—and the fried salami. This dish is a perfect example of how simple cooking can be when you utilize a few well-chosen, high-impact ingredients.

---

6 tablespoons blended oil or neutral oil such as canola

1½ shallots, thinly sliced, divided into thirds

3½ garlic cloves, thinly sliced, with the ½ clove kept separate

1 cup preserved lemons (store-bought or homemade, see page 40), thinly sliced

1 cup chicken stock, preferably homemade (page 366)

2 tablespoons (packed) light brown sugar

Finely grated zest and juice of 1 lemon

Kosher salt

Freshly ground white pepper

2 cups (loosely packed) coarsely chopped Tuscan kale

½ cup thick salami matchsticks

1 Honeycrisp apple, thinly sliced

4 skin-on striped bass fillets, about 6 ounces each

1 tablespoon unsalted butter

1 thyme sprig

To make the preserved lemon sauce: Heat 1 tablespoon of the oil in a medium, heavy saucepan over medium heat. When the oil is shimmering, add two-thirds of the shallots and 3 garlic cloves and cook, stirring, until softened but not browned, about 1 minute. Add the preserved lemons and chicken stock and bring to a simmer. Simmer for 15 minutes to mingle the flavors, then transfer the contents of the pan to a blender and blend until smooth. Add the sugar, lemon zest and juice, and 2 to 3 tablespoons water if the sauce seems too thick, and season with salt and pepper. Strain through a fine-mesh strainer over a medium bowl. The sauce should be sour, bitter, and slightly sweet.

▶ To make the braised kale: Heat 1 tablespoon of the oil in a Dutch oven or large pot over medium heat. When the oil is shimmering, add the remaining one-third of the shallots and ½ clove garlic and cook, stirring, without browning, for 1 minute. Add the kale and season with salt and pepper. Cook, stirring, until the kale is soft, about 7 minutes. Transfer to a colander and set in the sink to drain until no more liquid is released, about 5 minutes.

▶ To prepare the salami: Heat 2 tablespoons of the oil in a medium sauté pan over high heat. Add the salami and cook, stirring, until golden and crisp on all sides, about

continued

2 minutes. Stir in the braised kale and cook, tossing, until the kale is warmed through, about 1 minute. Toss in the apple and season with salt and pepper. Remove the pan from the heat and set aside, covered to keep warm.

▸ To prepare the bass: Preheat the oven to 425°F. Line a plate with paper towels and set aside. Score the bass's skin with a paring knife, taking care not to cut into the meat. Season the bass on both sides with salt and pepper. Heat the remaining 2 tablespoons oil in a medium, ovenproof sauté pan over medium-high heat. When the oil is shimmering, add the fish, skin side down, and lower the heat to medium. Sear until the skin is golden brown, about 2 minutes, then transfer the pan to the oven and roast until the flesh is opaque and the fish is cooked through, about 5 minutes. Remove the pan from the oven and place on the stovetop over low heat. Add the butter and thyme, allow the butter to melt, and use a tablespoon to baste the bass for 1 minute. Use a spatula to turn the fillets over, and continue to baste for 1 minute more. Transfer the fish to the prepared plate and lightly blot with additional paper towels. Discard the thyme sprig.

▸ To serve, spoon sauce onto the bottom of each of 4 dinner plates. Top with vegetables, then a piece of fish.

Fried Salami

I grew up eating cured meats like soppressata and Genoa salami and loving their blend of meat, fat, and spice. Whenever we topped our homemade pizzas with salami, the meat was cooked so long and hard that it got crusty, which gave me the idea of frying it. Frying cured meats obviously makes them crunchy, but it also brings their seasoning to the foreground, whereas they can sometimes be muted by the meat's fat content when eaten raw. In addition to the suggested uses below, garnish other dishes with it as the sea bass is garnished on page 231.

PANZANELLA: For another variation on the Italian bread salad (see page 133), toss croutons (page 363), sliced red onion, diced tomatoes, diced cucumbers, red wine vinegar, and extra-virgin olive oil in a bowl. Just before serving, toss in freshly fried salami.

SALAMI BURGER: Top a burger with fried salami for a spicy take on a bacon burger. To up the ante even more, add fried cubanelle peppers and melted aged provolone.

FRIED SALAMI CALZONE: Add fried salami to your favorite calzone recipe, in addition to, or replacing, the ham.

EGGS WITH FRIED SALAMI AND MOZZARELLA: This combination can be applied three ways: Render sliced salami in a hot pan, then remove the salami and scramble or fry eggs in the pan. Serve the eggs and salami alongside each other, grating mozzarella over them, or on your favorite toasted bread or roll, topping the eggs and salami with a slice of cheese for a breakfast sandwich. Alternatively, after removing the rendered salami from the pan, make an omelet in the pan, filling it with the salami and diced mozzarella.

Triggerfish

with Quinoa, Oyster Mushrooms, Marinated Grape Tomatoes, and Sweet-and-Sour Eggplant-Basil Sauce

SERVES 4

Triggerfish is one of my favorite fish. It's a sort of poor man's Dover sole because it has a similar shape and texture—thin but firm, and very succulent when cooked properly. Because of its understated elegance, triggerfish is complemented by a full spectrum of vegetables and sauces. Here it's paired with earthy mushrooms as well as acidic tomatoes and a sweet-and-sour eggplant-basil sauce.

Kosher salt

1 cup quinoa

2 Italian eggplants, halved lengthwise, flesh side scored with a paring knife

Freshly ground white pepper

4 garlic cloves, thinly sliced

1 shallot, thinly sliced

3 cups chicken stock, preferably homemade (page 366)

¼ cup palm sugar or turbinado sugar such as Sugar in the Raw

¼ cup Thai basil

2 tablespoons fermented yellow soybean paste (see Sources, page 370)

2 tablespoons fish sauce

3 tablespoons plus 2 teaspoons freshly squeezed lime juice

1 pint halved grape tomatoes

1 cup plus 1 tablespoon extra-virgin olive oil

1 cup black rice vinegar (balsamic vinegar may be substituted)

½ cup quartered oyster mushrooms

1 cup chicory

3 tablespoons unsalted butter

1 tablespoon minced chives

2 tablespoons blended oil or neutral oil such as canola

4 skinless triggerfish fillets, about 6 ounces each

1 cup Wondra flour

Bring a small pot of salted water to a boil over high heat, then add the quinoa and cook for 20 minutes. Drain and set aside.

▶ To make the eggplant-basil sauce: Heat a grill over high heat, or preheat a grill pan or sauté pan over high heat for 5 minutes. Season the eggplant halves with salt and pepper, and place on the grill, flesh side down. Cook until completely charred, about 8 minutes, then use tongs to turn the eggplant over and grill until the flesh is very soft, about 5 minutes more. Set aside to cool slightly for 7 minutes, then remove and discard the skin and transfer the eggplant flesh to a large saucepan. Add the garlic, shallot, and stock and bring to a boil over high heat. Lower the heat so the liquid is simmering, and continue to simmer for 20 minutes to develop the flavors. Transfer the contents of the pan to a blender and add the sugar, basil, soybean paste, fish sauce, and 3 tablespoons of the lime juice. Blend until a smooth purée forms, about 30 seconds. Strain through a fine-mesh strainer set over a bowl, pressing on the purée with a rubber spatula or the bottom of a ladle

continued

to extract as much flavorful liquid as possible. Season with salt and pepper.

▶ To make the marinated grape tomatoes: Put the tomatoes, 1 cup of the olive oil, and the vinegar in a large bowl and toss to incorporate. Season with salt and pepper, and set aside at room temperature.

▶ To make the quinoa and mushrooms: Heat the remaining 1 tablespoon olive oil in a large sauté pan over high heat. When the oil is shimmering, add the mushrooms and chicory and cook for 2 minutes. Lower the heat to medium and add the quinoa and 1 tablespoon of the butter. Season generously with salt and pepper. Fold in the remaining 2 teaspoons lime juice and the chives.

▶ To prepare the triggerfish: Heat the blended oil in a medium sauté pan over high heat. Season the fillets on both sides with salt and pepper. Put the flour in a bowl and dredge the fillets, coating lightly with the flour, gently shaking off any excess. Place the fish in the sauté pan, skinned side down, and lower to medium heat. Sear for 3 minutes, until golden brown. Add the remaining 2 tablespoons butter, allow it to melt, and use a tablespoon to baste the triggerfish for 2 minutes. Carefully turn the fish over and continue to baste for 1 minute more.

▶ To serve, spoon sauce onto each of 4 dinner plates. Top with a fish fillet and spoon the tomatoes over and around the fish.

Eggplant - Basil Combinatins

Eggplant and basil are both late-summer crops and they get along in a way that's unique in this season, when most ingredients are light. Eggplant actually has a dense texture and an almost meaty presence on any plate, but the basil provides an essential herbal lift.

EGGPLANT PARMESAN: Top fried eggplant slices (see Notebook, page 277 for breading and frying instructions) with tomato sauce and basil leaves and serve plated with spaghetti, or on an Italian hero. You can also top the slices with pesto rather than fresh basil slices.

EGGPLANT *NAM PLA*: For an Asian spin on what most consider a Mediterranean combination, split Japanese eggplant lengthwise, score the flesh with a paring knife, rub with canola oil, season with salt and pepper, and grill until soft and lightly charred. When cool enough to handle, remove and discard the skin, dice the flesh, put it in a bowl, and add 2 teaspoons fish sauce (nam pla), 1 teaspoon lime juice, and 1 torn Thai basil leaf. Toss and serve as a starter or side dish.

CAPONATA WITH BASIL: To make 2 cups of this Italian condiment, heat ¼ cup extra-virgin olive oil in a wide, deep sauté pan or skillet. When the oil is shimmering, add ¼ cup pine nuts and cook, stirring, until golden, about 1½ minutes. Add 1 diced Spanish onion, 1 tablespoon minced garlic, ¼ cup golden raisins, and 1 tablespoon anchovy paste (or minced anchovy fillet). Cook, stirring occasionally, for 3 minutes, then add 1 diced Italian eggplant, 3 diced plum tomatoes (with their seeds), and 1 teaspoon crushed red pepper flakes. Gently simmer until the liquid has almost completely evaporated, about 20 minutes. Taste and adjust the seasoning with salt and pepper if necessary. Stir in 2 tablespoons flat-leaf parsley leaves and 2 tablespoons basil chiffonade (see page 362). Chill and serve within 2 days as part of an antipasto spread, tossed with hot pasta for a quick sauce, or with grilled fish or meats.

PENNE ALLA NORMA: Toss tomato sauce (such as the one on page 147), finished with a last-second addition of basil, with hot penne and plate it. Top with fried eggplant slices (see the recipe on page 277 for breading and frying instructions).

Roasted Tilefish "*Vitello Tonnato*"
with Sweetbreads, Beans, Tapenade, and Tuna Belly Sauce

Vitello tonnato is a classic Italian dish of roasted, chilled veal sauced with a thick dressing made by puréeing preserved tuna—it sounds crazy until you taste it and realize that it's perfection. When you think about it, it was surf and turf before surf and turf was cool. This dish is a riff on that combination (the Notebook entry on page 241 features more), substituting sweetbreads for veal breast, and weaving in elements of another tuna classic, salad Niçoise—namely, via green beans and olives. The tilefish, a lean whitefish, offers a somewhat neutral base for all these big flavors to play out on.

¼ cup thinly sliced cipollini onions

¼ cup plus 4 tablespoons extra-virgin olive oil

2 tablespoons balsamic vinegar

2 garlic cloves, thinly sliced

1 shallot, thinly sliced

6 ounces preserved tuna, preferably Italian or Spanish

1 cup dry white wine

1 cup chicken stock, preferably homemade (page 366)

¼ cup mayonnaise

2 tablespoons freshly squeezed lemon juice

2 teaspoons capers (preferably brine packed; do not rinse)

2 cornichons

Kosher salt

Freshly ground white pepper

2 tablespoons thinly sliced green Sicilian olives

2 tablespoons thinly sliced black olives

2 tablespoons diced plum tomatoes, with their seeds

1 cup all-purpose flour

2 large eggs, beaten

1 cup panko bread crumbs

8 ounces veal sweetbreads, cut into small nuggets

Canola oil or corn oil, for frying

2 large fingerling potatoes, blanched (see page 362) and sliced into rounds

½ cup green beans, trimmed, blanched, and shocked (see page 362)

1 tablespoon thinly sliced flat-leaf parsley

2 tablespoons blended oil or neutral oil such as canola

4 skinless tilefish fillets, about 6 ounces each

About 1 cup Wondra flour

1 tablespoon unsalted butter

Put the onions, 2 tablespoons of the olive oil, and the balsamic vinegar in a medium bowl, toss to coat the onions, and set aside to marinate at room temperature for 1 hour.

▸ Meanwhile, to make the *tonnato* sauce: Heat ¼ cup of the olive oil in a large saucepan over medium heat. When the oil is shimmering, add the garlic and shallot and cook, stirring, for 1 minute. Add the preserved tuna and cook, breaking it apart with a spoon, for 2 minutes. Pour in the wine and cook until the liquid has reduced by half, about 5 minutes. Pour in the stock and bring to a simmer. Simmer for 15 minutes to mingle the flavors. Transfer the contents of the pan to a blender and add ¼ cup water, the mayonnaise, lemon juice, capers, and cornichons. Season with salt and pepper and blend until smooth. Strain through a fine-mesh strainer into a bowl, pressing down on the solids with a rubber spatula or the bottom of a ladle to extract as much sauce as possible, and set aside.

▸ To make the tapenade: Put the green and black olives, plum tomatoes, and 1 tablespoon of the olive oil in a medium bowl and stir them together. Set aside.

▸ To prepare the sweetbreads: Put the all-purpose flour in a medium bowl, the eggs in another medium bowl, and the panko in a third bowl. Dip the sweetbreads first into the flour, shaking off any excess, then into the eggs to coat, and finally into the panko.

▸ Pour canola oil into a deep fryer, or wide, deep pot, to a depth of 4 inches. Heat the oil to 350°F. Line a plate with paper towels and set it aside. Carefully lower the sweetbreads into the fryer and fry until golden and crispy, about 3 minutes. Use a slotted spoon to transfer them to the prepared plate to drain, and season immediately with salt and pepper.

▸ To cook the vegetables: Heat the remaining 1 tablespoon olive oil in a large saucepan over medium heat. When the oil is shimmering but not smoking, add the potato slices and cook until crispy, about 3 minutes per side. Remove the onions from the marinade and add them to the pan. Add the green beans and cook, tossing or stirring, to heat through, about 1 minute. Season with salt and pepper and add the sweetbreads. Stir in the parsley.

▸ Preheat the oven to 450°F. Heat the blended oil in a large, ovenproof sauté pan over medium heat. Season the tilefish fillets generously with salt and pepper and coat the bottom of each fillet with Wondra flour. When the oil is shimmering, add the fillets to the pan, floured side down, and cook until lightly golden brown, about 4 minutes. Transfer the pan to the oven and cook for 5 minutes more. Remove the pan from the oven, return to the stovetop over low heat, and add the butter, allow it to melt, and use a tablespoon to baste the fish with the butter for 2 minutes.

▸ To serve, spoon sauce into the center of each of 4 dinner plates and top with the sweetbread mixture. Set a tilefish fillet on top of the sweetbread mixture on each plate, and garnish with the tapenade.

Veal and Tuna Pairings

Vitello tonnato's central combination of veal and tuna, in both raw and cooked forms, can pay dividends with results that add up to more than the sum of their parts. Incorporating *tonnato* sauce (see recipe on page 239) often helps unify the veal and tuna.

TRADITIONAL *VITELLO TONNATO*: For a traditional *vitello tonnato*, arrange thin slices of roasted, chilled veal breast on a salad plate, sauce with the *tonnato* sauce, and garnish with capers or caper berries. If desired, mound a simple arugula salad, dressed with lemon juice and olive oil, in the center of the plate.

VEAL SANDWICH WITH *TONNATO* SAUCE: Make a sandwich of thinly sliced, roasted, chilled veal breast, dressing it with *tonnato* sauce, on rye toast.

GRILLED VEAL-WRAPPED TUNA: Wrap super-thin slices of veal breast around tuna steaks and grill them together. Be sure to grill on the seam side first to seal the veal around the tuna, and be sure the grill is super-hot to keep the veal from sticking and pulling away from the tuna.

TUNA AND VEAL CANAPÉS: Roll raw, sushi-grade tuna, cut into ½-inch dice and dressed with olive oil, inside thin slices of roasted, chilled veal breast. If desired, build out the tuna, tossing with capers, diced tomato, minced red onion, and/or fresh herbs before rolling it inside the veal. You might also spread *tonnato* sauce (see recipe on facing page) on the inside of the veal before topping it with the tuna and rolling it.

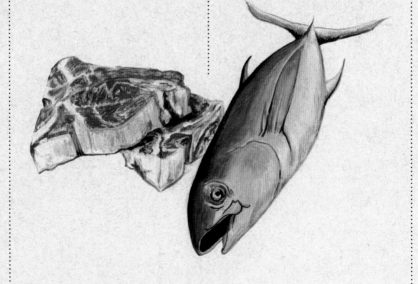

6
Poultry and Game Birds

Thai-Style Fried Chicken
with Sweet Lime-Fish Sauce

The chicken in this recipe is marinated for several hours in a mixture of oyster sauce, ginger, garlic, fermented shrimp paste, and water. During that time, it drinks up an obscene amount of flavor. It is then coated with a combination of all-purpose flour and rice flour for a delicate result when fried. This dish is for all kinds of entertaining, from sports-viewing parties to potlucks. Leftover fried chicken is also delicious cold on its own or sliced and tossed into a salad.

5 garlic cloves, peeled

1 tablespoon peeled, sliced fresh ginger, plus 2 tablespoons thin ginger matchsticks

¼ cup shrimp paste

¼ cup plus 2 tablespoons fish sauce

¼ cup oyster sauce

2 chickens, about 3 pounds each, broken down by your butcher into 8 pieces each

Canola oil or corn oil, for frying

2 cups rice flour

2 cups all-purpose flour

¼ cup kosher salt

½ cup coarsely ground black pepper

1 cup palm sugar or turbinado sugar such as Sugar in the Raw

2 tablespoons freshly squeezed lime juice

2 Thai red chiles, thinly sliced

2 Thai green chiles, thinly sliced

Put the garlic, sliced ginger, shrimp paste, ¼ cup of the fish sauce, the oyster sauce, and ½ cup water in a blender and blend until smooth, about 20 seconds. Put the chicken pieces on a large baking sheet in a single layer and pour the marinade over them, turning the chicken to coat evenly. Cover with plastic wrap and refrigerate for at least 6 hours or overnight.

▶ Pour oil into a deep fryer, or wide, heavy pot, at least 12 inches deep, to a depth of 6 inches. Heat the oil to 325°F. Line a plate or platter with paper towels and set it aside. Put the rice flour, all-purpose flour, salt, and pepper in a large, wide bowl, and stir them together. Remove the chicken pieces from the marinade, allowing excess to drip off, and discard the marinade. Dredge the chicken pieces in the flour mixture, then carefully lower them into the oil. Fry until golden brown and crispy and a meat thermometer inserted into the center of the chicken registers 160°F, about 15 minutes. When the chicken is done, use a slotted spoon to transfer it to the prepared plate to drain.

▶ Meanwhile, stir the sugar, ½ cup water, and the remaining 2 tablespoons fish sauce together in a medium saucepan and bring to a simmer over medium heat. Stir in the lime juice, red and green chiles, and ginger matchsticks. Remove the pan from the heat and transfer the sauce to a heatproof serving vessel.

▶ To serve, divide the chicken among 4 plates and pass the fish sauce alongside.

Fish Sauce

In the Thai cooking that I love, salinity is usually delivered not by salting food but rather by seasoning with fish sauce. (Soy sauce is also used, but mostly in marinades and stir-fries.) Fish sauce can also be ap- plied to other cooking when a more complex salinity is desired—for example, it brings a distinct fermented quality to curries. The label in the illustration below is a nod to my favorite brand, Three Crabs Fish Sauce.

VINAIGRETTES AND DRESSINGS: Add ½ to 1 teaspoon fish sauce to vinaigrettes for an extra dimension of flavor. It's also good in combination with lime juice as a quick dressing for greens or for tomato-and-watermelon salads— a good rule of thumb is 2 parts canola oil to 1 part lime juice and 1 part fish sauce.

FISH SAUCE GASTRIQUE: For a modern treatment of fish sauce, make a gastrique (see page 98) using palm sugar or light brown sugar in place of granulated sugar, and 1 cup rice vinegar for the vinegar. Reduce it until thick and caramel-like; stir in ¼ cup fish sauce and ½ cup tamarind concentrate, varying the liquids to taste, and cook, stirring, until a syrupy consistency is achieved. Finish with 2 tablespoons lime juice and coarsely ground black pepper.

Roasted Whole Chicken
with Spaetzle, Chestnuts, and Persimmons

SERVES 4

This autumnal main course is beautiful and elegant enough for a holiday dinner. The chestnuts are as seasonal as it gets; their earthy quality is offset and brightened by the tart, colorful persimmons. The roasted chicken boasts a crackling, crispy skin, arrived at by starting it at a low temperature, then finishing the cooking at a higher heat.

2 chickens, 2½ to 3 pounds each, washed and patted dry with paper towels

Kosher salt

Freshly ground white pepper

2 tablespoons extra-virgin olive oil

6 garlic cloves, 4 smashed with the side of a chef's knife and peeled, 2 thinly sliced, plus 2 tablespoons minced garlic

1 lemon, thinly sliced into rounds

2 thyme sprigs

3 tablespoons blended oil or neutral oil such as canola

2 shallots, thinly sliced

1 cup peeled, diced persimmons

¼ cup (packed) light brown sugar

1 tablespoon ground cinnamon

½ teaspoon freshly grated nutmeg

½ teaspoon ground cloves

½ teaspoon ground star anise

1 cup chicken stock, preferably homemade (page 366)

3 tablespoons unsalted butter

2 tablespoons pumpkin seed oil (page 105)

1 tablespoon rice wine vinegar

2 cups cooked quark spaetzle (see Notebook, page 248)

¾ cup roasted, thinly sliced chestnuts (from about 12 chestnuts) (see Note opposite)

2 cups (loosely packed) baby arugula

1 tablespoon thinly sliced flat-leaf parsley leaves

1 tablespoon minced chives

To roast the chickens: Preheat the oven to 400°F. Season the inside and outside of the chickens with salt and pepper. Rub all over with the olive oil, and stuff the cavities with the 4 smashed garlic cloves, lemon slices, and thyme sprigs. Truss the chickens with butcher's twine and transfer to a roasting pan or a rimmed baking sheet fitted with a roasting rack. Roast in the oven until a meat thermometer inserted into the thigh registers 150°F, about 40 minutes.

▶ Meanwhile, to make the persimmon purée: Heat 1 tablespoon of the blended oil in a medium saucepan over medium heat. When the oil is shimmering, add the sliced garlic, half of the sliced shallots, and persimmons and cook, stirring, until the garlic and shallots are softened but not browned, about 2 minutes. Stir in the brown sugar, cinnamon, nutmeg, cloves, and star anise and cook, stirring, for 1 minute. Pour in the stock and bring to a simmer, then lower the heat and continue to simmer until the persimmons are soft to a knife tip, about 10 minutes.

▸ Transfer the contents of the pan to a blender and blend to a smooth purée. Add 2 tablespoons of the butter, the pumpkin seed oil, and vinegar and blend until smooth. Season with salt and pepper and set aside, covered, to keep warm.

▸ To cook the spaetzle: Heat the remaining 2 tablespoons blended oil in a large sauté pan over high heat. When the oil is shimmering, add the spaetzle and cook, stirring, until they just begin to lightly brown all over, 2 to 3 minutes. Stir in the remaining 1 tablespoon butter, the minced garlic, the remaining 1 sliced shallot, and the chestnuts, and season with salt and pepper. Continue to cook and stir until the vegetables are softened but not browned and the spaetzle are golden brown, about 3 minutes more. Add the arugula, parsley, and chives and season with salt and pepper.

▸ To finish the chicken: When the internal temperature of the chicken reaches 150°F, increase the oven temperature to 500°F and continue to roast until the meat thermometer registers 160°F, about 5 minutes. Remove the chicken from the oven, tent with foil, and allow it to rest for 15 minutes.

▸ To serve, cut the chickens in half along the breastbone. Spoon persimmon purée onto each of 4 dinner plates. Top with the spaetzle and add half a chicken to each plate.

NOTE: To roast and peel chestnuts, preheat the oven to 400°F. Cut a shallow "X" on the flat side of each chestnut. Arrange the chestnuts in a single layer on a rimmed baking sheet and roast until they crack open, about 20 minutes. Let cool, then peel.

Spaetzle

Spaetzle are my favorite dumplings. They remind me of my grandmother, who made them with an old-fashioned spaetzle maker, but you can push them through the holes of a colander as most American home cooks do. They are a perfect match for schnit-zel (see page 277), especially duck, pork, or chicken. My basic spaetzle recipe includes an unconventional addition of quark for a light tang; it's easily adapted to make other varieties (see below).

MAKES 2 CUPS

2 large eggs

⅓ cup plus 1 teaspoon quark or fromage blanc

⅔ cup all-purpose flour

⅔ teaspoon freshly grated nutmeg

Kosher salt

Freshly ground white pepper

Put the eggs and quark in a mixer fitted with a paddle attachment and mix until incorporated. Put the flour and nutmeg in a medium bowl and season with salt and pepper. Whisk to incorporate; then, with the mixer running, slowly add the flour and nutmeg to the egg-quark mixture, paddling until they come together in a smooth batter, about 1 minute. Cover loosely with plastic wrap and chill in the refrigerator for 1 hour.

▸ Bring a large pot of salted water to a boil. Working in batches, put the batter in a colander, and use a dough scraper or rubber spatula to press it through the holes of the colander into the boiling water in roughly ½-inch strands. Cook until the spaetzle float, about 1 minute. Use a slotted spoon to transfer to a rimmed baking sheet. Allow the spaetzle to cool about 6 minutes, then cook according to individual recipes. In most cases, you will want to sauté the spaetzle in oil, then finish with butter until lightly golden brown, just before serving.

CARAWAY SPAETZLE: Replace the all-purpose flour with caraway flour, made by whisking together 1 tablespoon ground caraway seed with 9 tablespoons all-purpose flour; serve with bratwurst.

WHOLE WHEAT SPAETZLE: Replace the all-purpose flour with whole wheat flour; serve with lean meats, or with roasted vegetables for a vegetarian main course.

PORCINI SPAETZLE: Replace the all-purpose flour with porcini flour, made by whisking together 1 tablespoon porcini powder (page 363) with 9 tablespoons all-purpose flour; serve with mushrooms and game dishes.

Roasted Game Hen
with Grilled Radicchio, Peaches, Croutons, Bagna Cauda, and Salsa Verde

SERVES 4

I have probably never crammed more preparations into one composition than I do in this main course, which features not one, but two classic Italian adornments: bagna cauda, a garlic-and-anchovy dip; and *salsa verde*, or green sauce, a piquant condiment. There are also luscious, sweet peaches; bitter, charred, grilled radicchio; and crunchy croutons, all tossed with the bagna cauda. Amazingly, this hodgepodge harmonizes beautifully and invites diners to mix and match bites and combinations as they eat their way through the dish.

½ cup extra-virgin olive oil

3 tablespoons minced garlic

1 tablespoon minced rosemary

4 Cornish game hens, broken down by your butcher into 4 bone-in breasts, 8 legs, and 8 thighs

Kosher salt

Freshly ground white pepper

2 peaches, halved and pitted

1 head radicchio, quartered through the root

½ cup balsamic vinegar

1 tablespoon minced anchovy fillets (about 2 fillets)

½ cup sourdough croutons (see page 363)

¼ cup freshly squeezed lemon juice

1 tablespoon flat-leaf parsley leaves

½ cup Salsa Verde (see Notebook, page 251)

Preheat the oven to 400°F. Put 2 tablespoons of the olive oil, 2 tablespoons of the garlic, and the rosemary in a bowl and stir to incorporate. Rub the inside and outside of the game hen breasts with the garlic mixture, season with salt and pepper, and place on a baking sheet. Season the legs and thighs with salt and pepper and place on a separate baking sheet. Put the breasts on the top rack of the oven and the legs and thighs on the bottom. Remove the leg and thigh pieces from the oven when a thermometer inserted into the center of the pieces registers 160°F, about 10 minutes. Roast the breasts for another 5 minutes, then increase the oven temperature to 500°F and continue to roast until the skin is golden brown and crispy and a thermometer inserted into the center of the pieces registers 160°F, about 4 minutes more.

▶ Meanwhile, put the peaches and 1 tablespoon of the olive oil in a bowl and season with salt and pepper. Heat a grill pan over high heat for 5 minutes. Once the pan is hot, add the peach halves and grill until grill marks form and the peaches have softened slightly but still hold their shape, about 2 minutes per side. Remove the pan from the heat, cut the peaches into bite-size pieces, and set aside.

continued

▸ Return the grill pan to the stovetop over high heat for 2 minutes. Meanwhile, put the radicchio, 3 table-spoons of the olive oil, and the vinegar in a bowl and toss to coat. Season the radicchio with salt and pepper and place on the grill pan. Grill until charred, about 3 minutes. Transfer the radicchio to a cutting board, cut it into bite-size pieces, and set aside.

▸ When the game hen has finished roasting, remove the baking sheet from the oven. Remove the meat from the leg and thighbones, leaving the breasts whole. Coarsely chop the thigh and leg meat.

▸ To make the bagna cauda: Heat the remaining 2 tablespoons oil in a large sauté pan over medium-high heat. When the oil is shimmering, add the anchovy and the remaining 1 tablespoon garlic and cook, stirring, until softened but not browned, 1 minute. Add the reserved peaches, radicchio, croutons, and thigh and leg meat and toss to incorporate. Add the lemon juice and parsley, season with salt and pepper, and toss again.

▸ To serve, smear salsa verde in the middle of each of 4 dinner plates. Add radicchio mixture to each plate and top with a breast.

Salsa Verde

Salsa verde, or green sauce, is a highly adaptable condiment made with garlic, a variety of herbs, and salty components such as capers and anchovies. You can tweak this base recipe depending on how it will be used—for example, using more delicate herbs for fish or making it more assertive by adding an-chovies and more garlic if saucing meat. My favorite uses for salsa verde are topping grilled meats and grilled vegetables; drizzling over soups; spreading on sandwiches (on its own or stirred into mayon-naise); tossing with boiled potatoes and olive oil; or mixing into mayonnaise as a dip for fries.

MAKES ½ CUP

¼ cup (loosely packed) flat-leaf parsley leaves

2 tablespoons tarragon

¼ cup chives

1 tablespoon chervil

¼ cup basil leaves

1 teaspoon capers

2 teaspoons minced garlic

¼ cup extra-virgin olive oil

Kosher salt

Freshly ground white pepper

Put the parsley, tarragon, chives, chervil, basil, capers, garlic, oil, and 2 tablespoons cold water in a blender and season with salt and pepper. Blend until smooth. Serve right away; otherwise, the colors and flavors will become murky.

Chicken Fricassee

with Crispy Chicken Skin, Spaghetti Squash, Potato Fondue, and Black Truffle–Madeira Jus

This dish has roots in a formative moment from my culinary school days, when I had no interest in cooking or eating chicken because I thought it was too boring for my developing palate. When one of my instructors demonstrated a chicken and mushroom fricassee and sensed my indifference, he scolded me: "You're a good German; you *should* eat chicken!" He then proceeded to put his hand in the hot stew and hand-feed it to me to show me its merits. Miraculously, despite the circumstances, I liked it, and in time I developed my own version of a fricassee featuring black truffles, potato fondue, and lip-smacking, addictively crispy chicken skin. Note that this recipe uses more butter than most others; it's an indulgence for sure, but one that I think is worth it.

---

2 chickens, about 2½ pounds each, broken down by your butcher into 8 pieces each

2 tablespoons blended oil or neutral oil such as canola

1 Spanish onion, thinly sliced

4 plum tomatoes, thinly sliced

4 cups Madeira

2 gallons chicken stock, preferably homemade (page 366)

6 thyme sprigs

2 pounds (8 sticks) unsalted butter, cut into small pieces, plus 15 tablespoons (1½ sticks plus 3 tablespoons) unsalted butter

½ cup black truffle peelings

1 shallot, thinly sliced

2 cups dry white wine

Kosher salt

Freshly ground white pepper

1 spaghetti squash (about 2½ pounds), halved lengthwise, seeds removed

¼ cup shiro dashi

2 tablespoons minced chives

2 cups Idaho potatoes, peeled and chopped

1 cup buttermilk

1 cup whole milk

4 pieces Crispy Chicken Skin (see Notebook, page 254)

Preheat the oven to 450°F. Remove the chicken skin, reserving it for the crispy chicken skin (see Notebook, page 254). Bone out the chicken breasts and thighs and set the breast and thigh meat aside. Put all the chicken bones, the legs, and wings in a large roasting pan and roast, shaking the pan periodically to ensure even cooking, until the bones and parts are golden brown, about 40 minutes. Remove the pan from the oven and set it aside.

▶ To make the sauce: Heat the oil in a large stockpot over high heat. When the oil is shimmering, add the onion and tomatoes and cook, stirring, until caramelized, about 8 minutes. Pour in the Madeira and cook, stirring to loosen any flavorful bits from the bottom of the pot. Bring to a simmer, and continue to simmer until the liquid is reduced by half, about 8 minutes. Add the roasted chicken parts and pour in the stock. Bring to a simmer and continue to simmer, adjusting the heat as necessary to prevent the liquid from boiling aggressively, until the liquid has reduced to 1 quart, about 2 hours. Use a slotted spoon to remove and discard the bones. Strain the liquid through a fine-mesh strainer set over a large bowl, pressing down with a rubber spatula or the back of a ladle to extract as much flavorful liquid as possible. Return the liquid to the pot, add 2 of the thyme sprigs, and return to a simmer. Simmer until the liquid has reduced to 1 cup and is thick enough to coat the back of a wooden spoon, 12 to 15 minutes. Use a slotted spoon to remove and discard the thyme. Swirl 1 tablespoon of the butter and the truffles into the sauce and set it aside.

▶ Put the shallot and white wine in a large, deep saucepan over high heat, bring to a simmer, then lower the heat and continue to simmer until the wine has reduced by a quarter, about 5 minutes. Remove the pan from the heat and gradually whisk in the 2 pounds (8 sticks) of cut-up butter, a few pieces at a time, until emulsified. Add the remaining 4 thyme sprigs and season with salt and pepper. Place the pan back over medium heat and bring the liquid to 190°F. Season the chicken breasts and thighs with salt and pepper and add them to the liquid, completely submerging them. Lower the heat and cook gently until a meat thermometer inserted in the thickest part of the chicken thighs registers 160°F, about 15 minutes. Use a slotted spoon to remove the breasts and thighs from the pot and cut them in half lengthwise.

▶ Meanwhile, to make the spaghetti squash: Lower the oven temperature to 425°F. Season the squash with salt and pepper and place on a rimmed baking sheet, flesh side down. Pour about 1 quart water onto the sheet and carefully place in the oven. Roast until strands can be easily pulled away from the skin with a fork, about 20 minutes. Remove the squash from the sheet and set aside to cool. Once the squash is cool enough to handle, about 12 minutes, use a fork to scrape the squash away from the skin to create spaghetti-like strands, and discard the skin. Melt 2 tablespoons of the butter in a large sauté pan over medium heat. Add the squash and cook, stirring, until the squash is cooked through. Stir in the shiro dashi and chives.

▶ To make the potato fondue: Put the potato, buttermilk, and whole milk in a large saucepan over medium-high heat and season with salt and pepper. Bring to a simmer and cook until the potatoes are tender to a knife tip, about 20 minutes. Run the potatoes through a food mill and return to the pot with the liquid. Add the remaining 12 tablespoons (1½ sticks) butter and stir to melt it. Season with salt and pepper. Strain through a fine-mesh strainer set over a large bowl; the fondue should have the texture of a loose purée.

▶ To serve, spoon potato fondue into the bottom of each of 4 dinner plates. Top with the squash and chicken pieces. Spoon the sauce over and around the chicken. Garnish each serving with a chicken skin tuile and serve.

Crispy Chicken Skin

Any lover of roasted chicken knows that, when properly cooked, the skin is the best part. In dishes like the one on page 252, it also adds necessary crunch. Use it to finish chicken main courses, salads, or dishes featuring steamed eggs (see page 259). For a decadent hors d'oeuvre, use it as a crostini base.

CHICKEN SKIN TUILES

MAKES 4

4 pieces chicken breast skin

Preheat the oven to 250°F. Line a baking sheet with parchment paper and set aside. Lay the skin flat on a cutting board and use a sharp knife to scrape away any excess fat, taking care to not tear the skin.

▶ Transfer the chicken skin to the prepared baking sheet and lay another piece of parchment on top. Set another baking sheet over the parchment to weigh down and flatten the skin. Put the stacked baking sheets in the oven and bake until the skin is golden and crispy, about 3 hours. The crispy skin pieces can be held for up to 24 hours in an airtight container at room temperature.

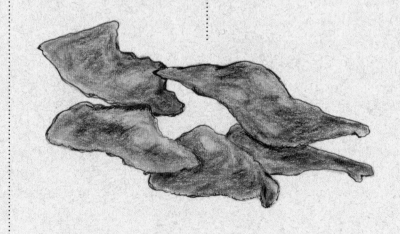

Khao Soi

with Roasted Chicken, Crispy Egg Noodles, Lime, and Peanuts

SERVES 4

My adaptation of the Chiang Mai curry noodle dish *khao soi* is a potently flavored, aromatic mixture of Thai flavors and textures, finished with crunchy fried noodles and served with a variety of garnishes that allow each diner to doctor his or her portion according to personal taste. I like mine with a lot of peanuts, especially roasted peanuts.

1 chicken, about 2½ pounds, washed and patted dry with paper towels

3 tablespoons blended oil or neutral oil such as canola

Kosher salt

Freshly ground white pepper

2 tablespoons garlic, 1 minced, 1 thinly sliced

1 tablespoon peeled, minced fresh ginger

5 kaffir lime leaves

1½ teaspoons coriander seeds

1½ teaspoons cardamom seeds

1½ teaspoons mace

1 tablespoon cumin seeds

½ stick cassia (cinnamon may be substituted)

½ cup dried Thai chiles, seeded and soaked in warm water for 5 minutes, then drained, soaking liquid reserved

3 tablespoons thinly sliced shallot

1 lemongrass stalk, thinly sliced (see page 362)

2 tablespoons peeled, chopped galangal

¼ cup peeled, chopped fresh turmeric

6 cilantro stems plus ¼ cup (loosely packed) cilantro leaves

6 cups coconut milk

4 ounces tamarind concentrate

¾ cup palm sugar or turbinado sugar such as Sugar in the Raw

Fish sauce

8 ounces fried chow mein noodles

2 limes, halved

1 hothouse cucumber, seeds removed, thinly sliced

1 cup bean sprouts

1 carrot, peeled and sliced into thin disks

½ cup roasted peanuts

¼ cup Thai basil

Preheat the oven to 425°F. Rub the chicken with 2 tablespoons of the oil and season generously inside and out with salt and pepper. Stuff the cavity with the minced garlic, ginger, and 2 of the lime leaves and truss the chicken with butcher's twine. Place in a roasting pan fitted with a rack and roast until a meat thermometer inserted into the thigh reaches 150°F, about 35 minutes.

▶ Meanwhile, to make the *khao soi* curry paste: Grind the coriander, cardamom, mace, cumin, and cas-sia in a spice or coffee grinder. Transfer the mixture to a blender and add the chiles, shallot, sliced garlic, lemongrass, galangal, turmeric, cilantro stems, and salt. Blend to a smooth purée, about 1 minute, adding some of the chile soaking liquid as needed to help the blender's blade catch.

▶ Heat the remaining 1 tablespoon oil in a medium saucepan over high heat. When the oil is shimmering,

continued

Peanuts

Often crushed and scattered over dishes as a finishing element in Thai cuisine, peanuts can also be the basis of high-impact, stand-alone preparations. Here are a few of my favorites:

THAI-STYLE ROASTED RED-SKIN PEANUTS: To make 1 quart of this spicy peanut snack, preheat the oven to 375°F. Heat 2 tablespoons blended oil or neutral oil such as canola in an ovenproof sauté pan over high heat. When the oil is shimmering, add 1 pound red-skin peanuts and cook, tossing every minute, for about 4 minutes. Season with salt and white pepper, and add 2 sliced garlic cloves, 1 tablespoon peeled, minced fresh ginger, and 5 whole Thai red chiles, and cook, tossing, for 2 minutes more. Toss in 2 kaffir lime leaves cut into chiffonade (see page 362), transfer the pan to the oven, and roast until golden brown, about 10 minutes. Drain on paper towels, allow to cool, and enjoy right away or store in an airtight container for up to 1 week.

These are especially good in place of regular roasted peanuts atop the Crispy Calamari and Watercress Salad on page 27.

SATAY MARINADE: Use this peanut-based marinade for grilled meats. Put 3 tablespoons roasted peanuts, 2 sliced shallots, 1 tablespoon toasted coriander seeds, 1 teaspoon cumin seeds, ½ cup coconut milk, 1 teaspoon turmeric powder, 2 tablespoons palm sugar, 2 tablespoons fish sauce, 1 tablespoon Mekhong or whiskey, and ¼ cup water in a blender and blend to a smooth purée. Marinate 8 ounces of chicken, beef, or pork in the purée for at least 1 hour before grilling.

PEANUT BUTTER: Use warm roasted peanuts to make your own peanut butter (page 349).

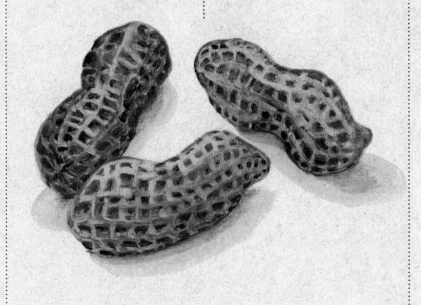

Chicken Chiang Mai Sausage

with Congee, Slow-Cooked Duck Egg, and Razor Clam Sauce

SERVES 4

The sausage here is based on one they make in Chiang Mai, Thailand, but the rest of the dish is my own concoction—a fantasy of a Thai breakfast dish. It may seem exotic, but its components harken back to American sausage, gravy, and egg dishes, and it's just as homey. The recipe calls for 4 duck eggs, but I suggest starting with a few extra to test for doneness as you steam them; you are looking for a soft white and molten, oozing yolk.

Canola oil or corn oil, for frying

1½ pounds Chiang Mai Sausage (page 215)

3 tablespoons blended oil or neutral oil such as canola

2 pounds razor clams, in their shells

Kosher salt

Freshly ground white pepper

3 garlic cloves, thinly sliced, 1 kept separate

1 shallot, thinly sliced

2 cups dry white wine

2 kaffir lime leaves

4 duck eggs

1½ cups Congee (see Notebook, page 262)

½ cup shellfish stock, preferably homemade (page 367)

1 tablespoon fish sauce

¼ cup chopped scallion greens

1 tablespoon Thai basil leaves

1 tablespoon fried shallots (see page 369)

1 tablespoon fried garlic (see page 369)

To fry the sausage: Pour canola oil into a deep fryer, or wide, deep, heavy pot, to a depth of 4 inches. Heat the oil to 350°F. Line a plate with paper towels and set it aside. Fry the sausage disks until crispy, about 4 minutes, then transfer to the prepared plate to drain.

▶ To prepare the clams: Heat 2 tablespoons of the blended oil in a wide pot over high heat. When the oil is shimmering, add the razor clams and season with salt and pepper. Cook, stirring, for 1 minute. Add 2 of the garlic cloves and the shallot and cook, stirring, for 1 minute. Pour in the white wine, add the lime leaves, and cover the pot. Cook, gently shaking the pot occasionally, until all the clams open, about 6 minutes. Discard any unopened clams. Strain the liquid through

a fine-mesh strainer set over a large bowl. Set the liquid aside and allow the clams to cool for 5 minutes. Remove the clams from the shells and slice the bottoms off the clams to remove the belly sack. Discard the sack. Return the clams to the reserved liquid in the bowl and set aside.

▶ To prepare the duck eggs: Bring a large pot of water to 140°F over medium-high heat and fill a large bowl halfway with ice water. Add the duck eggs to the hot water and gently cook for 40 minutes, adjusting the heat to maintain the water temperature. Transfer the eggs to the ice bath to stop the cooking.

continued

▸ Warm the congee and shellfish stock in a small sauce-pan over medium heat. When they are warmed though, about 3 minutes, stir in the fish sauce and scallions.

▸ Heat the remaining 1 tablespoon blended oil in a medium sauté pan over medium heat. When the oil is shimmering, add the remaining garlic clove and cook, stirring, until golden brown, about 3 minutes. Stir in the reserved clams and 1 cup of their liquid, the sausage, and basil. Cook, stirring, until the sausage is warmed through, about 4 minutes.

▸ To serve, divide the congee among 4 bowls. Spoon the clam and sausage stew around the congee. Use the back of a spoon to make a small divot in the congee. Crack an egg into each divot and garnish with fried shallots and fried garlic.

Congee

Congee is a porridge-like Asian dish made by recooking rice in water until the grains break down and the rice turns thick and creamy. To me, it's one of the ultimate comfort foods: simple, soothing, and nourishing.

MAKES 1½ CUPS

1 cup jasmine rice, cooked
  (½ cup rice and 1 cup water, simmered together for about 35 minutes)
1½ cups water

Heat a medium saucepan over medium heat. Add the rice and water and cook, stirring occasionally, until the rice breaks down and the mixture turns thick and porridge-like, about 5 minutes.

VIETNAMESE BREAKFAST: Serve congee for breakfast with grilled pork and eggs cooked your favorite way. I like to treat this in street-food style, serving it all in the same bowl, topping the congee with the pork and eggs.

VIETNAMESE BREAKFAST, PART 2: For an oatmeal-like treatment of congee, serve the congee with milk, brown sugar, granola, and/or fruit stirred into it.

CONGEE-BRAISED PORK: For a spin on the Italian tradition of braising meats in polenta, braise pork shoulder in gently simmering congee for about 3 hours. Set aside until cool enough to handle, about 15 minutes. Remove and shred the meat and serve it scattered over the congee, reheating both just before serving.

Crispy Duck Confit

with Brazil Nuts, Bulgur Wheat, Celery, and Mango–"Gin-Ger" Sauce

SERVES 4

Once turned to as a means of preservation, confit—or cooking something in its own fat—remains a potent method for imparting tremendous flavor to a variety of poultry and meats and is sometimes used to cook fish as well. The most common variety is duck confit, and the method here is traditional, curing the duck in a mixture of salt and herbs, then slow-cooking it in fat. The duck meat is then sautéed and served with a bulgur wheat salad and mango sauce that's enlivened by the addition of ginger and gin.

4 cups kosher salt, plus more for seasoning

3 cups sugar

8 thyme sprigs, plus 1 teaspoon thyme leaves

16 garlic cloves, sliced

4 duck leg-thigh pieces

2 quarts plus 1 tablespoon duck fat (see Sources, page 370)

½ cup bulgur wheat

2¼ cups sherry vinegar

¼ cup high-quality gin such as Hendrick's

½ cup puréed mango, plus ½ cup diced mango

Freshly ground white pepper

4 tablespoons (½ stick) unsalted butter

¼ cup peeled, julienned fresh ginger

Freshly ground black pepper

½ cup sliced celery

½ cup crushed roasted Brazil nuts

¼ cup extra-virgin olive oil

1 tablespoon minced shallot

To cure the duck: Put the salt, 2 cups of the sugar, the thyme sprigs, and garlic in a large bowl and stir them together. Arrange the duck leg-thigh pieces in a shallow baking vessel in a single layer and pour the mixture over them, turning the pieces in the mixture to coat them. Cover the vessel with plastic wrap and place in the refrigerator to cure for 12 to 24 hours.

▸ When the duck has been cured, preheat the oven to 275°F. Remove the duck pieces from the cure, rinse them, and pat them dry with paper towels. Heat 2 quarts of the duck fat in a Dutch oven or other large, wide pot over high heat. When the fat reaches 180°F, carefully lower the duck pieces in, cover the pot with

aluminum foil, and cook in the oven until tender and cooked through, 2 to 3 hours. (The confit can be made up to 3 days in advance, cooled, and refrigerated in an airtight container, covered with its cooking fat.)

▸ Meanwhile, to cook the bulgur wheat: Put the wheat in a medium, heatproof bowl. Bring 1 cup water to a boil and pour it over the wheat. Add a pinch of salt, stir, and cover with a tight-fitting lid or plastic wrap and set aside for 7 minutes. Fluff the wheat with a fork and carefully pour off any excess water. Allow it to cool to room temperature while you finish preparing the dish.

continued

To make the mango sauce: Cook 2 cups of the vinegar and the remaining 1 cup sugar in a saucepan over medium-high heat, whisking, until the sugar has dissolved and the mixture has reduced by half, about 5 minutes. Stir in the gin and mango purée, and simmer until reduced by half, about 5 minutes. Season with salt and white pepper, then fold in the butter, diced mango, and ginger.

Increase the oven temperature to 475°F. Season the duck generously with salt and black pepper. Heat the remaining 1 tablespoon duck fat in a wide, deep, oven-proof sauté pan over medium-high heat. When the fat is shimmering, add the duck pieces to the pan and cook for 3 minutes. Transfer the pan to the oven and cook for another 8 minutes.

Add the celery, nuts, remaining ¼ cup vinegar, the extra-virgin olive oil, shallot, and remaining 1 teaspoon thyme leaves to the bowl with the cooled bulgur wheat, season with salt and black pepper, and gently toss.

To serve, spoon bulgur salad onto each of 4 dinner plates. Lay 1 duck leg-thigh piece alongside the salad, and finish with the mango sauce.

Gin

Gin is, by far, my favorite spirit, with a flavor conjured by juniper berries and other aromatics. I love it so much that rather than gin and tonics, I drink gin and soda so as not to obscure the flavor of the gin itself. My go-to gin is Hendrick's, for its clean, floral character and pronounced juniper flavor. Here are some popular cocktails from my restaurants, and a recipe that uses gin flavors to produce a unique assortment of pickled vegetables.

Many of these recipes call for a homemade syrup; see page 363 for guidance in making them.

PERILLA 75

1 ounce high-quality gin, preferably Plymouth

¾ ounce perilla syrup (see page 363)

1½ ounces freshly squeezed grapefruit juice

Prosecco, as needed

Put the gin, syrup, and grapefruit juice in a shaker with ice. Strain into a champagne flute and top with prosecco or other sparkling wine.

GIN AND TONIC

3 hothouse cucumber slices

¼ ounce freshly squeezed lime juice

4 cilantro leaves

1½ ounces high-quality gin

½ ounce St. Germain elderflower liqueur

Scoop of ice

Tonic water, as needed

Muddle the cucumber, lime juice, and cilantro together. Add the gin, St. Germain, and a scoop of ice. Lightly shake and pour into a highball glass. Top with tonic water.

GIN AND GINGER

1½ ounces high-quality gin

½ ounce Domaine de Canton ginger liqueur

½ ounce freshly squeezed lime juice

½ ounce mint syrup (see page 363)

Scoop of ice

Soda water, as needed

1 piece candied ginger (store-bought or homemade; see page 116)

In a shaker, combine the gin, Domaine de Canton, lime juice, mint syrup, and a scoop of ice. Lightly shake and pour into a highball glass. Top with soda water and garnish with a piece of candied ginger.

SAGE 75

1½ ounces high-quality gin

¾ ounce freshly squeezed lemon juice

1 sage leaf

½ ounce sage syrup (see page 363)

Scoop of ice

Sparkling wine, as needed

In a shaker, muddle together the gin, lemon juice, sage, and sage syrup. Add a scoop of ice, and lightly shake. Strain into a flute and pour sparkling wine over the top.

THE BERLINER

1½ ounces high-quality gin

½ ounce dry vermouth

½ ounce freshly squeezed lemon juice

½ ounce Combier kümmel

Scoop of ice

1 lemon twist

Put the gin, vermouth, lemon juice, and Combier kümmel in a shaker with ice. Shake and pour into a martini glass. Garnish with a twist of lemon.

GIN AND SAFFRON PICKLED PLATTER

¼ cup quartered baby cauliflower

¼ cup halved baby carrots

2 tablespoons peeled pearl onions

2 tablespoons halved baby radishes

¼ cup quartered baby cucumbers such as Kirbys

2 cups rice vinegar

2 tablespoons mustard seeds

1 tablespoon juniper berries

½ cup high-quality gin

1 tablespoon saffron threads

⅓ cup sugar

1 tablespoon kosher salt

Put the cauliflower, carrots, onions, radishes, and cucumbers in a heat-proof vessel.

▶ Put the vinegar, mustard seeds, juniper berries, gin, saffron, sugar, and salt in a medium pot and bring to a boil over high heat. Pour the liquid over the vegetables, and allow to cool to room temperature, about 20 minutes. Cover with a tight-fitting lid and refrigerate for 48 hours. Serve the vegetables within 1 week.

Whole Roasted Duck

with Toasted Almonds, Balsamic Vinegar, Wild Rice, and Bing Cherry Sauce

SERVES 4

As far as I'm concerned, duck ought to be as popular all over the world as it is in China, and as chicken is in the United States. It's very easy to cook, with a high fat content that makes it very forgiving; it almost bastes itself as it roasts or even as it is sautéed. To balance the richness of its fat, duck is usually served with sweet or tart accompaniments (the ultimate example being the French staple duck à l'orange), such as the Bing cherry sauce here. The wild rice and nuts here are also very traditional pairings.

---

2 Pekin (Long Island) ducks, about 6 pounds each

Kosher salt

2 tablespoons cracked black pepper, plus freshly ground black pepper for seasoning

8 garlic cloves, smashed with the side of a chef's knife

1 cup wild rice

1 cup sugar

1 cup sherry vinegar

1½ cups pitted Bing cherries

¾ pound (3 sticks) unsalted butter, cut into small pieces

¼ cup honey

¼ cup balsamic vinegar

½ cup thinly sliced shallots

1 cup slivered almonds, toasted (see page 362)

Zest and juice of 2 oranges

½ cup thinly sliced Belgian endive

¼ cup (loosely packed) basil chiffonade (see page 362)

Preheat the oven to 375°F. Season the ducks inside and out with salt and coarsely ground black pepper. Divide the garlic cloves between the duck cavities and truss both ducks with butcher's twine. Place in a roasting pan fitted with a roasting rack, breast side up. Place in the oven and roast until nicely burnished, about 50 minutes.

▸ Meanwhile, bring 2 cups water to a boil in a medium pot over high heat. Stir in the rice, season with salt, cover, and lower the heat. Simmer until the rice is al dente, about 40 minutes.

▸ While the duck and rice cook, make the Bing cherry sauce: Cook the sugar and 2 tablespoons water in a medium saucepan over medium-high heat, stirring, until the sugar has caramelized, about 7 minutes. Pour in the sherry vinegar and stir vigorously to incorporate. Bring to a simmer and continue to simmer until reduced by half, 5 to 6 minutes. Add 1 cup of the cherries and season with salt. Cook for 5 minutes, then add 12 tablespoons (1½ sticks) of the butter, a few pieces at a time, whisking constantly, until incorporated. Transfer the contents of the pan to a blender and blend until smooth. Strain through a fine-mesh strainer set over a bowl. Stir in the remaining ½ cup cherries and the 2 tablespoons cracked black pepper.

▸ Put the honey and balsamic vinegar in a small bowl and stir together. Use a pastry brush to brush the mixture all over the ducks, and return them the oven.

continued

Cook for 5 minutes more, then brush the ducks again and cook for another 5 minutes. Brush the ducks once more and set aside to rest for 30 minutes.

▸ Melt the remaining 12 tablespoons (1½ sticks) butter in a medium sauté pan over medium heat. Add the shallots and cook, stirring, until softened but not browned, about 2 minutes. Put the rice, almonds, orange zest and juice, endive, and basil in a large bowl. Season with salt and pepper and stir to incorporate. Pour the hot butter-shallot mixture over the rice mixture, and toss to incorporate.

▸ When the duck is rested, preheat the broiler to high. Remove the duck meat from the carcass, leaving only the wing bones and leg bones. Transfer the duck meat to a baking sheet, skin side up, and brush again with the honey-balsamic mixture. Place in the oven and broil until the skin is crisp, 3 to 4 minutes.

▸ To serve, divide the wild rice among 4 dinner plates. Top the rice on each plate with ½ crispy duck, and spoon the Bing cherry sauce around the duck and rice.

Cherries

Ever since my first taste of Breyers cherry-vanilla ice cream, I've been hooked on cherries. When summer rolls around, I can't get enough of them, and I love using them in savory and sweet dishes as well as in cocktails. With one exception, all of the following preparations use Bing cherries, which are consistently my favorite for their juicy sweetness.

CANDIED CHERRIES: Toss cherries with simple syrup (page 363), spread them out on a baking sheet, and bake in a 200°F oven until the syrup crystallizes, about 8 hours. Serve in sundaes or over chocolate cake.

PICKLED CHERRIES: Pickle cherries following the pickled onion recipe on page 100. Toss them in salads or use them to garnish fatty meats such as duck or squab.

CHERRY-TOPPED COOKIES: For Italian Americans like me, there's only one way to top butter cookies—with a sweet maraschino cherry. The contrast between the crumbly dough and crunchy, preserved fruit is one of those combinations that adds up to more than the sum of its parts.

CHERRY AND SPINACH SALAD: Make a salad of spinach leaves, pitted and halved Bing cherries, crumbled feta cheese, sliced red onion, and a brown butter–balsamic vinaigrette.

BRANDIED CHERRIES: For a potent cocktail garnish, soak cherries in a small amount of brandy at least overnight or up to 24 hours.

Grilled Quail

with Grilled Pineapple, Cashew Butter, and Baby Bok Choy Salad

SERVES 4

This dish is very playful—one doesn't expect to find a rustic game bird paired with a sweet tropical fruit. The juxtaposition works because the pineapple proves to be an ideal foil for the quail, a fowl many people feel has a livery flavor, but I love it—especially meaty semi-boneless quail, which I eat with my hands even in the fanciest of restaurants. Baby bok choy adds a pleasing crunch.

4 tablespoons (½ stick) unsalted butter

1 cup whole cashews, plus 1 tablespoon chopped toasted cashews (see page 362)

½ cup Madras curry powder

Kosher salt

1 tablespoon freshly ground white pepper, plus more for seasoning

1 tablespoon rice vinegar

8 semiboneless quail, about 4 ounces each

2 tablespoons minced shallot

1½ teaspoons minced garlic

1 teaspoon peeled, minced fresh ginger

½ teaspoon minced lemongrass (see page 362)

3 tablespoons blended oil or neutral oil such as canola

¼ pineapple, peeled, cored, and cut lengthwise into 4 wedges

1 tablespoon freshly ground pink peppercorns

Canola oil or corn oil, for frying

4 baby bok choy, quartered through the root

¼ cup basil leaves

2 tablespoons fish sauce

2 tablespoons freshly squeezed lime juice

To make the curry cashew butter: Melt the butter in a medium sauté pan over medium heat. Once the butter is melted, add the whole cashews and the curry powder and cook, tossing gently, until the cashews are caramelized, 2 to 3 minutes. Remove the pan from the heat, pour in 1 cup water, and season with salt and pepper. Transfer the contents of the pan to a blender and blend until smooth. Stir in the vinegar and add more water as needed to yield a smooth purée. Strain through a fine-mesh strainer set over a bowl, pressing down with a ladle or the back of a spoon, and refrigerate until chilled, at least 1 hour.

▸ Put the quail in a large mixing bowl. Scatter 2 teaspoons of the minced shallots, the garlic, ginger, lemongrass, 2 tablespoons of the blended oil, and 1 tablespoon white pepper over them. Season with salt and toss to coat. Heat a grill over high heat, or heat a grill pan over high heat for 5 minutes. (See pages 274–75 for grilling guidelines.) Add the quail to the grill and cook until they are browned and a thermometer inserted into the quail registers 125°F, about 3 minutes per side. Remove the quail from the grill and let rest for 2 minutes, then use a sharp, heavy knife to split them, slicing down the center of each breast.

▶ Put the pineapple, pink peppercorns, and the remaining 1 tablespoon blended oil in a medium bowl, season with salt, and toss to coat the pineapple. Arrange the pineapple on the grill and grill until it is lightly caramelized and nice grill marks form, turning once, about 3 minutes on each side. Remove from the heat and cut the pineapple into bite-size pieces.

▶ Pour canola oil into a deep fryer, or wide, deep, heavy pot, to a depth of 6 inches. Heat the oil to 350°F. Add the bok choy and fry until crispy, about 2 minutes.

Use a slotted spoon to transfer the bok choy to a large bowl and add the grilled pineapple, remaining 4 teaspoons shallots, basil, fish sauce, lime juice, and chopped cashews. Toss to combine. The mixture should be sour and salty; add more lime juice (sour) or fish sauce as needed.

▶ To serve, smear chilled cashew butter onto the center of each of 4 dinner plates. Stack 2 quail halves on top of the butter and spoon salad over and around the quail.

Grilling

Since many of the recipes in this book involve grilling, I wanted to share some tips about this technique. Grills come in so many sizes, shapes, and levels of complexity today—from old-fashioned charcoal grills with nothing but a coal bed and a grate all the way to super-sophisticated gas grills—that it's impossible to address every option out there in a Notebook entry, but a few principles apply universally to grilling:

▸ Gas grills are more convenient than charcoal grills, but charcoal grills are truer to the original spirit of the technique and produce a superior flavor. When you grill over charcoal, the fats and juices from your food drip down onto the coals, then are returned in the smoke that rises, creating intensely flavored char. Gas grills provide heat and grill marks but simply cannot match that flavor.

▸ If you are using a charcoal grill, do not use lighter fluid or self-starting briquettes, which are treated with chemicals that will impair the flavor of the food. The best, most reliable way to light charcoal is with a chimney starter, a cylindrical ventilated tool that holds the charcoal in an upper compartment and newspaper or other flammable material below. When you light the paper, the contained heat ignites the charcoal; then you dump it into the grill's coal bed.

▸ Be sure your grill is clean. The best way to do so is by brushing it with a dedicated grilling brush just after using it, when it's still hot. If food dries and cools on the grate, it becomes much more difficult to remove.

▸ When grilling, be sure the grill is properly heated. With a gas grill, this means preheating it as you would an oven. With a charcoal grill, it means allowing the coals to burn until covered with white ash, which can take up to 45 minutes. A great, low-tech test to gauge if the grill is at the right temperature is the 5-second test. Hold your hand about 6 inches over the grate. If you can leave it there for 5 seconds, the grill is ready for use; if you can leave it longer, it's not hot enough; if you cannot leave it for 5 seconds, it's too hot. (In cases where a grill pan or cast-iron pan are being used in place of the real deal, I suggest preheating them on the stovetop over high heat for 5 minutes, but no longer, to get them hot enough to produce grill marks or charring.)

▸ It's often not necessary to pre-oil a grill. If the food being cooked has been marinated with oil or is naturally fatty or oily, that should be sufficient. If, however, you are grilling, say, a lean piece of fish, then it's useful to oil the grill. The best way to do so is by bringing a small bowl of canola or corn oil out with you when you grill. Grab a clean kitchen towel with long tongs and, leaning away from the grill, use the tongs to dip the towel in the oil, just moistening it, then quickly rub it over the grate.

▸ If a flare-up occurs when grilling, don't panic. Calmly use tongs or a long spatula to pick up the food that's in the line of fire and move it to another part of the grill.

▸ It's fun to add flavor to grilled food, especially meats, with different types of wood chips, although lava rocks are better on a gas grill because they won't incinerate. That said, some gas grills have special built-in areas for wood or smoking elements.

▸ It's important to know the difference between direct and indirect heat. Both are just what they sound like. Direct heat means grilling right over the heat source, and it's how most grilling is done. Indirect heat means grilling to the side of that source and is generally used to gently or slowly grill some foods or to keep grilled foods warm as you cook other items. To achieve indirect heat with charcoal, bank the coals to one side of the coal bed; with gas, simply make one side of the grill hotter than the other.

Turkey Schnitzel

with Cucumber Salad, Dill, and Lingonberries

This simple dish—namely, the schnitzel and the dill and lingonberries that are part of the cucumber salad—is based on Germanic Alsatian techniques and flavors. It's handy to have in your repertoire for a quick weeknight dinner, and the schnitzel can be adapted to many variations (see Notebook on the facing page).

2 hothouse cucumbers, halved lengthwise, seeded, and thinly sliced

½ medium red onion, thinly sliced

1 shallot, minced

2 tablespoons minced dill

¼ cup cider vinegar

2 tablespoons extra-virgin olive oil

Kosher salt

Freshly ground white pepper

4 pieces boneless turkey breast, about 6 ounces each

1 cup all-purpose flour

4 large eggs

2 cups finely ground panko bread crumbs

2 cups blended oil, or other neutral oil such as canola

4 tablespoons (½ stick) unsalted butter

½ cup lingonberries

½ lemon, cut into wedges

Put the cucumbers, onion, shallot, dill, cider vinegar, and olive oil in a large bowl. Season with salt and pepper and toss. Set aside.

▸ To prepare the schnitzel: Preheat the oven to 425°F. Line a large plate with paper towels.

▸ Working with one piece of turkey at a time, place the meat between 2 pieces of plastic wrap and lightly pound with a meat mallet or the bottom of a heavy pan to an even thickness of 1 inch.

▸ Put the flour in a medium bowl. Put the eggs in a second bowl and beat them to blend. Put the bread crumbs in a third bowl. Dredge the turkey breasts first in the flour, then the eggs, and finally the panko, gently shaking off any excess.

▸ Heat the blended oil in a large, ovenproof sauté pan over high heat. When the oil is shimmering, add the schnitzels to the pan without crowding (you may need to work in two batches, or use two pans and extra oil) and sear until golden on one side, about 5 minutes. Turn them over and cook until golden on the second side, about 5 minutes more. Add the butter to the pan and put the pan in the oven. Cook for 3 minutes to heat the schnitzel through, then remove the pan from the oven and use a spoon to baste the turkey with the melted butter. Transfer the schnitzels to the prepared plate to drain and immediately season generously with salt and pepper.

▸ To serve, place 1 turkey schnitzel in the center of each of 4 plates, top with lingonberries, and spoon cucumber salad alongside. Garnish each plate with a lemon wedge for squeezing over the schnitzels.

Schnitzel

Schnitzel is my favorite German dish, and I'm equally fond of other cultures' versions of pounded, breaded meats, such as the Italian Milanese. Some deep-fry their schnitzel, but I'm strictly against that technique because it threatens to incinerate the breading and can also overcook the meat within. Pan-frying and finishing with a basting of butter is the way to go for a crispy, golden result. To make the variations below, follow the instructions on the facing page, replacing the turkey with these proteins.

FLUKE OR FLOUNDER: Serve like a piccata with a butter-caper sauce made by heating 2 tablespoons olive oil in a large sauté pan, then sautéing 1 sliced shallot and ¼ cup diced sweet bell peppers until softened but not browned, about 4 minutes. Stir in ½ cup dry white wine and simmer until reduced by half, about 6 minutes. Finish off the dish by swirling in 2 tablespoons unsalted butter, melting it, then adding 1 tablespoon sliced flat-leaf parsley leaves and a few drops of lemon juice. Serve with mashed potatoes.

CHICKEN: Serve Marsala-style with a sauce of Marsala and mushrooms. Heat ¼ cup olive oil in a sauté pan over medium-high heat. When the oil is shimmering, add 1 cup of your favorite sliced wild mushrooms, season with salt and black pepper, and sauté until softened, about 5 minutes, depending on mushroom type. Add 1 cup Marsala and simmer until reduced by half, about 8 minutes. Off heat, swirl in 1 tablespoon unsalted butter, melting it to emulsify the sauce. Finish with 2 tablespoons sliced flat-leaf parsley leaves. Spoon over the chicken schnitzel.

VEAL: Serve like veal Milanese, with a tomato and arugula salad, and finish the dish with Parmesan shavings.

PORK: Serve Japanese-style with teriyaki sauce, or make an Italian hero with it, along with sautéed broccoli rabe and marinara sauce on a seeded roll.

Grilled Guinea Hen

with Scallions, Hedgehog Mushrooms, and Local Creamed Corn

This summery main course takes advantage of the natural affinity between hedgehog mushrooms and corn, as well as the seasonal associations of the grill. Scallions add a light, oniony presence to the plate. Note that the guinea hens must be brined for 12 to 24 hours.

2 guinea hens, about 2½ pounds each

Brine (see Notebook, page 280)

½ cup blended oil or neutral oil such as canola

4 garlic cloves, thinly sliced

3 shallots, 2 thinly sliced, 1 minced

4 cups fresh corn kernels (from about 4 large ears)

Kosher salt

Freshly ground white pepper

1 cup whole milk

1 cup heavy cream

4 cups hedgehog mushrooms

4 tablespoons (½ stick) unsalted butter

2 bunches scallions, ends trimmed

¼ cup minced garlic chives

To brine the guinea hens: Use a sharp knife to cut down the length of the guinea hens' breastbones and remove the breast, leg, and thigh from each hen in one piece. French the wing bone, cutting away the skin and meat, then using your knife tip to scrape a 2-inch length of bone clean, exposing it. Remove the leg and thighbones. Put the hen pieces in a large glass baking dish or other vessel large enough to hold them in a single layer, and pour the brine over them. Cover and refrigerate for 12 to 24 hours.

▶ To make the creamed corn: Heat 2 tablespoons of the oil in a medium saucepan over medium heat. When the oil is shimmering, add the garlic and the sliced shallots and cook for 1 minute. Add 2 cups of the corn and cook, stirring, for about 2 minutes. Season with salt and pepper and pour in the milk and heavy cream. Bring to a simmer and cook, stirring occasionally, until the milk has thickened, about 15 minutes. Transfer the contents of the pan to a blender and blend to a smooth purée,

about 1 minute. Return the purée to the pan over medium heat and add the remaining 2 cups corn. Simmer gently until the corn is soft, about 10 minutes. Season with salt and pepper and remove the pan from the heat. Set aside, covered to keep warm.

▶ To make the roasted hedgehog mushrooms: Heat ¼ cup of the oil in a large sauté pan over high heat. When the oil is shimmering, add the mushrooms and cook, stirring, until golden brown, about 4 minutes. Add the minced shallot and butter and cook until the butter melts. Season with salt and pepper. Remove the pan from the heat and set aside, covered to keep warm.

▶ Heat a grill, setting one side to high heat and the other to low. (See pages 274–75 for grilling guidelines; if using a charcoal grill, bank the coals to one side.) Remove the hens from the brine and pat them dry with paper towels. Season with salt and pepper and place on the low side of the grill, skin side down. Grill until the skin is golden and crispy, about 20 minutes. Turn the hens

over and continue to cook until a meat thermometer inserted into the thigh registers 160°F, 7 to 10 more minutes. Transfer the hens to a plate and allow to rest. Put the scallions into a large bowl and drizzle with the remaining 2 tablespoons oil. Season with salt and pepper and place the scallions on the hot side of the grill. Grill, turning, until lightly charred all over, about 6 minutes.

▸ To serve, stir the garlic chives into the creamed corn, and divide the corn among 4 plates. Place a hen half on top of each and divide the mushrooms and scallions on top of and around the hens. Serve.

Brine

If you've ever been frustrated by the tendency of lean proteins to dry out when roasted, then you should give brining a try. Brining imparts crucial moisture and salinity, as well as additional, herbaceous flavor, to proteins. I especially like brining pork, chicken, rabbit legs, and turkey. You can vary this basic recipe, customizing the brine for different proteins and specific recipes by adding herbs that echo or complement other ingredients that will be served with them. Also, be sure to soak according to the weight and size of what's being brined: small cuts such as fish fillets require minimal brining, no more than 30 minutes; the time needed for a pork chop or chicken breast can range anywhere from 45 minutes to a few hours, depending on size and thickness; larger proteins such as whole turkeys call for longer soaking times, up to 4 hours for a whole chicken or up to 2 days for a 14- to 18-pound bird.

1 cup kosher salt

¾ cup sugar

5 garlic cloves, smashed with the side of a chef's knife

1 bunch thyme

¼ cup crushed red pepper flakes

Put 1 gallon water in a large pot. Add the salt, sugar, garlic, thyme, and pepper flakes and bring to a boil. Remove the pot from the heat and allow to cool to room temperature before using with your protein, submerging the meat.

Roasted Duck Breast

with Duck-Fat Popcorn, Collard Greens, Roasted Plums, and Spicy Almond Sauce

SERVES 4

This dish is founded on the contrast between what goes on in the oven and what happens on the stovetop. The duck and plums are roasted, intensifying their flavor by the patient reduction of their water content. Meanwhile, sautéed collard greens and a spicy almond sauce—quickly cooked on the stovetop—bring bolder, fresher flavors to the plate. All of that said, the popcorn steals the show here because it is a surprising finishing touch for any plated dish. Cooking it in duck fat makes it a true gourmet flourish.

---

2 tablespoons unsalted butter

2½ cloves garlic, thinly sliced, ½ clove kept separate

1½ shallots, thinly sliced, ½ shallot kept separate

3 cups coarsely chopped collard greens

Kosher salt

Freshly ground white pepper

¼ cup almond oil

½ tablespoon cayenne

2 tablespoons whole blanched almonds

1 cup almond milk

¼ cup rice vinegar

2 tablespoons sugar

4 Pekin (Long Island) duck breasts, 10 to 12 ounces each, trimmed

Freshly ground pink peppercorns

½ cup chopped duck skin (from trimmings)

Freshly ground black pepper

2 red plums, halved and pitted

2 tablespoons blended oil or neutral oil such as canola

1 cup Duck-Fat Popcorn (see Notebook, page 283)

To prepare the collard greens: Melt the butter in a medium saucepan over medium heat. When the butter has melted, add 2 of the sliced garlic cloves and 1 of the sliced shallots and cook, stirring, for 1 minute. Stir in the collard greens and ½ cup water, season with salt and white pepper, and cook, stirring occasionally, until tender, about 30 minutes. Drain the greens in a colander and set aside.

▶ Meanwhile, to make the almond sauce: Heat the almond oil in a large sauté pan over medium heat. When the oil is shimmering, add the remaining ½ clove sliced garlic, remaining ½ sliced shallot, and the cayenne and cook, stirring, for 1 minute. Add the almonds and

season with salt and white pepper. Pour in the almond milk, bring to a simmer, and continue to simmer for 15 minutes to mingle the flavors. Transfer the contents of the pan to a blender and blend until smooth. Add ¼ cup water, the vinegar, and sugar, and season with salt and white pepper. Set aside in the blender.

▶ Preheat the oven to 450°F. Season the duck breasts generously with salt on the flesh and skin sides and ground pink peppercorns on the flesh side only. Put the ducks, skin side down, in a large, ovenproof sauté pan over low heat. Cook until the skin is golden brown, 8 to

continued

10 minutes. Transfer the pan to the oven and roast for 7 minutes. Remove the ducks from the oven and set aside to rest for 7 minutes.

▸ To make the duck cracklings: Line a plate with paper towels and set it aside. Put the duck skin in a medium sauté pan and cook over medium heat until crispy, about 10 minutes. Transfer the duck skin to the prepared plate and season with salt and black pepper.

▸ To prepare the plums: Preheat the oven to 425°F. Put the plums and blended oil in a medium bowl and season with salt and white pepper. Scatter the plums on a rimmed baking sheet and bake until they begin to blister, about 8 minutes. Remove the sheet from the oven and set aside to cool for 6 minutes. Cut the plums into bite-size pieces.

▸ To serve, heat the collard greens in a medium sauté pan over medium heat until warmed through, about 2 minutes. Fold in the plums and popcorn. Spoon spicy almond sauce into the bottom of each of 4 dinner plates. Divide the collard green-plum mixture among the plates. Slice each duck breast in half lengthwise and place over the collard greens. Garnish with duck cracklings and serve.

Duck Fat

Super-flavorful duck fat is an alternative to other fats such as oil and butter. Because it has a high smoke point, you can get it nice and hot without it scalding, which means you can use it for just about anything you like. Save your own duck fat when rendering duck for recipes, or purchase it (see Sources, page 370). Here are some of my favorite applications.

DUCK-FAT POPCORN

To make 1 cup duck-fat popcorn, heat 2 tablespoons duck fat in a deep sauté pan over high heat until shimmering. Add 1 tablespoon popcorn kernels and cover the pan with a tight-fitting lid. Cook, shaking occasionally to prevent scorching, until almost all the kernels are popped, about 3 minutes. Pour the popcorn into a strainer set over a pot to drain off any excess fat. Season the popcorn with salt and pepper and toss.

POACHING FISH: Heat a few inches of duck fat to 95°F in a large pot, adding garlic and herbs for more flavor, if desired. Gently lower skinless fish fillets such as salmon, sturgeon, or monkfish into the fat, remove the pot from the heat, and poach until cooked through, 10 to 15 minutes, depending on the type of fish.

CURRY PASTES: For a richer flavor, fry the ingredients for curry paste (see pages 57–60) in duck fat instead of in oil.

FRIED POTATOES: For an incomparably decadent result, fry potatoes in duck fat. My favorite version is to dice baked potatoes, with the skin on, then fry them in duck fat and season generously with salt and pepper. Serve with mayonnaise and/or ketchup alongside.

Roasted Squab
with Foie Gras, Roasted Salsify, Tatsoi, and Fish Sauce Gastrique

Truth be told, the inspiration for this dish was visual; I came up with a more elaborate version of it for a photo shoot for the graphically oriented magazine *Art Culinaire*. Despite its roots, the result is delicious. The squab, salsify, and tatsoi (a member of the mustard family) are sandwiched together in a beautiful roulade that shows off their disparate colors. The fish sauce gastrique, made with tamarind and lime juice, offers essential relief to the gamy squab, fatty foie gras, and intensified flavor of roasted salsify.

4 squabs, 16 to 18 ounces each

1 cup whole milk

3 salsify roots, 2 cut crosswise into 4 (6-inch) pieces, 1 thinly sliced crosswise

2 tablespoons unsalted butter

1 tablespoon minced garlic

1 tablespoon minced shallot

4 cups (loosely packed) tatsoi

Kosher salt

1 tablespoon coarsely cracked black pepper, plus freshly ground black pepper for seasoning

1 cup palm sugar or turbinado sugar such as Sugar in the Raw

¼ cup fish sauce

¼ cup tamarind concentrate

2 tablespoons freshly squeezed lime juice

4 squares caul fat (see Sources, page 370)

Wondra flour, as needed

¼ cup plus 2 tablespoons blended oil or neutral oil such as canola

1 cup (about 6 ounces) diced foie gras (see Notebook, page 287)

Use a sharp knife to remove the breasts, legs, and thighs from the squabs. Separate the breasts from the wings. Reserve the legs and thighs separately.

▸ Heat a small saucepan over medium-high heat. Add the milk and the 6-inch salsify pieces and bring to a simmer. Braise until the salsify is tender to a knife tip, about 10 minutes. Transfer the milk and salsify to a bowl and chill in the refrigerator.

▸ Melt 1 tablespoon of the butter in a large sauté pan over high heat. Add the garlic and shallot and cook, stirring, until softened but not browned, about 1 minute. Add 2 cups of the tatsoi and season with salt and ground pepper. Cook, stirring, until the tatsoi is wilted,

about 2 minutes. Transfer the tatsoi to a colander and let rest in the sink or suspended over a bowl until no more liquid drains out.

▸ To make the fish sauce gastrique: Heat a large saucepan over medium heat. Add the palm sugar and 2 tablespoons water and cook without stirring until caramelized, 8 to 10 minutes. Stir in the fish sauce and tamarind. Bring to a simmer and stir in the lime juice and the cracked black pepper. Set aside to cool to room temperature.

▸ Preheat the oven to 425°F. Season the squab legs and thighs with salt and ground pepper and place on a baking sheet. Roast until heated through, about

continued

15 minutes. (The meat will be further cooked in the oven, so it's not necessary to measure the exact internal temperature.) Pick the meat from the bones and discard the bones.

▸ Lay the squab breasts, flesh side up, on a work surface. Place wilted tatsoi on top of each breast and place 1 piece of braised salsify in the center of each breast. Place another breast on top of each to form four "sandwiches" (roulades) with the salsify in the middle. Wrap the roulades in the caul fat, making sure the fat wraps around the meat twice. Put the flour in a medium bowl and season the roulades with salt and ground pepper. Dredge in the flour, gently shaking off any excess.

▸ Heat ¼ cup of the oil in a large, ovenproof sauté pan over medium-high heat. Add the roulades to the pan and cook until golden brown on all sides, 3 to 4 minutes per side, turning the roulades as they brown. Transfer the pan to the oven and cook until a meat thermometer inserted in the center of the roulades registers 120°F, about 5 minutes. Transfer the roulades to a plate and let rest for 5 minutes. Slice each roulade into 4 even disks (the squab should be served rare).

▸ Heat a large sauté pan over high heat. Add the remaining 2 tablespoons oil and tilt the pan to coat it; heat until the oil is shimmering but not smoking. Add the thinly sliced salsify and cook, stirring, until the salsify is golden brown, about 4 minutes. Add the remaining 1 tablespoon butter, season with salt and ground pepper, and cook for 1 minute to incorporate the flavors. Transfer the mixture to a bowl.

▸ Heat another large sauté pan over high heat. Season the foie gras cubes with salt and ground pepper and add them to the pan. Sear until the foie gras is golden brown on all sides, just a few seconds per side, working quickly to keep the foie gras from melting. Add the browned salsify, the remaining 2 cups tatsoi, and the reserved squab leg and thigh meat and heat until warmed through.

▸ Drizzle fish sauce gastrique over each of 4 plates. Arrange the foie gras–squab mixture along the center of each plate, and set a roulade on the mixture on each plate. Serve.

Foie Gras

Foie gras is one of the most decadent, luxurious ingredients we have. It comes from duck or geese that are fed a high-calorie diet (*foie gras* is French for "fat liver") and has a peerless luscious texture and rich flavor. Many home cooks have never worked with foie gras, so here are a few guidelines.

▸ It's not that easy to find fresh foie gras in markets—some butchers and specialty markets may carry it, but you will likely have to mail-order it to get a high-quality, fresh foie gras. See Sources, page 370.

▸ When buying foie gras, select grade A, which will be free of bruises and is the easiest to clean.

▸ To clean foie gras, rinse it and pat it dry with paper towels or a clean kitchen towel. Working on a kitchen towel to keep the foie gras from sliding around, pull the two lobes apart. Use a paring knife to remove any fat and green spots. Pull off the membranes.

▸ When cooking foie gras, it's essential that you work over very high heat so that you can sear the exterior before the rest of it melts away. If grilling foie gras, be especially careful of flare-ups (see pages 274–75).

▸ Because it's so rich, foie gras almost has to be paired with a sweet or tart component to offer relief to the palate. Compotes, chutneys, caramelized onions, and balsamic vinegar reductions are a few popular accompaniments.

FOIE GRAS MOUSSE: In addition to sautéing foie gras as I do in several dishes in this book, one of my favorite ways to enjoy it is in a mousse. Sear 1 cup diced foie gras in a hot pan until golden brown, about 1 minute. Season with salt and pepper, then transfer the foie gras to a plate. Add 1 sliced shallot to the pan with the foie gras fat, and sauté until slightly softened, about 1 minute. Add ¼ cup Madeira and cook until the Madeira completely reduces, about 3 minutes. Remove the pan from the heat and let its contents cool to room temperature. Transfer to a blender with the foie gras and blend, adding 8 tablespoons (1 stick) softened unsalted butter, a tablespoon at a time, until it forms a smooth purée. Let cool to room temperature, about 30 minutes. The mousse can be refrigerated in an airtight container for up to 2 days; let come to room temperature before serving. Spread the mousse on toasts and top with caramelized onions, or fill doughnuts with it (see page 330) for a decadent savory treat.

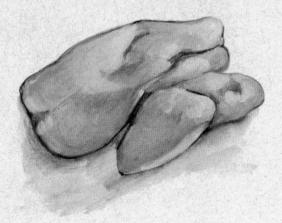

7

Meats and Game

Grilled Beef Hanger Steak
with Sunchoke Creamed Spinach, Hen of the Woods Mushrooms, and Red Shallot Purée

SERVES 4

My take on some traditional steakhouse combinations, slightly reimagined: hanger steak is used in place of more popular cuts such as New York strip and porterhouse, bringing a more mineral flavor to the plate, and the shallot purée is a cross between a vegetable and a condiment, with some of the same flavors found in steak sauce.

---

4 tablespoons (½ stick) unsalted butter

6 garlic cloves, thinly sliced

6 medium shallots, thinly sliced, keeping 2 separate from each other and the rest

1½ pounds baby spinach

Kosher salt

Freshly ground white pepper

3 tablespoons olive oil

1 pound sunchokes, thinly sliced

2 cups chicken stock, preferably homemade (page 366), plus more as needed

1 cup heavy cream

2 cups dry red wine

2 cups ruby port

8 ounces hen of the woods mushrooms, cut into bite-size pieces

4 prime hanger steaks, preferably dry-aged, about 8 ounces each

Freshly ground black pepper

Maldon sea salt

To make the sunchoke creamed spinach: Melt 2 tablespoons of the butter in a large sauté pan over medium heat and continue to cook until it browns slightly, about 4 minutes. Add half of the garlic and 1 of the sliced shallots and cook, stirring, until softened but not browned, about 1 minute. Stir in the spinach, season with salt and white pepper, and cook, stirring, until the spinach is wilted and soft, about 3 minutes. Remove the pan from the heat and set aside while you cook the sunchokes.

▶ Heat 1 tablespoon of the oil in a large saucepan over medium heat. When the oil is shimmering, add the remaining half of the garlic and 1 of the sliced shallots and cook, stirring, until the shallots and garlic are lightly browned, about 2 minutes. Add the sunchokes and cook, stirring, for 3 minutes; season generously with salt and white pepper. Pour in the stock and cream and bring to a simmer, keeping the sunchokes just covered with liquid at all times. If the liquid reduces too much, stir in a few tablespoons more stock (or water). Simmer until a paring knife slides easily into the sunchokes, about 25 minutes. Transfer the contents of the pan to a blender and blend until smooth, about 45 seconds. Add the sunchoke purée to the spinach in its pan and place over medium heat. Heat until the mixture is warmed through, about 1 minute, then set aside, covered, to keep warm.

▶ To make the shallot purée: Put the wine, port, and remaining 4 shallots in a medium saucepan and bring to a simmer over medium heat. Lower the heat and continue to simmer until the liquid has almost evaporated, about 30 minutes. Transfer the contents

continued

of the pan to a blender and blend until smooth, about 20 seconds. Season with salt and white pepper. Strain the shallot purée through a fine-mesh strainer set over a bowl, pressing down with a rubber spatula or the bottom of a ladle to extract as much purée as possible. If the mixture is too loose, return it to the saucepan and reduce over medium-low heat until thickened. (It should stand up a bit when spooned.) Set the purée aside, covered to keep warm.

▸ To prepare the mushrooms: Heat the remaining 2 tablespoons oil in a wide sauté pan over medium-high heat. When the oil is shimmering, add the mushrooms and season with salt and white pepper. Cook, tossing, until they start to brown, about 3 minutes; add the remaining 2 tablespoons butter and cook, tossing, until the butter melts and the mushrooms are crispy around the edges, about 5 minutes. Remove the pan from the heat and set aside, covered to keep warm.

▸ To cook the steaks: Heat a grill over high heat. (See pages 274–75 for grilling guidelines.) Season the steaks generously with salt and black pepper. Place the steaks on the grill and grill on one side until they begin to char and grill marks form, about 3 minutes. Turn the steaks over and continue to grill until charred and a meat thermometer inserted into the center registers 135°F, about 3 minutes more. Transfer the steaks to a large plate, cover loosely with aluminum foil, and allow to rest for 5 minutes.

▸ To serve, reheat the sunchoke creamed spinach, shallot purée, and mushrooms in their pans over medium heat for a minute or two, if necessary. Slice the steaks diagonally, divide among 4 plates, season with sea salt, and serve with the creamed spinach, mushrooms, and shallot purée.

Sunchokes

Sunchokes, also known as Jerusalem artichokes, are a versatile tuber that can be cooked and served in just about any style, from rustic to elegant, or even raw. They have a special place in my heart because they feature prominently in the sunchoke creamed spinach that helped me win the grand finale episode of season 1 of *Top Chef*. With the unusual combination of a meaty texture and sweet flavor, they are a valuable ingredient to add to your repertoire and experiment with.

SUNCHOKE CREAMED SPINACH PURÉE: Adapt the sunchoke creamed spinach on page 289 to make a purée by reducing the amount of liquid, or make a sunchoke soup by thinning it with vegetable stock and puréeing to your desired consistency.

FRIED SUNCHOKE CHIPS: For a garnish or snack, slice sunchokes and deep-fry them, along with whole garlic cloves and a few rosemary sprigs, in canola oil heated to 325°F, until golden brown. Use a slotted spoon to transfer the chips to paper towels to drain, and season immediately with salt and pepper.

ROASTED SUNCHOKES: Cut sunchokes into bite-size pieces and pan-roast, along with sliced shallots and garlic, in olive oil in a heavy skillet. Serve with roasted meats and poultry.

SUNCHOKE SALAD: Shave raw sunchokes on a mandoline and dress with olive oil and lemon juice. Toss with mixed greens and season with salt and pepper.

Roasted Rib Roast of Beef

with Radish Salad, Bone Marrow Yorkshire Pudding, and Natural Jus

When my family celebrates Christmas, this dish is how we do it—a slightly tweaked but mostly traditional version of the British beef classic. Of course, Yorkshire pudding isn't really a pudding, but more of a dense, decadent popover baked in tins coated with the beef drippings. We Dieterles go one step further, coating the tin with bone marrow fat. Serve this with a bottle of red wine that you've been saving for a special occasion.

1 prime rib roast (2 bones), 3 to 4 pounds

2 tablespoons blended oil or neutral oil such as canola

4 tablespoons minced garlic

½ teaspoon kosher salt, plus more for seasoning

Freshly ground black pepper

3 large eggs

¾ cup whole milk

¾ cup all-purpose flour

2 tablespoons Roasted Bone Marrow fat (see Notebook, page 295)

1 tablespoon extra-virgin olive oil

1 shallot, thinly sliced

¼ cup quartered breakfast radishes

1 cup diced Roasted Bone Marrow (see Notebook, page 295)

2 tablespoons flat-leaf parsley leaves

1 tablespoon freshly squeezed lemon juice

2 cups veal stock, preferably homemade (page 368)

1 rosemary sprig

Maldon sea salt

Rub the rib roast on all sides with the blended oil, then season all over with 2 tablespoons of the minced garlic, kosher salt, and pepper. Set aside, at room temperature, for 30 minutes. Preheat the oven to 500°F. Transfer the roast to a roasting pan fitted with a rack, bone side down. Roast in the oven to sear the exterior, then lower the temperature to 325°F and continue to roast until a meat thermometer inserted into the center reads 135°F for medium rare, about 90 minutes. Remove the roasting pan from the oven, transfer the roast to a rack or inverted plate, tent loosely with aluminum foil, and set aside to rest while you continue cooking. Do not clean the roasting pan.

▶ Raise the oven temperature to 450°F. Put the eggs and milk in a medium mixing bowl and whisk together until smooth. Slowly add the flour and the ½ teaspoon kosher salt, whisking constantly until smooth. Put a muffin tin in the oven and heat until warm, about 5 minutes. Add ½ tablespoon of the bone marrow fat to each of 4 of the muffin wells and return to the oven. Once the marrow fat begins to smoke, about 2 minutes, remove the tin from the oven and ladle the batter into the 4 greased wells. Return to the oven and bake until the puddings have risen over the top of the tin and appear set and golden brown, 15 to 20 minutes.

continued

Remove the tin from the oven and set aside to cool slightly for 5 minutes.

▸ To make the radish salad: Heat the olive oil in a medium saucepan over medium heat. When the oil is shimmering, add the shallot and cook, stirring, until softened but not browned, about 1 minute. Add the radishes and cook, stirring, without browning, for 1 minute. Stir in the bone marrow and heat through, about 2 minutes. Season with kosher salt and pepper and stir in the parsley and lemon juice. Remove the pan from the heat and set aside, covered to keep the salad warm.

▸ To make the jus: Place the roasting pan over medium heat across 2 burners. When the drippings just begin to simmer, add the remaining 2 tablespoons minced garlic and cook, stirring, for 1 minute. Pour in the stock, stirring with a wooden spoon to loosen any flavorful bits from the bottom of the pan. Transfer the liquid and any bits to a small saucepan and set over medium-high heat. Bring to a boil, then lower the heat and simmer until the liquid reduces by one-quarter, 3 to 4 minutes. Remove the pan from the heat and swirl in the rosemary. Season with kosher salt and pepper and set aside to steep for 20 minutes. Strain through a fine-mesh strainer set over a bowl.

▸ To serve, slice the roast between the bones and place a slice on each of 4 plates. Season with sea salt and pour the jus over the meat. Finish each plate with a bone marrow Yorkshire pudding, topping it with the radish salad.

Roasted Bone Marrow

Bone marrow is about the beefiest thing known to humankind, the very essence of meat, obtained by roasting halved bones, then removing the marrow from within. Until a savvy meat merchant starts selling roasted marrow, roasting the bones yourself is the only way to obtain it. Bone marrow can be enjoyed virtually unadorned on toast or can be used to garnish meat and even some fish dishes. Some other possibilities follow after the recipe below.

MAKES ABOUT 1 CUP DICED MARROW

2 beef marrow bones, split lengthwise by your butcher

Kosher salt

Freshly ground black pepper

Preheat the oven to 425°F. Season the exposed marrow in each bone half generously with salt and pepper and place the halves, marrow side up, in a single layer on a rimmed baking sheet. Roast until the color of the marrow turns grayish-brown and the marrow is soft to a knife tip, about 15 minutes. Remove the baking sheet from the oven and pour any fat that has dripped onto it into a small bowl, reserving it, if desired, for certain recipes such as the Yorkshire pudding on page 293, or the vinaigrette, at right. Set the bones aside to cool for 7 minutes. Once they have cooled, use a tablespoon to scoop the marrow from the bones and cut into small dice. Discard the bones. The bone marrow may be refrigerated in an airtight container for 2 to 3 days.

BONE MARROW STUFFING: Fold the bone marrow cubes into your favorite stuffing just before baking.

BONE MARROW TOAST: For a steakhouse classic, serve bone marrow on toast, topped with sliced raw shallots and flat-leaf parsley.

BONE MARROW BUTTER: Fold equal quantities of bone marrow and unsalted butter together with a rubber spatula until well incorporated; season with salt and pepper. Roll the butter in plastic wrap and refrigerate for up to 1 week. Slice and serve over rib roasts, steaks, and grilled dry-aged meats.

BONE MARROW VINAIGRETTE: Whisk 1 tablespoon bone marrow with 1 tablespoon champagne vinegar, then whisk in the bone marrow fat. (If there's not enough fat to finish the vinaigrette, add extra-virgin olive oil.) Finish by stirring in minced shallot, finely grated lemon zest, minced parsley, and minced chives, and season with salt and pepper.

BONE MARROW GOUGÈRES: To make a rich variation on the famous French pastry puffs, preheat the oven to 400°F. Put ½ cup water, ½ cup milk, and ½ cup (1 stick) butter, diced, in a medium saucepan and bring to a boil over high heat. Season with salt and pepper and whisk in 1 cup all-purpose flour. Stir with a wooden spoon until the mixture is smooth and pulls away from the sides of the pan. Remove the pan from the heat and, working with 1 egg at a time, beat 4 eggs into the dough. Stir in ¾ cup grated Emmental cheese, transfer the mixture to a pastry bag, and pipe tablespoon-size mounds about 2 inches apart onto a parchment-lined baking sheet. Sprinkle with ¼ cup grated cheese and bake until golden and puffy, about 20 minutes. Serve piping hot.

Grilled Rack of Lamb

with Swiss Chard, Fava Beans, and Orzo Risotto

If you live in an Italian American household as I did growing up, Easter Sunday means one thing and one thing only: lamb. This dish is a revved-up version of a typical Italian American Easter supper, in which the meat would likely be served with spring vegetables, such as the fava beans here, and a pasta, such as the orzo. The other adjustment in my version is that this is a composed plate, whereas most Easter meals would be served family-style.

½ cup thinly sliced Swiss chard stems, plus 3 cups Swiss chard leaves, in bite-size pieces

½ cup rice wine vinegar

1 tablespoon sugar

2 teaspoons kosher salt, plus more for seasoning

1½ pounds fava beans, in the pod

6 tablespoons (¾ stick) unsalted butter

1 shallot, thinly sliced

2 garlic cloves, thinly sliced, plus 1 tablespoon minced garlic

Freshly ground black pepper

2 cups blanched orzo

1½ cups chicken stock, preferably homemade (page 366)

2 tablespoons goat cheese

2 tablespoons thinly sliced mint leaves

1 Colorado rack of lamb, about 1½ pounds, chine bone removed, rack split and frenched by your butcher

1 tablespoon extra-virgin olive oil

1 tablespoon minced rosemary

First, to make the pickled Swiss chard: Put the Swiss chard stems in a temperature-proof medium bowl and set aside. Heat the vinegar in a medium saucepan over medium heat. When the vinegar begins simmering, stir in the sugar and the 2 teaspoons kosher salt and whisk until they dissolve, about 1 minute. Pour the hot vinegar mixture over the stems and chill in the refrigerator until cold, at least 4 hours or overnight. Allow to come to room temperature for a few minutes before serving.

▶ To prepare the fava beans: Fill a medium pot halfway with water and bring to a boil over high heat. Fill a medium bowl halfway with ice water and set aside. Snap the fava bean pods in half and remove the "string"

that runs along the seam of the pods. Remove the individual favas. Blanch them in the boiling water for 1 minute, then drain in a colander and shock in the ice water. Drain again and peel the individual favas by gently tearing off the end of their outer white shells and pushing the fava out with your thumb. Dry the bowl that held the ice water and collect the shelled favas in the bowl. Set aside.

▶ To make the orzo risotto: Melt 4 tablespoons of the butter in a large sauté pan over high heat and continue to cook until it turns light brown, about 3 minutes. Add the shallot and sliced garlic and cook, stirring, for

continued

296   **HAROLD DIETERLE'S** KITCHEN NOTEBOOK

1 minute. Stir in the Swiss chard leaves and cook, stirring, until the chard is soft, about 4 minutes. Season with kosher salt and pepper. Transfer the mixture to a colander and drain.

▸ Put the orzo and chicken stock in a medium saucepan over medium-high heat and stir to incorporate. Bring to a simmer and cook, stirring occasionally, until most of the liquid is evaporated, about 8 minutes. Stir in the Swiss chard leaves and fava beans and heat until warmed through, about 1 minute. Stir in the remaining 2 tablespoons butter and the goat cheese and stir vigorously until melted and incorporated. Stir in the mint and season with salt and pepper. Remove the pan from the heat and set aside, covered with a lid, to keep it warm.

▸ To prepare the lamb chops, preheat a grill or grill pan over medium-high heat. (See pages 274–75 for grilling guidelines.) Rub the lamb all over with olive oil, then with the minced garlic and rosemary, and season generously with salt and pepper. Wrap the exposed bones in aluminum foil and place the lamb on the grill, fat side down. Cook until the fat begins to render and nice dark grill marks form, about 10 minutes. Use a meat fork to turn the lamb over, and grill until a meat thermometer inserted into the center of the rack registers 135°F, about 10 minutes more. Transfer the lamb to a plate or platter, tent loosely with aluminum foil, and set aside to rest for 5 to 7 minutes. Remove the aluminum foil and slice the rack between the bones to make 8 chops.

▸ Divide the orzo among 4 bowls. Top each with 2 lamb chops, crossing the bones. Sprinkle the meat of each chop with the sea salt, top each serving with pickled Swiss chard stems, and serve.

Risotto

Usually made with rice such as Arborio, Carnaroli, or Vialone Nano, risotto is one of the most versatile recipes there is. (I also like rice alternatives such as orzo and farro because they are sturdier than rice and don't break down as much when cooked.) Once you understand how to make a basic risotto, you can adapt it to make just about any type you like.

For shellfish risottos, omit the cheese, use fish stock or shellfish stock, and stir sautéed shellfish into the risotto just before serving; for vegetables, use vegetable stock or stocks specific to the vegetables you are adding (e.g., mushroom stock), and stir in sautéed vegetables just before serving; for a change of pace, replace the white wine with a red wine such as Amarone. You can also augment risottos with fresh herbs and compound butters to enhance their flavor.

Adapt risotto into cakes or balls, rolling it into desired shapes, finishing them with ingredients such as diced prosciutto or blanched peas, dusting them with flour, and pan-frying them. Make a rice pudding based on this risotto recipe by omitting the garlic, shallot, and wine, cooking the rice with water rather than stock, and finishing it with a blend of pastry cream (page 330) and whipped cream. If you have leftover risotto, enjoy it for breakfast by making a frittata: cook the risotto in a pan until almost crunchy, then pour beaten eggs over it and cook until set.

Here is my basic recipe for risotto.

1 tablespoon extra-virgin olive oil

1 shallot, minced

1 cup risotto rice, such as Arborio

1 cup dry white wine

3 cups stock, preferably home-made (see pages 365–68), simmering in a pot over low–medium heat

½ finely cup grated Parmigiano-Reggiano cheese

4 tablespoons (½ stick) unsalted butter

Kosher salt

Freshly ground white pepper

Heat the oil in a medium saucepan over medium heat. When the oil is shimmering, add the shallot and cook, stirring, until softened but not browned, about 1 minute. Stir in the rice and cook without browning, coating with the oil, until the rice turns opaque, about 1 minute. Stir in the wine and cook, continuing to stir, until the wine has evaporated and been absorbed by the rice, 3 to 4 minutes. Pour in 1 cup of the hot stock and cook, stirring, until the stock is almost completely absorbed by the rice, about 6 minutes. Add the remaining 1 cup stock in small increments, stirring constantly, waiting until all the stock is absorbed before adding the next small increment. It should take about 10 more minutes to incorporate the remaining stock. When the risotto is done, stir in the cheese and butter. Season generously with salt and pepper and stir vigorously one last time.

Lamb Rib Sauerbraten

with Caraway Yogurt, *Stumpf*, and Cured Red Cabbage

SERVES 4

German comfort food and a perfect Sunday dinner: braised lamb ribs fried before serving, caraway-accented yogurt, a purée of root vegetables, and quick-cured red cabbage. (The vegetables are based on *stumpf*, a German dish of mashed root vegetables that my grandmother used to make.) In many ways, this is an alternate-universe version of *choucroute garni*—the Alsatian meat, sauerkraut, and potato platter—a timeless answer to the chill of winter.

1 cup thinly sliced red cabbage

1 tablespoon kosher salt, plus more for seasoning

1 tablespoon rice vinegar

2 teaspoons sugar

1 cup full-fat Greek yogurt

1 tablespoon freshly squeezed lemon juice

3 tablespoons ground caraway seed

Freshly ground black pepper

1 carrot, peeled and coarsely chopped

1 parsnip, peeled and coarsely chopped

½ rutabaga, peeled and coarsely chopped

½ celery root, peeled and coarsely chopped

2 cups whole milk

½ pound (2 sticks) unsalted butter

Freshly grated nutmeg

2 tablespoons thinly sliced flat-leaf parsley leaves

Canola oil or corn oil, for frying

2 cups all-purpose flour

Lamb Sauerbraten (see Notebook, page 302)

To make the cured red cabbage: Put the cabbage, 1 tablespoon salt, vinegar, and sugar in a large bowl and toss to coat. Set aside to marinate for at least 2 hours or up to 12 hours.

▸ To make the caraway yogurt: Put the yogurt, lemon juice, and 1 tablespoon of the caraway seeds in a medium bowl. Stir to incorporate and season with salt and pepper. Set aside.

▸ To make the *stumpf*: Put the carrot, parsnip, rutabaga, and celery root in a large, deep pot. Add enough water to cover, season with salt, and set over medium-high heat. Bring the water to a simmer and continue to simmer until all the vegetables are fork-tender, 6 to 8 minutes. Strain through a fine-mesh strainer and transfer the vegetables to a large bowl.

▸ Heat the milk and butter in a medium saucepan over medium heat until the milk is warm and the butter melts, about 4 minutes. Pass the vegetables through a food mill set over a large bowl and stir in the milk-butter mixture. (The mash should not be completely smooth.) Stir in the nutmeg, season with salt and pepper, then scatter the parsley over the *stumpf*.

▸ To fry the lamb sauerbraten: Pour the canola oil into a deep fryer, or wide, deep, heavy pot, to a depth of at

least 6 inches. Heat the oil to 350°F. Line a large plate with paper towels. Put the flour and the remaining 2 tablespoons caraway seeds in a medium bowl. Add the ribs to the bowl with the flour, and toss to coat. Carefully lower the ribs into the oil and fry until golden brown and crispy, 4 to 5 minutes, using a slotted spoon to turn the lamb as it fries, ensuring even crisping. Use the spoon to transfer the ribs to the prepared plate; season with salt and pepper.

▸ To serve, smear caraway yogurt on each of 4 plates. Rest a serving of ribs on the yogurt and spoon *stumpf* and cured cabbage alongside, or present the ribs family-style (as pictured), presenting the yogurt, *stumpf*, and cabbage alongside in individual serving vessels.

Sauerbraten

Sauerbraten, or "sour meat," is meat that's been marinated in pickling liquid, then braised. Like many braised dishes, it's usually made with tough, fatty cuts that soften over a long, slow cooking time. Often, the braising liquid is reduced to make a sauce, but I find it cloyingly sweet so usually skip it. You can use this recipe, which features lamb, for other types of meat so long as you vary the cooking times. My favorites are beef brisket (braise for 3 to 3½ hours); pork shoulder (braise for about 4 hours); chicken legs (braise for about 40 minutes); and lamb shank (braise for 3½ to 4 hours).

LAMB SAUERBRATEN

SERVES 4

2 cups red wine vinegar

5 garlic cloves, smashed with the side of a chef's knife

1 bay leaf

2 tablespoons kosher salt

20 whole black peppercorns

10 whole juniper berries

2 racks lamb ribs, about 2 pounds each

Put 2 cups water, the vinegar, garlic, bay leaf, salt, peppercorns, and berries in a large saucepan over medium-high heat. Put the ribs in a large, ovenproof, stovetop-safe baking dish. When the liquid in the pan boils, pour the hot mixture over the ribs and cover with aluminum foil. Refrigerate for at least 6 hours or up to 24 hours.

▶ Preheat the oven to 300°F. Uncover the racks and place the baking dish over medium-high heat. Bring the mixture to a simmer, then re-cover with aluminum foil and place in the oven. Braise until the meat is tender, about 1½ hours. Set aside to cool, then cut the racks into individual ribs.

Pancetta-Wrapped Pork Tenderloin

with Asian Pear, Pecans, and Rutabaga Purée

SERVES 4

A lot of pork dishes win us over with the succulence of their charred fat, which has incredible natural flavor. But pork tenderloin is a very lean cut, almost completely lacking in fat, that we love for its silky texture. Here I augment that texture with the fat of pancetta, an effect I talk more about in the Notebook (see page 305). This dynamic allows pork tenderloin to get along with lighter accompaniments than we sometimes think of as pork-appropriate, such as the sweet, crunchy Asian pear and rutabaga purée.

2 cups peeled, diced rutabaga

Kosher salt

1 cup whole milk

1 cup (2 sticks) unsalted butter

Freshly ground white pepper

1 cup roasted pecans

½ cup wood chips, such as apple, cherry, or pecan

2 pork tenderloins, about 1 pound each

12 thin slices pancetta (about 4 ounces)

Freshly ground black pepper

2 tablespoons blended oil or neutral oil such as canola

1 Asian pear, thinly sliced

1 head Belgian endive, thinly sliced lengthwise (about 2 cups slices)

1 shallot, minced

3 tablespoons freshly squeezed lemon juice

2 tablespoons extra-virgin olive oil

1 tablespoon thinly sliced flat-leaf parsley leaves

To make the rutabaga purée: Put the rutabaga in a medium saucepan. Add enough water to cover it, and set the pan over high heat. Salt the water and bring it to a boil. Cook until fork-tender, about 20 minutes. Use a slotted spoon to transfer the rutabaga to a food processor and blend to a smooth purée. Blend in the milk and butter and season with salt and white pepper. Strain through a fine-mesh strainer set over a large bowl. Set aside, covered to keep warm.

▸ To make the smoked pecans: Using a smoking device fitted with the wood chips (see Note, page 304), smoke the roasted pecans for about 30 minutes.

▸ To make the pancetta-wrapped pork tenderloin: Preheat the oven to 450°F. Wrap the pork tenderloins entirely with the sliced pancetta. Season with salt and black pepper, bearing in mind that the pancetta is salty.

▸ Heat the blended oil in a medium, ovenproof sauté pan over high heat. When the oil is shimmering, add the tenderloins to the pan, seam side down, and cook until the pancetta is crispy on all sides, about 8 minutes to-tal cooking time. Transfer the pan to the oven and cook, turning the tenderloins halfway through, until a meat thermometer inserted into the center registers 135°F, about 16 minutes. Remove the pan from the oven and set aside to rest for 5 minutes.

continued

▶ Meanwhile, to make the Asian pear salad: Put the pear, endive, smoked pecans, shallot, lemon juice, olive oil, and parsley in a medium bowl. Season with salt and white pepper and toss.

▶ Divide the rutabaga purée among 4 plates. Slice the pork tenderloins crosswise into 8 slices each and set 2 slices on top of the purée on each pate. Spoon salad onto each plate and serve.

NOTE: If you don't own smoking equipment, you can easily create it: Use a large pot with a metal steaming basket, pasta insert, or colander suspended over it, allowing it to hang high enough to leave several inches of space between the wood chips and the food being smoked. Light the chips (see pages 13–14) and set them in the bottom of the pot, set the food in the basket, and cover with the lid.

Pork Wrapping

Wrapping ingredients with pork products such as pancetta, prosciutto, or plain old bacon is a surefire way to add salt, fat, and crunch (and, in the case of bacon and speck, smoke) to a variety of foods. The combination of flavor and fat produced by the curing process packs those qualities into thin slices. Here are some of my favorite applications; in all cases, be sure to sear the seam side of the wrapping first to seal it in place, and if possible use a nonstick ovenproof pan to help prevent the pork from fusing to the metal.

PROSCIUTTO-WRAPPED CHICKEN BREAST: Roll chicken breasts in overlapping layers of prosciutto, sear on both sides in an oven-proof pan, and finish in an oven preheated to 425°F until the chicken is cooked through, about 15 minutes. Serve with sautéed broccoli rabe.

BACON-WRAPPED SEA SCALLOPS: Wrap sea scallops around their sides with bacon, and sear in a pan on the stovetop, turning until the bacon is crisped all around and the scallops are cooked, about 6 minutes. Serve with cauliflower purée (page 91).

SPECK-WRAPPED FIGS: Wrap pitted figs with speck (smoked prosciutto), folding it over to completely encase them, and hold the speck in place with a toothpick. Cook under the broiler until the speck is slightly crispy, 1 to 2 minutes. Serve on their own as a canapé (for extra flavor, set a nugget of blue cheese in the fig's center before wrapping), or plated and sauced with reduced balsamic vinegar or saba.

PANCETTA-WRAPPED HALIBUT: Wrap 6-ounce halibut fillets with pancetta and cook, following the instructions for the chicken at left, reducing the oven cooking time to 6 minutes. Serve with creamed corn (page 278).

Roasted Veal Chop

with Parmesan Butter Beans, and Escarole

This composition is another one inspired by my half–Italian American upbringing. Though not a mainstream meat in the United States, veal is very popular in communities like the one I grew up in in West Babylon, right up there with beef, pork, and lamb. The accompaniments here are jazzed-up versions of traditional veal-friendly vegetables, namely, the strudy green escarole and creamy butter beans.

2 cups Parmesan Broth (page 138)

1 cup dry butter beans, soaked overnight in cold water and drained

¼ cup plus 2 tablespoons extra-virgin olive oil

1 cup diced Spanish onion

½ cup red wine vinegar

1 tablespoon sugar

1 red bell pepper, roasted, peeled, seeded, and diced (page 362)

2 tablespoons thinly sliced caper berries

2 tablespoons thinly sliced peperoncini

Kosher salt

Freshly ground white pepper

1 garlic clove, sliced

2 cups bite-size escarole slices

2 tablespoons unsalted butter

1 tablespoon thinly sliced basil, plus 2 basil stems

2 tablespoons blended oil or neutral oil such as canola

4 bone-in veal chops, 12 to 14 ounces each, frenched by your butcher

Heat the broth and beans in a large saucepan over medium-high heat. Bring to a simmer and continue to simmer, stirring occasionally, until the beans are softened but still al dente, about 30 minutes.

▸ Meanwhile, to make the peperonata: Heat 1 tablespoon of the olive oil in a medium saucepan over high heat. When the oil is shimmering, add the onion and cook, stirring, until it is softened but not browned, about 2 minutes. Pour in the red wine vinegar and the sugar and cook until the wine has evaporated and the mixture is sticky, about 10 minutes. Transfer the onion mixture to a temperature-proof medium bowl and add

¼ cup of the olive oil, the red pepper, caper berries, and peperoncini. Season with salt and white pepper and refrigerate until chilled, about 1 hour.

▸ To make the ragù: Heat the remaining 1 tablespoon olive oil in a large, deep sauté pan over medium heat. When the oil is shimmering, add the garlic and cook, stirring, until lightly toasted, 3 to 4 minutes. Stir in the escarole and season with salt and white pepper. Cook until the escarole is soft, about 2 minutes, then stir in the butter beans and their broth. Bring to a simmer and cook until the liquid is almost evaporated, about 6 minutes. Stir in 1 tablespoon of the butter and the sliced

continued

basil and season with salt and white pepper. Remove from the heat and set aside, covered to keep warm.

▸ To roast the veal chops: Preheat the oven to 425°F. Heat the blended oil in a large, ovenproof sauté pan over high heat. Season the veal chops with salt and white pepper. When the oil in the pan is shimmering, add the veal chops to the pan. Cook until the chops are golden brown on the bottom, about 4 minutes. Turn the veal chops over and cook until golden brown on the other side, about 4 minutes more. Transfer the pan to the oven and cook until a meat thermometer inserted into the center of the veal chops registers 140°F, about 8 minutes. Remove the pan from the oven and return to the stovetop over low heat. Add the remaining 1 tablespoon butter and the basil stems to the pan, allowing the butter to melt, and use a spoon to baste the chops with the butter for 3 minutes. Transfer the chops to a large plate, cover with foil, and set aside to rest for 5 minutes before serving.

▸ To serve, spoon ragù into the bottom of 4 bowls. Top each with a veal chop and garnish with the peperonata.

White Beans

White beans are popular in Mediterranean cooking. With a pleasing creamy texture and the useful ability to take on the flavor of whatever they are cooked with or in, they are an easy way to add starch and texture to salads, soups, and stews. They are also helpful for more than just eating—you can use dried beans instead of kitchen weights to fill in tart shells while blind baking them. Or call on them as a perfect base for raw oysters on the half shell—just cover a plate or platter with an even layer of dried white beans and set the oysters on top to keep them from sliding around.

WHITE BEAN SALAD: Toss about 2 cups cooked, cooled white beans with 2 tablespoons minced red onion, ¼ cup minced celery, 1 tablespoon red wine vinegar, and ¼ cup extra-virgin olive oil. Top with chopped fresh oregano. Serve as a side dish to grilled fish, or tossed with 6 ounces drained high-quality Spanish or Italian preserved tuna.

WHITE BEAN PURÉE: Process 2 cups freshly cooked white beans in a food processor, adding 2 teaspoons lemon juice, then ¼ to ½ cup olive oil until a smooth, creamy purée is achieved. Pulse in 2 teaspoons thyme leaves and season with salt and white pepper. Use as a dip for chips, or spread on croutons for crostini.

WHITE BEAN SOUP: Heat 2 tablespoons olive oil in a large pot over medium-high heat. When the oil is shimmering, add 1 sliced garlic clove, ½ minced Spanish onion, 1 minced celery stalk, and 1 minced small carrot. Cook, stirring, until the vegetables are softened, about 4 minutes. Stir in 2 cups coarsely chopped escarole and cook, stirring, just until wilted, about 1 minute. Add 1½ cups cooked white beans and cook, stirring, for 2 minutes to mingle the flavors. Add 2 quarts chicken stock and 2 thyme sprigs, bring to a simmer, and continue to simmer for 30 minutes. Remove and discard the thyme. Season with salt and white pepper, and ladle into bowls. Drizzle with extra-virgin olive oil and, if desired, float croutons (page 363) on the surface.

Grilled Venison Sirloin

with Potato-Leek Gratin, Asparagus, and Huckleberry Sauce

The main thing when cooking venison is to not overcook it; because of its relatively low fat content, it goes from tender and faintly gamy to dry and flavorless in a very short time. I don't usually like pairing berries with meat, but huckleberries are an exception (see Notebook, page 312), and venison and huckleberry are an especially successful combination because, here, the berry behaves almost like a wine sauce. In the fall, when most of us confine our cooking to the indoors, you can roast the venison, rather than grilling it, and serve it the same way. The gratin is a fun variation on the potato-leek theme that's better known as a soup.

1 quart heavy cream

2 leeks, white parts only, thinly sliced and well washed

Nonstick cooking spray

2 pounds Idaho potatoes, peeled and thinly sliced crosswise

Kosher salt

Freshly ground white pepper

1 cup cider vinegar

½ cup sugar

1 quart veal stock, preferably home-made (page 368)

1 teaspoon whole black peppercorns

1 teaspoon whole cloves

1 cinnamon stick

1 whole star anise

2 tablespoons extra-virgin olive oil

2 garlic cloves, minced

2 tablespoons finely grated lemon zest

1 tablespoon freshly ground black pepper, plus more for seasoning

1 bunch asparagus, stalks peeled, tough ends trimmed and discarded

4 venison sirloins, 12 to 14 ounces each

½ cup huckleberries

To make the potato-leek gratin: Preheat the oven to 400°F. Put the cream and leeks in a large saucepan and set it over low heat. Cook until the leeks are slightly softened and the cream has reduced and thickened slightly, about 8 minutes. Spray four 1-cup earthenware or cast-iron crocks with nonstick cooking spray and set them on a baking sheet without crowding. Fill them with alternating layers of the cream-leek mixture and potatoes (in that order), seasoning each layer with salt and white pepper. Cover the crocks individually with aluminum foil and bake until the potatoes are soft and a paring knife slides easily through to the center, about 40 minutes.

▸ Meanwhile, to make the spiced huckleberry jus: Cook the cider vinegar and sugar in a large saucepan over high heat, stirring occasionally, until the sugar has dissolved and the mixture has reduced by half, about 6 minutes. Add the veal stock, peppercorns, cloves, cinnamon stick, and star anise, bring to a simmer, and continue to simmer until reduced to about 1 cup, about

12 minutes. Strain through a fine-mesh strainer set over a medium bowl. Cover to keep warm and set aside.

▸ To prepare the asparagus: Put the olive oil, garlic, lemon zest, and black pepper in a medium bowl. Season with salt and add the asparagus. Toss to coat.

▸ To prepare the venison sirloins: Heat a grill over high heat. (See pages 274–75 for grilling guidelines.) Season the venison sirloins with salt and black pepper and place on the hot grill. Cook until they are charred and a meat thermometer inserted into the center of the sirloins registers 135°F, about 5 minutes per side. Transfer to a large plate, tent loosely with foil, and allow to rest for 5 minutes. While the sirloins rest, place the asparagus on the grill and grill, turning the stalks as grill marks form, until marks have formed all around, about 4 minutes.

▸ Reheat the jus on the stove, if necessary, and stir in the huckleberries.

▸ To serve, place 1 venison steak on each of 4 plates, and spoon the huckleberry jus over the steak. Stack the grilled asparagus on top of the steaks and serve with the gratin alongside.

Huckleberries

Huckleberries are like a tarter, smaller version of blueberries. For such a tiny fruit, they have incredible flavor and a nice pop when you bite into them. I especially love them with rich, gamy meats such as wild boar, duck, and squab. (If you can't find huckleberries—their season is limited to late summer and early fall—you can substitute blueberries, especially small, wild blueberries, for them in recipes.)

HUCKLEBERRY GASTRIQUE: Stir ¼ cup huckleberries into a gastrique (see page 98) along with the sugar and vinegar. Serve with duck or foie gras.

HUCKLEBERRY SYRUP: Warm maple syrup in a small saucepan over low heat. Add huckleberries and allow them to infuse the syrup for 5 to 10 minutes. Serve over pancakes or waffles.

HUCKLEBERRY COULIS: Cook 2 parts huckleberries to 1 part sugar together in a saucepot over medium heat, stirring, until the huckleberries break down and the sugar dissolves. Blend with an immersion blender or in a stand blender, allow to cool, and serve over sundaes.

HUCKLEBERRY PANCAKES: Add huckleberries to pancakes as they cook.

Braised Goat Neck

with Mustard Greens, Purple Yams, and Massaman Curry

SERVES 4

Is anybody reading this? You didn't turn the page after you saw "goat neck" at the top? I hope you're still with me because I love goat neck and want you to try it. It may seem off-putting if you're not used to eating goat, but if you think about it, it's really just another type of meat. To me it has an appealing, lamb-like flavor and melting texture when braised. Here it is sauced with curry and served with slightly spicy mustard greens and sweet purple yams, which provide such big, bold ambient flavors that this is a perfect "starter" goat dish. Though it's the most consumed meat in the world, your butcher may need to special order goat's neck for you, so plan ahead.

2 tablespoons unsweetened coconut flakes

4 center-cut goat necks, about 12 ounces each

Kosher salt

Freshly ground black pepper

2 tablespoons blended oil or neutral oil such as canola

8 garlic cloves, 4 minced and 4 thinly sliced

3 shallots, thinly sliced, 1 kept separate

1 lemongrass stalk, coarsely chopped

1 (2-inch) piece fresh ginger, peeled and coarsely chopped

1 kaffir lime leaf

1 cup dry white wine

1 gallon chicken stock, preferably homemade (page 366)

1 tablespoon olive oil

2 cups (loosely packed) coarsely chopped mustard greens

Freshly ground white pepper

1 cup peeled, diced purple yams

1 tablespoon minced dried shrimp

1 tablespoon sliced fried shallots (see page 369)

1 quart Massaman Curry (page 57)

Preheat the oven to 300°F. Spread the coconut flakes out in an even layer on a baking sheet and toast in the oven until golden and fragrant, about 5 minutes. Remove the sheet from the oven and set aside to cool.

▶ Raise the oven temperature to 325°F. Season the goat necks generously with salt and black pepper. Heat the blended oil in a Dutch oven or similar vessel over medium-high heat. When the oil is shimmering, add the necks and sear them, turning occasionally, until they are golden brown on all sides, about 8 minutes total

cooking time. Use tongs to transfer the necks to a large plate. Add the minced garlic, 1 of the sliced shallots, the lemongrass, ginger, lime leaf, and white wine to the Dutch oven, and cook for 2 minutes, stirring to loosen any flavorful bits from the bottom. Pour in the stock and return the necks to the Dutch oven. Bring to a simmer, cover tightly with aluminum foil, place in the oven, and braise until tender to a knife tip, about 2½ hours, periodically checking to ensure that the liquid

continued

is barely simmering. If it is bubbling too aggressively, lower the oven temperature by 25 degrees; if it is not simmering at all, raise it by 25 degrees.

▸ Meanwhile, to prepare the mustard greens: heat the olive oil in a large sauté pan over medium heat. When the oil is shimmering, add the sliced garlic and remaining 2 sliced shallots and cook, stirring, until softened but not browned, about 1 minute. Stir in the mustard greens and season with salt and white pepper. Cook, stirring occasionally, until the greens have wilted, about 10 minutes. Transfer the mustard greens to a colander and drain.

▸ Fill a large bowl halfway with ice water. Bring a large pot of salted water to a boil. Add the yams to the boiling water and blanch until softened, about 3 minutes. Drain the yams and transfer them to the ice water to stop the cooking. Drain again. Put the drained mustard greens and yams in a large bowl and toss together.

▸ Put the coconut flakes, dried shrimp, and fried shallots in a small bowl and stir to incorporate.

▸ To serve, place a goat neck on each of 4 plates. Top with the mustard green–yam mixture and curry, and finish with a sprinkle of the fried coconut mixture.

Mustard Greens

Peppery mustard greens bring heat and crunch to both hot and cold dishes. They are part of a diverse family of greens that also includes tatsoi, which is used in the dish on page 284. Part of the charm of mustard greens is the element of surprise: they aren't as common as, say, spinach or arugula, so they bring an unfamiliar but relatable flavor to any dish they are a part of.

STIR-FRIED MUSTARD GREENS: Heat 2 tablespoons olive oil in a sauté pan over high heat. When the oil is shimmering, add 4 cups (loosely packed) mustard greens, season quickly with salt and pepper, and quickly toss or move around with tongs to keep the greens from scorching. When they are lightly crispy, about 1 minute, transfer them to a bowl. If you like extra texture, stir in 2 teaspoons toasted white sesame seeds after cooking. Serve alongside roasted fish or poultry.

MUSTARD GREEN KIMCHI: Use mustard greens in the recipe for kimchi (see page 75). Serve with grilled duck or pork.

MUSTARD GREEN CAESAR SALAD: Replace the romaine in the HD Caesar Salad (page 45) with mustard greens to underscore the dish's peppery quality.

CREAMED MUSTARD GREENS: Heat 1 tablespoon olive oil in a sauté pan over medium-high heat. Add 2 cups (loosely packed) mustard greens, season with salt and white pepper, and cook, stirring, until wilted, about 2 minutes. Add ½ cup vegetable stock, chicken stock, or water, and simmer until the greens are tender, about 8 minutes. Meanwhile, melt 2 tablespoons butter in a medium pot over medium heat, then whisk in 2 tablespoons flour, cooking for 1 minute. Whisk in about 1¼ cups simmering whole milk, a few tablespoons at a time, until the mixture becomes a thick and creamy sauce (béchamel), about 5 minutes. When the greens are done braising, fold them into the béchamel. Serve with steaks or other grilled or roasted beef dishes.

Braised Beef Braciole
with Pesto, Prosciutto, Tomato, and Polenta

This dish easily could have been a Sunday supper in the home I grew up in: braciole, a stuffed, rolled cut of meat (also sometimes called "involtini"), is as traditional Italian as it gets, and so are the polenta, prosciutto, and pesto. I love making it at home on a night off because I'm fond of the steps for braising meat: sautéing the vegetables, deglazing with wine, adding stock, and then slowly cooking the meat, filling your home with delicious aromas. When making braciole, try to avoid the fatty deckle part of the brisket and instead obtain the leaner, inside cut.

¾ cup extra-virgin olive oil, plus more for serving

¼ cup thinly sliced garlic, plus 2 whole garlic cloves

1 cup minced Spanish onion

2 tablespoons crushed red pepper flakes

1 tablespoon fennel seeds

8 cups whole canned plum tomatoes with their juices

1 quart chicken stock, preferably homemade (page 366)

Kosher salt

Freshly ground white pepper

2 cups (loosely packed) basil leaves, plus 12 hand-torn basil leaves

½ cup grated pecorino Romano cheese, plus a piece for grating

1 piece lean-cut beef brisket, 2 to 3 pounds, butterflied

10 thin slices prosciutto (about 4 ounces total)

Freshly ground black pepper

Polenta (see Notebook, page 319)

To make the tomato sauce: Heat ¼ cup of the oil in a medium saucepan over medium heat. When the oil is shimmering, add the sliced garlic, onion, red pepper flakes, and fennel seeds, and cook, stirring frequently, until the garlic and onion are softened but not browned, about 2 minutes. Stir in the tomatoes and stock and season with salt and white pepper. Bring to a simmer and cook, stirring occasionally, until the flavors are mingled, about 30 minutes. While the sauce is simmering, continue cooking. Preheat the oven to 300°F.

▸ Put the 2 cups basil leaves, grated pecorino, whole garlic cloves, and ¼ cup of the oil in a blender and pulse to a smooth, slightly coarse purée. Season with salt and white pepper.

▸ Lay the beef out on a clean work surface and score it with a paring knife, taking care not to cut through the meat. Spread the pesto over it. Layer the prosciutto on top of the pesto and drizzle with 1 tablespoon of the oil. Grate pecorino over the prosciutto and roll the meat into a tight round, encasing the prosciutto, pesto, and pecorino, securing it with butcher's twine. Season the braciole with salt and black pepper.

▸ Heat the remaining 3 tablespoons oil in a wide, deep sauté pan over medium-high heat. When the oil is shimmering, add the braciole and cook until it is golden brown on all sides, turning it as it browns, about 8 minutes total cooking time.

continued

▶ When the sauce is done simmering, remove the pot from the heat and use an immersion blender or food mill to purée the sauce until smooth. Season with salt and white pepper and stir in the torn basil leaves. Transfer the sauce to a large braising dish or Dutch oven and bring it to a simmer over medium-high heat. Transfer the braciole to the tomato sauce, being sure the braciole is completely submerged. Cover the dish and braise in the oven until fork-tender, about 3 hours, periodically checking to ensure that the liquid is barely simmering. If it is bubbling too aggressively, lower the oven temperature by 25 degrees; if it is not simmering at all, raise it by 25 degrees.

▶ To serve, use a slotted spoon to transfer the braciole from the pot to a cutting board, and cut away the butcher's twine. Slice the meat into 4 equal roulades. Spoon the polenta into the center of 4 plates. Top each with a slice of the braciole and spoon the tomato sauce over the meat. Grate more cheese over each serving, and drizzle with olive oil.

Polenta

Polenta is white or yellow cornmeal cooked in water, stock, or milk, or some combination of those liquids, and served as a side dish with meats and poultry. Like mashed potatoes, it's especially good with rich sauces or meats that give off juices, which the polenta soaks up. I always make my polenta with milk and finish it with mascarpone and pecorino Romano for a rich, sweet result—if you like, you can vary the amounts of these ingredients, leaving them out or reducing them for a more understated polenta, or adding more for a decadent result.

2½ cups whole milk

Kosher salt

Freshly ground white pepper

¾ cup yellow cornmeal

3 tablespoons unsalted butter

3 tablespoons mascarpone cheese

¼ cup grated pecorino Romano cheese

Bring the milk to a simmer in a medium saucepan over medium-high heat. Season with salt and pepper and gradually whisk in the cornmeal. Lower the heat to low and cook, stirring often, until the mixture thickens and the cornmeal is tender, about 15 minutes. Turn off the heat and fold in the butter, mascarpone, and pecorino until melted and incorporated. Season with salt and pepper. Finished polenta can be kept covered for up to 2 hours; reheat just before serving.

POLENTA FRIES: Shape cooled polenta into sticks, flour them with all-purpose flour, and deep-fry them.

POLENTA CAKES: Pour hot polenta onto a rimmed baking sheet and use a rubber spatula to spread it into an even layer. Once cool, cut or punch it into desired shapes and grill or pan-fry in butter.

BRAISED VEAL AND POLENTA: Add extra stock to your favorite braised veal recipe and stir raw polenta (cornmeal) into the braising liquid just before adding the veal. Braise them together and the polenta will become rich with the flavor of the veal. (Think of this as a variation on a Crock-Pot recipe.) Serve the meat, braising vegetables, and polenta together.

Veal Cheek Saltimbocca

with Sautéed Broccoli Rabe and Hot Cherry Peppers

SERVES 4

Saltimbocca means "jump in the mouth," a reference to how the Tuscan preparation of prosciutto-wrapped veal meets the palate. The name has never been more true than when you serve *this* saltimbocca, which is made with braised cheeks rather than with, say, a cutlet, and paired with bitter broccoli rabe livened up with hot cherry peppers, a supermarket item that is vastly underappreciated (see Notebook, page 322).

---

8 veal cheeks (about 2 pounds)

Kosher salt

Freshly ground white pepper

¼ cup plus 2 tablespoons blended oil or neutral oil such as canola

8 garlic cloves, thinly sliced, 2 kept separate

1 Spanish onion, diced

2 cups dry white wine

2 quarts chicken stock, preferably homemade (page 366)

1 thyme sprig

¼ cup plus 2 tablespoons extra-virgin olive oil

1 bunch broccoli rabe, tough stems trimmed and discarded

½ cup diced hot cherry peppers (see Notebook, page 322), plus ¼ cup juice

8 fresh sage leaves

8 slices prosciutto (about 2 ounces)

About 1 cup Wondra flour

1 lemon, halved, seeds removed

Preheat the oven to 300°F. Season the veal cheeks generously with salt and pepper. Heat ¼ cup of the blended oil in a Dutch oven or similar vessel over high heat. When the oil is shimmering, add the veal cheeks to the pan and cook until golden brown on one side, about 2 minutes. Turn the veal cheeks over, and cook until golden brown on the other side, about 2 minutes more. Transfer them to a large plate and set aside.

▸ Add 6 of the garlic cloves and the onion to the pan and cook, stirring, until softened but not browned, about 2 minutes. Pour in the wine and cook, stirring with a wooden spoon to loosen any flavorful bits from the bottom of the pan, and simmer until the liquid has reduced by half, about 4 minutes. Pour in the stock and bring to a simmer. Return the veal cheeks to the pan

and add the thyme. Cover the pan with aluminum foil and place in the oven. Braise until fork-tender, about 2 hours, periodically checking to ensure that the liquid is barely simmering. If it is bubbling too aggressively, lower the oven temperature by 25 degrees; if it is not simmering at all, raise it by 25 degrees.

▸ When the veal is braised, use a slotted spoon to transfer the cheeks to a baking sheet. Cover with plastic wrap or aluminum foil and refrigerate until chilled, about 90 minutes.

▸ Heat ¼ cup of the olive oil in a large sauté pan over high heat. When the oil is shimmering, add the broccoli rabe and season with salt and pepper. Cook, stirring, for 4 minutes, then add the remaining 2 garlic cloves and cook, stirring, until the broccoli is al dente, about

4 more minutes. Stir in the cherry peppers, pepper juice, and 2 tablespoons water and cook, stirring, until the liquid is evaporated, about 2 minutes more. Season with salt and pepper. Remove from the heat, cover to keep warm, and set aside.

▸ Preheat the oven to 425°F. Line a large plate with paper towels. Place a sage leaf on the center of each chilled veal cheek. Wrap each in a slice of prosciutto and season with salt and pepper. Lightly dust the cheeks with flour. Heat the remaining 2 tablespoons blended oil in a large ovenproof sauté pan over high heat. When the oil is shimmering, add the veal cheeks and sear until golden brown on one side, about 3 minutes. Turn the cheeks over and sear on the other side until golden brown, about 3 more minutes. Transfer the sauté pan to the oven and roast until the cheeks are hot through the middle, about 5 minutes. Remove the pan from the oven and transfer the veal cheeks to the prepared plate to drain.

▸ To serve, divide the broccoli rabe among 4 plates and top each with 2 veal cheeks. Drizzle with the remaining 2 tablespoons olive oil and squeeze lemon juice over each serving.

Hot Cherry Peppers

Hot cherry peppers are small, spicy peppers that you can easily find in glass jars in the supermarket. They pack an enormous punch that can be somewhat moderated by removing the seeds. The brine is also versatile: use a little to add heat to a martini; add it to the base of a vinaigrette (omitting some of the vinegar); or add it to marinades.

A FRESH ALTERNATIVE TO CRUSHED RED PEPPER FLAKES: Add thinly sliced cherry peppers to pasta sauces, such as the tomato sauce on page 147, at the beginning of the cooking process, along with the garlic and/or onions. Or use them as a pizza topping, right after the pizza comes out of the oven, in place of red pepper flakes.

SPICY BEAN RAGÙ: To bring bursts of heat and acid to white bean ragùs, fold diced cherry peppers in during the final 5 minutes of cooking. For a basic ragù, heat 2 tablespoons olive oil in a sauté pan over medium-high heat. When the oil is shimmering, add 2 sliced garlic cloves, 1 minced shallot, 1 minced celery stalk, and 1 minced small carrot. Cook, stirring, until the vegetables are softened, about 2 minutes. Add 2 cups cooked white beans and stir with the vegetables to mingle the flavors. Add 1½ cups chicken or vegetable stock, bring to a simmer, and continue to simmer until the stock is reduced and the mixture is thick and creamy, about 15 minutes. Season with salt and white pepper. Serve alongside grilled fish or pork.

CHERRY PEPPER STEAK: Use sliced cherry peppers in place of fresh bell peppers in your favorite pepper steak recipe. Or simply heat 2 tablespoons olive oil in a sauté pan over medium-high heat. When the oil is shimmering, add 2 sliced garlic cloves and 2 cups drained, sliced cherry peppers (for a less spicy dish, remove the seeds; for a spicier dish, leave them in) and cook, stirring, just until slightly softened, about 1 minute. Add 1½ cups vegetable or chicken stock and simmer until the peppers are softened but still al dente and the stock has reduced by nearly one-third, about 6 minutes. Spoon over just-grilled steaks, preferably New York strips.

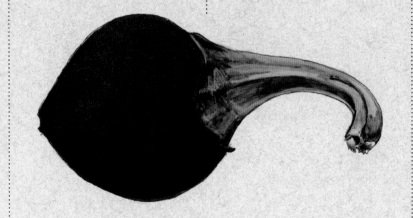

Grilled Pork Chop

with Lavender, Baby Arugula, Lychee, and White Bean–Robiola Purée

This dish may seem like a bit of a hodgepodge: grilled pork chops with a fragrant, almost floral, lavender marinade; a baby arugula salad featuring the distinctly Asian ingredient lychee; and a white bean purée flavored and thickened with the soft Italian cheese robiola. The components sound incompatible, but when you alternate bites of each, they play off each other beautifully, entertaining the palate from start to finish.

---

1 cup kosher salt, plus more
    for seasoning

¼ cup sugar

1 lavender sprig, plus 2 tablespoons
    minced lavender

4 double-cut pork chops, about
    1 pound each

¾ cup plus 2 tablespoons extra-
    virgin olive oil

3 garlic cloves, 2 thinly sliced,
    1 minced

2 teaspoons fennel seeds

2 shallots, thinly sliced

1 cup dried cannellini beans, soaked
    overnight

1 cup chicken stock, preferably
    homemade (page 366)

1 thyme sprig

Freshly ground white pepper

¼ cup robiola cheese (reblochon
    may be substituted)

3 cups (loosely packed) baby
    arugula

½ cup peeled, pitted fresh lychees,
    plus 1 tablespoon freshly
    squeezed lychee juice

1 radish, thinly sliced

2 teaspoons fresh ginger juice
    (see page 116)

1 teaspoon rice vinegar

Freshly ground black pepper

To brine the pork chops: Put 1 gallon water, 1 cup salt, the sugar, and the lavender sprig in a large pot and set over high heat. When the liquid boils, remove the pot from the heat and set aside to cool to room temperature. Put the pork chops in a large container and pour the liquid over the pork chops. Cover and refrigerate for 6 to 12 hours.

▸ Remove the pork chops from the brine and pat dry with paper towels. Put ½ cup of the olive oil, the minced lavender, minced garlic, and fennel seeds in a large bowl and stir to combine. Add the pork chops to the bowl and turn to coat. (You can cook the chops right away, or refrigerate in the marinade overnight to deepen the flavor.)

▸ To make the bean purée: Heat ¼ cup of the olive oil in a large saucepan over medium heat. When the oil is shimmering, add the sliced garlic and 1 of the sliced shallots and cook, stirring, for 1 minute. Add the beans, stock, and thyme, and season with salt and white pepper. Bring to a simmer, then lower the heat and continue to simmer until the beans are very soft, about 40 minutes. Remove and discard the thyme sprig and transfer the contents of the pan to a blender. Add the robiola and blend to a loose purée. Season with salt

continued

and white pepper. Strain through a fine-mesh strainer set over a medium bowl and cover to keep warm until ready to serve.

▸ To make the salad: Put the arugula, lychees, radish, and remaining shallot in a large bowl. Put the lychee juice, ginger juice, rice vinegar, and the remaining 2 tablespoons olive oil in a separate small bowl and whisk together. Pour the vinaigrette over the arugula mixture, season with salt and black pepper, and toss to coat.

▸ Heat a grill over high heat, or heat a grill pan for 5 minutes over high heat. (See pages 274—75 for grilling guidelines.) Season the pork chops with salt and black pepper and place on the grill. Cook until grill marks form and the pork is cooked through to an internal temperature of 135°F, about 8 minutes per side. Transfer the chops to a platter and set aside to rest for 5 minutes.

▸ To serve, divide the bean purée among 4 plates. Top the purée on each plate with a pork chop and spoon salad over the chops.

Lychees

Lychee nuts, or just "lychees" if you like, are popular in many Asian countries. They are distinctly sweet and fragrant, so are best suited to desserts, but they can also be used in cocktails and some savory cooking, especially as an accompaniment to foie gras and fatty meats such as duck, pork, and lamb. When using them, be sure to peel off the rind, which is inedible.

GRIDDLED LYCHEES: Cook lychees in a cast-iron pan or griddle until lightly charred. Toss into salads for a burst of flavor and texture—they go especially well with sturdy greens and balsamic vinaigrette.

LYCHEE MARTINI: Put 2 ounces high-quality vodka, 1½ ounces freshly squeezed lychee juice, and a splash of dry vermouth in a shaker over ice. Shake and strain into a martini glass. Garnish with a fresh lychee.

LYCHEE CHUTNEY: Cook 3 cups peeled, halved, pitted lychees on a grill pan over high heat until they begin to break down, about 3 minutes, then remove the pan from the heat. Heat 2 tablespoons blended oil or canola oil in a large saucepan over medium heat. When the oil shimmers, add 1 thinly sliced shallot, 4 thinly sliced garlic cloves, and the griddled lychees and cook, stirring, until the lychees soften further but still hold their shape, about 6 minutes. Stir in ¼ cup palm sugar or turbinado sugar such as Sugar in the Raw and cook, stirring, until the sugar melts. Transfer the mixture to a food processor and add 2 tablespoons fish sauce, 2 tablespoons freshly squeezed lime juice, and 2 tablespoons fermented yellow bean sauce. Stir in basil and serve alongside poultry and meats. Makes 3 cups.

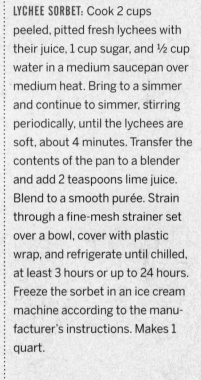

LYCHEE SORBET: Cook 2 cups peeled, pitted fresh lychees with their juice, 1 cup sugar, and ½ cup water in a medium saucepan over medium heat. Bring to a simmer and continue to simmer, stirring periodically, until the lychees are soft, about 4 minutes. Transfer the contents of the pan to a blender and add 2 teaspoons lime juice. Blend to a smooth purée. Strain through a fine-mesh strainer set over a bowl, cover with plastic wrap, and refrigerate until chilled, at least 3 hours or up to 24 hours. Freeze the sorbet in an ice cream machine according to the manufacturer's instructions. Makes 1 quart.

8

Desserts

Vanilla-Scented Doughnuts
with Meyer Lemon Curd and Chocolate Ganache

MAKES ABOUT 12 DOUGHNUTS

There's nothing like homemade doughnuts, freshly cooked and still warm from the fryer. I'm so fond of them that at my first restaurant, Perilla, we always have some kind of doughnut on the menu. This version is simple and satisfying, filled with Meyer lemon curd, dusted with vanilla sugar, and plated atop a streak of chocolate ganache. These never fail to elicit smiles and can be easily adapted to accommodate other fillings and finishing touches (see Notebook, page 330). The vanilla sugar can also be used to dust other baked goods and can be made in greater quantities; 1 bean will infuse up to 3 cups sugar.

---

1 vanilla bean, split and scraped

2 cups granulated sugar

¾ pound (2½ sticks) plus 1 tablespoon unsalted butter

2 cups whole milk

3 tablespoons plus ¼ teaspoon active dry yeast

1 large egg, plus ½ cup large egg yolks (about 8 yolks)

1 teaspoon pure vanilla extract

5 cups cake flour, plus more for dusting

1⅓ cups all-purpose flour

1 tablespoon kosher salt, plus more as needed

Nonstick cooking spray

Finely grated zest and juice of 2 Meyer lemons

8 ounces coarsely chopped semisweet chocolate (about 1 cup chopped)

1 cup heavy cream

Canola oil or corn oil, for frying

Put the vanilla bean pods and seeds and 1 cup of the sugar in an airtight container. Cover and shake vigorously. Allow to rest overnight to flavor. The sugar may be kept in the container for up to 1 month.

▸ Melt 1 stick of the butter in a small saucepan over low heat; do not allow it to brown. Once it has melted, after about 4 minutes, remove the pan from the heat and set aside. Heat the milk in a medium saucepan over medium heat. When just slightly warmed, pour the milk into the bowl of a stand mixer fitted with the paddle attachment, and add the yeast, the whole egg, and the vanilla extract. Paddle for 1 minute. Meanwhile, put the cake flour, all-purpose flour, ½ cup of the sugar, and

1 tablespoon salt in a large bowl and whisk them together. Gradually add the flour mixture to the milk mixture, paddling just until combined. Add the melted butter, paddling on low speed until all the butter is incorporated. Increase the speed slightly, and mix until a dough begins to form and stick to the paddle, pulling away from the sides of the bowl, about 10 minutes. Grease a large bowl with nonstick cooking spray and transfer the dough to the bowl. Cover with plastic wrap and refrigerate for 20 minutes, but no longer than 30 minutes.

▸ Meanwhile, to make the Meyer lemon curd: Put the lemon zest and juice, the remaining ½ cup sugar, and a

continued

pinch of salt in a large bowl and whisk them together. Set the bowl over a double boiler filled with an inch or two of simmering water and slowly whisk in the egg yolks, a little at a time. Cook, whisking frequently, until the curd is thick and the whisk leaves a mark in it, 3 to 4 minutes. Remove the curd from the heat. Cut 1½ sticks of the butter into cubes and whisk the cubes, a few at a time, into the curd until incorporated. Line a baking sheet with plastic wrap and strain the curd through a fine-mesh strainer over the baking sheet, pressing on it with a rubber spatula to obtain as much curd as possible. Cover with additional plastic wrap, letting it touch the surface of the curd to prevent a skin from forming, and refrigerate until chilled, about 1 hour, or up to 24 hours.

▶ To make the chocolate ganache: Put the chocolate in a medium heatproof bowl and set aside. Bring the cream to a simmer in a small saucepan over medium heat. Stir the cream into the chocolate and set aside until the chocolate melts, about 5 minutes. Stir in the remaining 1 tablespoon butter until the mixture is smooth. Allow to cool slightly before using.

▶ Pour oil into a deep fryer or large, deep pot to a depth of 6 inches, and heat to 355°F. Line a large plate with paper towels and set aside. Put the lemon curd in a pastry bag fitted with a large, plain tip and set aside.

▶ Dust a clean work surface with cake flour and turn the dough out onto it. Flour the top of the dough, and very gently roll out the dough to an even thickness of 1 inch. Punch out the dough using a square cookie cutter to make 12 doughnuts. Carefully lower the doughnuts into the oil and fry on one side for 30 seconds, then turn with a slotted spoon and fry on the other side for 30 seconds more. Use the spoon to transfer the doughnuts to the prepared plate to drain briefly, then toss the doughnuts in the vanilla sugar to coat them.

▶ While the doughnuts are still warm, working with one doughnut at a time, insert the pastry bag into the edge of a doughnut and pipe it full of curd.

▶ Smear chocolate ganache on each of 4 dessert plates and top each with 3 doughnuts. Serve.

Doughnuts

Doughnuts have had a special place in my heart dating back to when I was a member of the Junior Fire Department in Long Island. I was a member of the Signal 8 Committee, in charge of refreshments, and usually brought doughnuts to the junior events. Those were store-bought, but when I became a professional cook and learned to make my own, I knew there was nothing else like it. Kids and adults both love fresh-fried doughnuts, and they're terrific for breakfast or an irresistible plated dessert as in the recipe on page 327. Once you've made these doughnuts, you can make just about any kind you can imagine. Here are some of my favorites:

PASTRY CREAM DOUGHNUTS: Make a variation on Boston cream doughnuts by filling doughnuts with pastry cream, warming ganache, and dipping the doughnuts into the ganache. To make pastry cream: In a medium bowl, whisk together 1 large egg, 1 egg yolk, 2½ tablespoons sugar, and 2 tablespoons cornstarch and set aside. Heat 1 cup whole milk and 2½ tablespoons sugar in a medium pot over medium heat, just until simmering and the sugar is dissolved, about 2 minutes. Whisk the hot milk mixture into the egg mixture slowly, to keep the eggs from scrambling. Pour the mixture into the same pot, add 1 teaspoon pure vanilla extract, and cook, whisking vigorously, over medium-high heat, until the mixture begins to thicken, about 5 minutes. Stir in 1 tablespoon unsalted butter, melting it, then pour the mixture into a heatproof container and cover with plastic wrap, letting the wrap touch the top of the cream to keep a skin from forming. Chill in the refrigerator for at least 2 hours or up to 24 hours.

JELLY DOUGHNUTS: Make jelly doughnuts by piping the blueberry preserves on page 339 or your favorite jelly into the doughnuts and omitting the ganache.

NUTELLA DOUGHNUTS: Pipe doughnuts full of the chocolate-hazelnut spread Nutella, or leave the doughnuts unfilled, warm the Nutella in a small pot over medium heat enough to melt it, and dunk the doughnuts in the Nutella.

FOIE GRAS DOUGHNUTS: For a savory option, pipe the doughnuts full of foie gras mousse (page 287) and serve them with a grape compote for a sophisticated, peanut-butter-and-jelly-like effect.

Steamed Passion Fruit Pudding Cake

with Passion Fruit Sauce, Hazelnut Brittle, and Buttermilk Sherbet

Early in my career, I was fortunate to work with the great pastry chef Karen DeMasco at Della Femina restaurant in midtown Manhattan. One of my favorite desserts in her repertoire was a steamed lemon pudding—a luscious, light-as-air treat that I can still taste to this day. This dessert is based on that one, with the vibrant sweetness of the passion fruit offset by buttermilk sherbet and a crunchy hazelnut brittle.

---

1 cup passion fruit purée

1½ cups plus 2 tablespoons granulated sugar, plus more for the molds

1½ tablespoons cornstarch

Kosher salt

Nonstick cooking spray

¼ cup light corn syrup

2 tablespoons unsalted butter

2½ cups roasted unsalted hazelnuts, halved

¼ teaspoon baking soda

½ teaspoon pure vanilla extract

2 tablespoons all-purpose flour

2 large eggs, separated

½ cup buttermilk

4 scoops Buttermilk Sherbet (page 358)

To make the passion fruit sauce: Heat ¾ cup of the passion fruit purée in a medium saucepan over medium heat until warmed, about 4 minutes. Meanwhile, put ¼ cup of the sugar, the cornstarch, and a pinch of salt in a medium bowl and whisk them together. Whisk a small amount of the warm purée into the sugar mixture, then whisk that mixture into the remaining purée. Raise the heat to medium-high and bring the mixture to a boil, then strain the sauce through a fine-mesh strainer into a bowl. Cover with plastic wrap and chill completely in the refrigerator, at least 1 hour or up to 24 hours.

▶ To make the hazelnut brittle: Spray a baking sheet with nonstick cooking spray and set aside. Put 1 cup of the sugar, ¼ cup water, and the corn syrup in a large saucepan and bring to a boil over medium heat. Stir in the butter, melting it, then cook, without stirring, until the mixture registers 260°F on a candy thermometer, 10 to 15 minutes. Add the hazelnuts and continue to cook, stirring, until the mixture reaches 300°F. Stir in the baking soda, vanilla, and ½ teaspoon salt. Pour the mixture onto the prepared baking sheet and use a rubber spatula to spread it into a thin, even layer. Set aside to cool, about 30 minutes, then break the brittle into pieces.

▶ To make the pudding cake: Preheat the oven to 325°F. Spray 4 (4-ounce) disposable aluminum molds with nonstick cooking spray. Put a few tablespoons of sugar in each mold, turning the molds to coat them with sugar, and pour out the excess sugar.

▶ Put the remaining ¼ cup plus 2 tablespoons sugar, the flour, egg yolks, buttermilk, remaining ¼ cup

continued

passion fruit purée, and a pinch of salt in a large bowl and whisk them together. Put the egg whites in the bowl of a stand mixer fitted with the whisk attachment, and whisk the whites until soft peaks form, about 7 minutes. Fold the whites into the batter in 3 additions until incorporated. (Note: Because of the acid in the buttermilk and passion fruit, the mixture will *not* emulsify.)

▸ Ladle the batter into the prepared molds, filling them to the top, and place them in a roasting pan. Pour enough hot water into the pan to come halfway up the sides of the molds. Cover the pan tightly with aluminum foil and bake in the oven for 15 minutes. Remove the aluminum foil and rotate the pan 180 degrees. Return the pan to the oven and continue baking until the tops of the cakes feel dry and a toothpick or cake tester inserted into the center of the cakes comes out clean, about 15 minutes more. Remove the pan from the oven and allow the cakes to rest in the water bath until they have cooled to room temperature, about 15 minutes.

▸ To serve, spoon passion fruit sauce into the bottom of each of 4 dessert plates. Unmold the cakes and top the sauce on each with a cake. Spoon sherbet alongside and stick a piece of brittle into the sherbet.

Passion fruit

Uniquely sweet and peerlessly vibrant, passion fruit brings a singular quality to any dish or drink it touches. To access the pulp, simply cut the fruit down the middle and spoon it out. Be sure to clean your knife immediately after cutting passion fruit; if the knife is forged from carbon steel, the juice will stain it. Here are some of my favorite ways to use this fruit.

SHISO CRAZY: This is a popular cocktail from Kin Shop. Put 2 ounces high-quality vodka, ¼ ounce maraschino liqueur, ½ ounce freshly squeezed lemon juice, and ½ ounce passion fruit purée in a shaker with ice. Shake and strain into a martini glass. Garnish with 1 shiso leaf cut into chiffonade (see page 362) and top with sparkling wine.

PASSION FRUIT SORBET: To make 1 quart sorbet, bring 2½ cups passion fruit juice, 1 cup granulated sugar, and ¼ cup freshly squeezed lime juice to a simmer in a medium saucepan over medium heat and cook, stirring, until the sugar is dissolved, about 1 minute. Transfer the contents of the pan to a large heatproof bowl and refrigerate until chilled, at least 3 hours or up to 24 hours. Freeze the sorbet in an ice cream machine according to the manufacturer's instructions.

PASSION FRUIT MOUSSE: Put the pulp from 8 large passion fruit, 14 ounces sweetened condensed milk, and 1 cup palm sugar in a large pot and cook over medium heat, stirring, until the passion fruit seeds turn dark black and the sugar has melted, about 7 minutes. Transfer to a large temperature-proof bowl and refrigerate until cold, about 30 minutes. Meanwhile, chill a separate large bowl in the freezer until cold, about 5 minutes. Whisk 2 cups heavy cream in the cold bowl until stiff peaks form, about 7 minutes. When the passion fruit mixture is cold, fold half of the whipped cream into it, then fold in the other half. Refrigerate for 1 hour, then serve alongside sliced tropical fruits or over tropical fruit salads.

Salted Caramel Apple Crisp

with Dried Cranberries, Almond Streusel, and Vanilla Bean Ice Cream

SERVES 4

The epitome of a seasonal fall dessert: an apple crisp with the fruit cooked in caramel and punctuated by dried cranberries, another autumnal touchstone. The vanilla bean ice cream functions almost as a sauce, offering a creamy counterpoint that brings the essence of the other ingredients into high relief.

¾ cup granulated sugar

2 tablespoons heavy cream

8 tablespoons (1 stick) unsalted butter

1 teaspoon kosher salt

3 apples, preferably Honeycrisp, peeled and sliced

2 teaspoons ground cinnamon

¼ teaspoon freshly grated nutmeg

¼ teaspoon ground cloves

½ cup dried cranberries

Almond Streusel (see Notebook, page 336)

4 scoops Vanilla Bean Ice Cream (page 359)

Preheat the oven to 375°F. Put the sugar and 2 teaspoons water in a large sauté pan over high heat and cook, stirring, until the mixture is golden brown, about 8 minutes. Slowly add the heavy cream and cook, stirring, for 1 minute. Stir in 4 tablespoons of the butter and season with the salt. Set aside.

▶ Melt the remaining 4 tablespoons butter in a medium saucepan and continue to cook until it begins to brown, about 4 minutes. Add the apples and cook, stirring occasionally, until they just begin to soften, about 3 minutes. Stir in the cinnamon, nutmeg, and cloves. Add the cranberries and transfer the mixture to a colander and drain. Fold the apples into the caramel mixture in its sauté pan.

▶ Divide the apple-caramel mixture among 4 individual baking dishes with about a 2-cup capacity. Sprinkle with the almond streusel and bake until golden brown on top and the liquid within is bubbling, about 10 minutes. Remove the baking dishes from the oven, let rest for 5 minutes, then serve, topping each serving with a scoop of ice cream.

Streusel

Streusel is a crumb topping that hails from my ancestral home of Germany. I've always been fond of it because of its buttery, crunchy qualities. The exact makeup of streusel varies from cook to cook; I like a crumble-type mixture of butter, oats, almonds, and cinnamon, which conjures a homey feeling as it bakes, filling your home with a sweet, spiced scent.

MAKES 1 QUART

Use the recipe below to top crisps and other desserts. You can also replace the almonds with toasted rice pearls (a great topping for savory Asian rice dishes), cocoa nibs (perfect for topping ice cream sundaes), yogurt-covered raisins (scatter over fruit and yogurt or ice cream sundaes), or granola (delicious over yogurt for breakfast).

1½ cups all-purpose flour

1½ cups granulated sugar

1 teaspoon ground cinnamon

½ cup coarsely chopped roasted, unsalted almonds

¼ cup rolled oats

12 tablespoons (1½ sticks) cold unsalted butter, cut into small pieces

Put the flour, sugar, cinnamon, almonds, and rolled oats in the bowl of a stand mixer fitted with the paddle attachment, and paddle, adding the butter a piece at a time, until the streusel comes together in a crumble-like mixture. Extra streusel can be frozen in an airtight container; let come to room temperature before using.

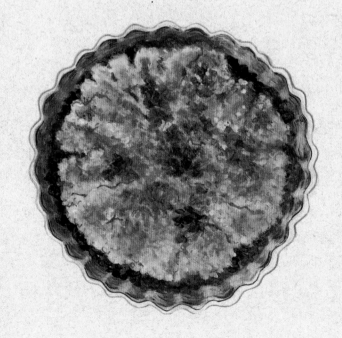

Blueberry Buckle

When summertime rolls around every year, one of the first cravings to hit me is for my mother's blueberry buckle, a very traditional version of the berry-studded cake, topped with a sugar-cinnamon crumble. This could not be easier to prepare and is one of my favorite show-cases for the charms of fresh blueberries. You can top it with ice cream or enjoy it for break-fast, either on its own or with a spoon-over of Greek yogurt, quark, or even crème fraîche.

½ pound (2 sticks) unsalted butter

2¼ cups granulated sugar

1 large egg

3 cups all-purpose flour

2 teaspoons baking powder

½ teaspoon kosher salt

¼ teaspoon baking soda

½ cup whole milk

Nonstick cooking spray

1 cup blueberries

1 teaspoon ground cinnamon

Preheat the oven to 375°F. Put 4 tablespoons of the butter, ¾ cup of the sugar, and the egg in a stand mixer fitted with the paddle attachment, and paddle until light and fluffy. In a medium bowl, whisk together 1½ cups of the flour, the baking powder, salt, and baking soda. Alternate adding the milk and the dry ingredients to the egg mixture, paddling just until a smooth batter forms.

▸ Spray an 8-inch round baking dish with nonstick cooking spray and use a rubber spatula to scrape the batter into the dish, shaking the dish slightly so the bat-ter is evenly distributed. Sprinkle the blueberries over the batter.

▸ To make the crumb topping, put the remaining 12 tablespoons butter, remaining 1½ cups flour, remaining 1½ cups sugar, and the cinnamon in a large bowl. Use clean hands to knead the ingredients together until the mixture comes together in pea-size bits. Scatter the crumb topping over the blueberries in the dish and bake in the oven until golden brown on top and the batter is set (a cake tester or toothpick inserted into the center will come out clean), 50 min-utes to 1 hour.

▸ To serve, slice the buckle and serve on 6 individual dessert plates.

Blueberries

Blueberries are, hands down, my favorite fruit. When I was a kid, we had a bush in our backyard and there were so many berries every summer that we couldn't eat them all, so we froze them and enjoyed them all year. Blueberries are wonderful in a variety of baked and griddled recipes, from muffins to pancakes to scones. You can also add frozen blueberries to cocktails instead of ice cubes. To extend your enjoyment of blueberries, you can freeze them as we did in resealable plastic bags. The preserves and sorbet below are another way to make them last.

BLUEBERRY PRESERVES: Cook blueberries and sugar together over low heat, stirring, until the berries break down and the sugar is dissolved, about 10 minutes. The amount of sugar will depend on how sweet the berries are (taste one or two to gauge this) and your own personal sweet tooth. I like to use as little sugar as possible to let the berry flavor shine through. You can use the preserves right away, or refrigerate in an airtight container for up to 1 week. Spread on toast and pastries or use it to fill doughnuts (see page 330).

BLUEBERRY SORBET: To make blueberry sorbet, put 1 pint blueberries, 1¼ cups granulated sugar, and ¾ cup water in a medium saucepan set over medium heat. Cook, stirring, until the blueberries are soft, about 2 minutes. Transfer the contents of the pan to a blender and add 1 tablespoon freshly squeezed lemon juice.

Blend to a smooth purée. Strain through a fine-mesh strainer set over a large bowl, pressing down with a rubber spatula, and refrigerate until chilled, about 1 hour. Freeze the sorbet in an ice cream machine according to the manufacturer's instructions. Makes about 1 quart.

Cornflake-Crusted Eggnog French Toast
with Rum-Raisin Syrup and Maple-Bacon Ice Cream

Like the doughnut recipe on page 327, this dessert reimagines a breakfast classic for dessert—actually, make that *four* breakfast classics: cornflakes, French toast, syrup, and bacon. It's an unapologetically indulgent treat in which each element builds on the others; get a little of each one in a mouthful and a veritable symphony of flavor takes place. Truth be told, this dish has a slightly shameful origin: it's my go-to dessert on Christmas morning, when I'm usually nursing a bit of a hangover from my celebration the night before.

1½ cups dark rum

½ cup golden raisins

6 large eggs

1 cup granulated sugar

1 teaspoon pure vanilla extract

1 teaspoon freshly grated nutmeg

2 cups heavy cream

2 cups whole milk

2 cups cornflakes

1 loaf challah, cut into ¼-inch-thick slices

2 tablespoons unsalted butter

2 cups maple syrup

Maple-Bacon Ice Cream (page 360)

To make the rum-raisin syrup: Put 1 cup of the rum and the raisins in a small saucepan and bring to a simmer over medium heat. Remove the pan from the heat and set aside to steep for 30 minutes.

▸ Meanwhile, to prepare the French toast: Whisk the eggs in a bowl till frothy, then add the sugar, vanilla, nutmeg, remaining ½ cup of rum, the cream, and milk. Lay the cornflakes out in a single layer on a dinner plate. Soak the bread in the milk mixture for 1 minute. Press each side of the moist bread onto the cornflakes to form a light crust. Heat a griddle or nonstick pan over medium heat. Working in batches, melt 1 teaspoon of the butter in the pan and cook each side of the bread until golden brown, 1 to 2 minutes per side; add more butter to the pan as necessary between batches.

▸ Pour the maple syrup over the raisins in their pan, and heat gently over low heat.

▸ To serve, divide the French toast slices among 4 plates and top each serving with a scoop of maple-bacon ice cream. Finish by drizzling the syrup over and around the ice cream and toast.

Cornflakes

The breakfast cereal cornflakes offers something irresistible to many chefs: a way to provoke a childhood memory, which often leads to a happy eating experience. We don't usually think of availing ourselves of cereal as a culinary ingredient, but cornflakes have great utility in the kitchen.

BREADING: Pulverize cornflakes to a fine powder by hand and use the powder instead of bread crumbs to crust fried fish. Season the flakes with salt and pepper as you would any other breading.

CORNFLAKE SHAKE: Add cornflakes to a vanilla shake before blending to mimic the flavor of cereal milk (Chef Christina Tosi has popularized an ice cream that goes by that name).

ICE CREAM TOPPING: Sprinkle whole or crushed cornflakes over ice cream and sundaes.

BAR SNACK: Toss cornflakes in a hot pan with canola oil and spice blends such as za'atar or *togarashi* and serve with beer, wine, or cocktails.

Banana and Milk Chocolate Financier

with Concord Grape Compote and Peanut Butter Ice Cream

Usually ice cream is the finishing touch for a dessert, but in this one, the ice cream dictates the other flavors, all of which complement the peanut butter: grape compote is the most obvious accompaniment, echoing a PB and J sandwich, but banana and chocolate is also a time-honored pairing. They all add up to a fun, decadent composition that would go well after just about any meal but will likely be most appreciated at gatherings where kids are present.

1 cup (2 sticks) unsalted butter

1¼ cups confectioners' sugar, plus more for dusting

⅓ cup all-purpose flour

½ cup almond flour

2 large eggs, plus 4 large egg whites

1 cup chopped ripe banana (about 1 large banana)

1 cup coarsely chopped milk chocolate

Nonstick cooking spray

1 cup Concord grapes

¼ cup granulated sugar

4 scoops Peanut Butter Ice Cream (page 360)

To make the financiers: Preheat the oven to 325°F. Melt the butter in a medium saucepan over medium heat, stirring, until browned, about 6 minutes. Set aside to cool to room temperature, about 6 minutes.

▶ Put the confectioners' sugar, all-purpose flour, and almond flour in a stand mixer fitted with the paddle attachment, and paddle to incorporate. Add the egg whites and paddle until a smooth batter forms. Add the cooled brown butter and paddle on low speed until just combined. Transfer the mixture to a large bowl and gently fold in the banana and chocolate.

▶ Line a baking sheet with parchment paper and spray 4 (6-inch) ring molds with nonstick cooking spray. Place the molds on the parchment and pour the batter evenly into the molds. Bake in the oven until set and a toothpick or cake tester inserted into the center of the cakes comes out clean, about 25 minutes. Remove the sheet from the oven and set aside to cool, about 12 minutes. When cool, use a paring knife to loosen around the sides of the molds. Carefully remove the financiers from the molds and let cool further on a cooling rack.

▶ To make the compote: Put the grapes and granulated sugar in a medium saucepan over medium heat and cook, stirring, until the grapes burst, about 5 minutes. Remove the pan from the heat, strain the compote through a fine-mesh strainer set over a bowl to remove the seeds, pressing down with a rubber spatula, and set aside to cool, about 10 minutes.

▶ To serve, spoon compote onto each of 4 dessert plates, top with a financier, and set a scoop of ice cream alongside. Dust the financier with confectioners' sugar.

Financiers

While my repertoire is made up mostly of Italian, German, and Thai reference points, once in a while I love classic French food as much as the next guy, especially because it harkens back to my culinary school days. I have a particular soft spot for traditional French baking and financiers; these small cakes, distinguished by the inclusion of brown butter and almond flour, really epitomize that style for me—simple, elegant, and delicious. Such simplicity is something of a white canvas that invites you to add other ingredients and flavoring agents to the batter. Here are some of my favorite adaptations.

WHITE CHOCOLATE–RASPBERRY FINANCIER: Replace the chocolate and banana with equal quantities of coarsely chopped white chocolate and stemmed raspberries. Serve with dark chocolate sorbet.

STRAWBERRY-RHUBARB FINANCIER: Replace the chocolate and banana with equal quantities of coarsely chopped, hulled strawberries and chopped rhubarb. Serve with vanilla ice cream or whipped cream.

BLUEBERRY-CINNAMON FINANCIER: Replace the chocolate and banana with 2 cups blueberries and 1 tablespoon ground cinnamon. Serve with citrus accompaniments such as lemon Chantilly, made by whisking a scant amount of lemon juice into whipped cream.

PEAR-WALNUT FINANCIER: Replace the chocolate and banana with equal quantities of peeled, coarsely chopped pears and chopped, toasted walnuts (see page 362). Serve with rum raisin ice cream.

Crème Caramel

with Caramel Corn, Hot Pecans, and Buttered Popcorn Sherbet

This dish was inspired by moviegoing memories and features riffs on buttered popcorn, caramel corn, and other snacks. Because the crème caramel and sherbet need to be made in advance, this is a wonderful choice for a dinner party; and if you host movie nights in your home, there's no more appropriate way to end the meal and start the viewing than with this irreverent dessert.

½ cup plus ⅔ cup granulated sugar

1⅓ cups whole milk

2 large eggs, plus 1 large egg yolk

½ teaspoon pure vanilla extract

¼ teaspoon kosher salt, plus more for seasoning

1 cup pecans

½ cup (packed) light brown sugar

2 teaspoons cayenne

Canola oil or corn oil, for frying

4 cups popped unbuttered, unsalted popcorn

2 tablespoons light corn syrup

2 tablespoons unsalted butter

¼ teaspoon baking soda

4 scoops Buttered Popcorn Sherbet (page 359)

To make the crème caramel: Put ½ cup of the granulated sugar and ¼ cup water in a medium saucepan over medium heat and cook, stirring, until the mixture thickens and turns amber, using a pastry brush to brush down the sides of the pan periodically, about 8 minutes. Divide the caramel among 4 (4-ounce) soufflé tins and set the tins in a roasting pan.

▸ Preheat the oven to 310°F. Bring the milk to a boil in a medium saucepan set over high heat. Remove the pan from the heat and set aside. Put the remaining ⅔ cup granulated sugar, the eggs, egg yolk, ¼ teaspoon of the vanilla extract, and a pinch of salt in a large bowl and whisk together. Slowly pour in the warm milk, whisking constantly to keep the eggs from scrambling. Strain the custard through a fine-mesh strainer into a large measuring cup or other spouted vessel, and divide among the soufflé tins over the caramel.

▸ Pour hot water into the roasting pan to come halfway up the sides of the tins. Loosely cover the roasting pan with aluminum foil and bake until the centers of the crème caramels are nearly set and a cake tester or toothpick inserted into the center of a crème caramel comes out clean, about 1 hour. Carefully remove the roasting pan from the oven and transfer the tins to a wire rack to cool to room temperature, about 20 minutes. Cover the crème caramels with plastic wrap and refrigerate overnight.

▸ To make the hot pecans: Put the pecans in a large heatproof container and cover with 4 cups hot water. Soak for 20 minutes. Drain through a fine-mesh strainer and transfer the pecans to a large bowl. Add ¼ cup of the brown sugar and the cayenne and toss to coat. Pour oil into a deep fryer, or wide, deep, heavy pot, to a depth of 4 inches. Heat the oil to 350°F. Line a plate with paper towels. Add the pecans to the hot oil and fry until golden brown, about 4 minutes. Use a slotted spoon to transfer the nuts to the prepared plate to drain and season immediately with salt. Set aside to cool slightly, about 5 minutes. Preheat the oven to 200°F. Put the pecans and popcorn in a large bowl and toss them together. Spread the mixture out in an even layer on a rimmed baking sheet and keep warm in the oven while you continue cooking.

▶ Put the remaining ¼ cup brown sugar, the corn syrup, butter, and ¼ teaspoon salt in a medium saucepan over medium heat. Bring to a boil, stirring constantly. Stop stirring and boil slowly for 5 minutes.

Remove the pan from the heat and stir in the remaining ¼ teaspoon vanilla extract and the baking soda. Remove the popcorn and pecans from the oven immediately and pour the caramel over the popcorn-pecan mixture. Mix until all the popcorn and pecans are coated. Return to the oven for 1 hour, until the popcorn and pecans dry out and the caramel hardens. Remove the pan from the oven and set aside to cool completely, about 30 minutes. Break apart the mixture and set it aside.

▶ To serve, unmold a crème caramel onto each of 4 dessert plates. Arrange caramel corn and pecans around the plate and finish with a scoop of popcorn sherbet. Serve immediately.

Popcorn

Because it's so closely associated with the escapist fun of moviegoing, popcorn always brings a smile to adult gatherings, whether in a savory or sweet context. I appreciate it for its crunch and potent, evocative aroma, and also for how well it gets along with a wide variety of other flavors. In addition to using popcorn in recipes such as the one on page 344, or popping it in duck fat as in the dish on page 283, try these wildly varied applications.

CURRIED POPCORN MIX: Pop buttered microwave popcorn following the package directions. While still hot, transfer 2½ cups of the popcorn to a heatproof bowl and add 1 cup salted pretzel sticks, ½ cup roasted peanuts, 3 tablespoons Madras curry powder, and 1 teaspoon kosher salt. Toss and serve right away as a party snack (it's especially good with ice-cold beers) or store for up to 2 days in an airtight container at room temperature.

POPCORN-BACON PUDDING: Sauté diced bacon and onions together until the bacon renders enough fat to coat the bottom of a sauté pan. Add popped popcorn and enough chicken stock to cover. Simmer for 10 minutes, then purée the mixture in a blender and season with salt and white pepper. Serve with rich gamy meats such as duck, pheasant, and squab, and with foie gras.

HERB-AND-CHEESE POPCORN: Toss hot, freshly popped popcorn with finely grated Parmesan cheese and minced rosemary for a savory snack and a wonderful accompaniment to wine and cocktails.

Warm Flourless Chocolate and Peanut Butter Soufflé Cake

with Coffee Crème Anglaise

Chocolate, peanut butter, and coffee conspire to create one of the richest desserts in this book. Serve this after a relatively light meal, or as the coda to a no-holds-barred, shamelessly decadent feast, such as the hanger steak dish on page 289.

1 cup (packed) chopped bitter-sweet dark chocolate

7 tablespoons unsalted butter

⅓ cup cocoa powder

6 large eggs, separated

¼ cup plus 3 tablespoons granulated sugar

Nonstick cooking spray

¼ cup creamy peanut butter

1 cup whole milk

1 tablespoon espresso powder

Kosher salt

Confectioners' sugar, for dusting

To make the soufflé cakes: Preheat the oven to 425°F. Put the chocolate, butter, and cocoa powder in the top of a medium double boiler set over simmering water. Heat, stirring, until melted, about 5 minutes, then remove the bowl from the heat. Set aside until lukewarm, about 4 minutes, then whisk in 3 of the egg yolks.

▶ Put ¼ cup of the granulated sugar and 3 of the egg whites in the bowl of a stand mixer fitted with the whisk attachment. Beat on medium speed until medium peaks form, about 7 minutes. Gently fold the egg white mixture into the chocolate mixture until just incorporated.

▶ Spray 4 coffee cups with nonstick cooking spray. Sprinkle with 1 tablespoon of the granulated sugar, turn to coat the interior, then pour out any excess sugar. Fill each cup halfway with batter. Add 1 tablespoon of the peanut butter to the center of each coffee cup and top with the remaining batter. Place on a baking sheet and bake until souffléd and slightly browned on top, about

10 minutes. Remove the sheet from the oven and set aside while you make the crème anglaise.

▶ To make the coffee crème anglaise: Put the milk and espresso powder in a large saucepan over high heat and cook, stirring occasionally, just until the liquid comes to a boil. Meanwhile, put the remaining 3 egg yolks, remaining 2 tablespoons granulated sugar, and a pinch of salt in a large bowl and whisk to incorporate. When the milk mixture boils, slowly add it to the egg mixture, whisking constantly to keep the eggs from scrambling. Return the milk-egg mixture to the saucepan over medium-low heat and cook, stirring constantly to be sure the mixture never boils, until the mixture thickens and reaches 170°F. Strain through a fine-mesh strainer set over a medium bowl and divide among 4 small sauce pitchers.

▶ Serve the cakes warm, dusted with confectioners' sugar, and invite your guests to break into the top with a tablespoon and pour the crème anglaise into the soufflé.

Peanut Butter

There are two schools of peanut butter love: creamy and chunky. Personally, I like creamy peanut butter, which delivers all its telltale flavors in a smooth, velvet package that also makes it easy to incorporate into recipes because it integrates better with other ingredients than do crunchy varieties. But do yourself a favor and avoid mass-produced supermarket brands in favor of the superior, often all-natural artisanal versions. Or, better still, make your own using the recipe below.

In addition to the Peanut Butter Ice Cream on page 360, you can make an Elvis sandwich with peanut butter and sliced bananas or a chocolate mousse, peanut butter, and Concord grape jam sandwich, or you can add some to the base of a sugar cookie recipe to make peanut butter cookies.

MAKES 2 CUPS

2 cups warm roasted peanuts

2 teaspoons kosher salt

2 teaspoons peanut oil

Put the peanuts and salt in a food processor and process to a coarse purée, about 1 minute. Turn the processor off and use a rubber spatula to scrape down the mixture from the sides. Turn the processor back on, slowly drizzle in the peanut oil, then continue to process until smooth, about 2 more minutes. Transfer to an airtight container and store for up to 1 week in the refrigerator.

Candy Bar Sundae

This sundae has evolved over the years at Perilla. It is based on the ingredients of a Take 5 candy bar, which features pretzels, peanuts, peanut butter, caramel, and chocolate—all that we look for in a dessert, sweet and bitter flavors, as well as salt, crunch, and chewiness—the only thing missing was the cool, creamy qualities of ice cream in the sundae.

2 (14-ounce) cans sweetened condensed milk

8 tablespoons (1 stick) unsalted butter

2½ cups heavy cream

2 cups granulated sugar

1 cup (packed) dark brown sugar

Kosher salt

⅓ cup cocoa powder, sifted

1 cup peanuts

2 tablespoons confectioners' sugar

1 cup crushed pretzels

20 small scoops Vanilla Bean Caramel Ice Cream (page 361)

To make the dulce de leche: Open the cans of milk, leaving the metal tops in place. Cover the tops with foil. Place the cans inside a pot and add water so that it's halfway up the sides of the cans. Cover the whole pot with aluminum foil. Set over medium heat, bring the water to a simmer, and simmer until the milk becomes a creamy, dark caramel, 4 to 5 hours, checking every hour to make sure the water remains halfway up the sides of the cans, replenishing it when necessary. Transfer to a blender and blend until smooth. Set aside.

▸ To make the chocolate sauce: Put the butter and 1½ cups of the heavy cream in a medium saucepan set over medium heat and cook until the butter has melted. Whisk in 1 cup of the granulated sugar, the brown sugar, a pinch of salt, and ¼ cup water. Whisk in the cocoa powder and slowly bring the mixture to a boil, taking care to not scorch the bottom. Strain through a fine-mesh strainer set over a medium heatproof bowl and allow the mixture to cool, about 20 minutes.

To prepare the peanuts: Line a baking sheet with parchment paper. Put the peanuts and remaining 1 cup granulated sugar in a sauté pan over medium heat. Cook, stirring constantly to keep the sugar from scorching. Once the sugar has completely caramelized and coated the peanuts, pour onto the prepared baking sheet and allow to cool, about 20 minutes.

▸ Transfer the peanuts to a food processor and pulse to chop them into small pieces. Add 1 tablespoon salt, pulse again, and transfer to a medium bowl.

▸ To make the Chantilly cream: Beat the remaining 1 cup heavy cream and the confectioners' sugar together in a stand mixer on high speed until the cream has thickened and has formed firm peaks, about 3 minutes.

▸ To serve, put 5 small scoops of ice cream in each of 4 sundae glasses. Top with pretzels, then a dollop of cream. Drizzle with the dulce de leche and chocolate sauces and finish with the peanuts.

Pretzels

With their signature mix of well-done dough, crunch, and salt, pretzels can bring unexpected dimensions to a variety of dishes. I also like occasionally using soft pretzels, as in the stuffing suggestion below, because they remind me of both a popular New York City street food and my German heritage. At my restaurants, we use Amish pretzels purchased at the Union Square Greenmarket in Manhattan, but for the following uses, any good-quality pretzel will do.

PRETZEL-SHERRY SAUCE: Heat ¼ cup blended oil or canola oil in a saucepan over high heat. Add ¼ cup diced pretzel bread and fry for 2 minutes. Add 1 sliced shallot, season with salt and white pepper, and sauté for another minute. Stir in 1 cup sherry and simmer until reduced by half, about 3 minutes. Add 2 cups chicken stock and 1 thyme sprig and simmer until thickened to a sauce consistency, about 15 minutes. Purée in a blender and spoon over poultry. Makes 2 cups.

PRETZEL STUFFING: For a surprising stuffing with a pronounced salinity and pleasingly toothsome texture, replace the bread cubes in your favorite recipe with cut-up soft pretzels.

PRETZEL-COATED FISH AND POULTRY: Pulverize hard pretzels by pulsing them in a food processor and transfer to a large bowl. Coat skinless fish fillets or chicken breasts by brushing them lightly with beaten eggs or Dijon mustard, then rolling them in the pretzel crumbs, pressing gently to be sure the crumbs adhere. Sauté in 1 tablespoon olive oil in a sauté pan over medium-high heat until the crumbs are lightly golden brown, about 4 minutes per side. Transfer to an oven preheated to 350°F and bake until cooked through, about 6 minutes for fish, or 12 for chicken, depending on thickness. Serve with spaetzle (page 248).

Cherry Clafouti

with Brandied Cherry Crème Anglaise

SERVES 4

For the most part, this dessert is a faithful rendition of the French dessert clafouti, which bakes cherries into a custardy batter, then tops it with confectioners' sugar and cream. Unlike some recipes, however, I use pitted cherries and underscore the fruit's flavor by adding brandied cherries to the crème anglaise. It's an elegant, understated dessert that's best in the summertime when cherries are at their peak.

⅔ cup granulated sugar	Kosher salt	10-X sugar, in a shaker
3 large eggs, beaten	1 tablespoon pure vanilla extract	Crème Anglaise (see Notebook, page 354) with 16 store-bought brandied cherries, plus 1 tablespoon of their liquid added after straining
½ cup all-purpose flour	Nonstick cooking spray	
1¼ cups whole milk	4 cups pitted fresh Bing cherries	

Preheat the oven to 350°F. Put ⅓ cup of the granulated sugar, the eggs, flour, milk, a pinch of salt, and the vanilla in a blender and blend them together.

▶ Generously spray the insides of 4 (6-inch) ring molds or 1 (8-cup) pan with nonstick cooking spray. If making individual desserts, set the molds on a parchment-lined, rimmed baking sheet and pour the batter into the molds to a depth of ¼ inch. If using the 8-cup pan, set it on a baking sheet and pour the batter into the pan to a depth of ¼ inch. Bake until the batter sets, 4 to 5 minutes.

▶ Meanwhile, toss the Bing cherries with the remaining ⅓ cup granulated sugar. Arrange the sugared cherries on top of the cake in the individual molds or larger pan, and pour the remaining batter over them. Bake until the clafoutis have risen and are golden brown and a toothpick or cake tester inserted into the center of a clafouti comes out clean, 25 to 40 minutes.

▶ Remove the clafoutis from the oven and allow to cool, about 12 minutes. If serving individual desserts, remove them from their molds and reheat briefly in the oven on a rimmed baking sheet. Serve, topped with confectioners' sugar and the crème anglaise.

Crème Anglaise

Crème anglaise is the base for ice creams and custards; it can also be infused and used on its own as a sauce for desserts from cakes to pies to ice creams. I especially enjoy it over apple strudel and chocolate soufflé. Try flavoring it with different liqueurs, especially when they echo the flavors of the dessert you'll top with the crème, such as Grand Marnier for orange desserts or coffee liqueur for desserts featuring coffee—just add a scant amount of the liqueur along with the milk in the first step. You can also bake the crème in custard molds for 40 to 50 minutes (depending on the depth of the molds) at 300°F, or freeze it in an ice cream machine according to the manufacturer's instructions, adding different ingredients and flavoring agents to create your own desserts.

MAKES ABOUT 1½ CUPS

1 cup whole milk

3 large egg yolks

2 tablespoons granulated sugar

Kosher salt

Bring the milk to a boil in a large saucepan over medium-high heat. Meanwhile, put the egg yolks, sugar, and a pinch of salt in a large heatproof bowl and lightly beat them together. As soon as the milk boils, remove it from the heat and add to the egg mixture in a thin stream, whisking constantly to keep the eggs from scrambling. Pour the mixture back into the pan and cook over low heat, stirring constantly, until it reaches 170°F, about 7 minutes. Do not allow the custard to boil. Strain the custard through a fine-mesh strainer into a clean medium bowl. Set a piece of plastic wrap on the surface of the crème anglaise to keep a film from forming and chill in the refrigerator until cold, at least 2 hours.

S'mores

with Chocolate Pudding, Graham Cracker Crumble, Marshmallows, and Chocolate Sorbet

A dessert for the kid in everybody, this deconstructed version of the campfire classic elevates the individual components of the original with unique versions, and brings them together with an arresting presentation. The chocolate is represented by pudding and sorbet, the graham cracker takes the form of a fresh-baked crumble, and the marshmallows are homemade ones that are brûléed with a torch to evoke the grill, where they would usually be toasted for traditional s'mores.

---

4 ounces dark chocolate, coarsely chopped

3 cups whole milk

¾ cup granulated sugar

Kosher salt

3 tablespoons cornstarch

4 large egg yolks

½ pound (2 sticks) unsalted butter, softened, plus 1 tablespoon unsalted butter, at room temperature

2 tablespoons honey

¾ cup (packed) dark brown sugar

1¼ cups all-purpose flour

½ teaspoon baking soda

½ teaspoon ground cinnamon

8 Homemade Marshmallows (see Notebook, page 357)

4 scoops Dark Chocolate Sorbet (page 358)

Maldon sea salt

To make the pudding: Melt the chocolate in a double boiler over simmering water and keep warm over low heat while you begin the pudding. Put 2¼ cups of the milk, 6 tablespoons of the granulated sugar, and ¼ teaspoon kosher salt in a pot and bring to a boil over medium-high heat.

▸ In a separate medium bowl, whisk together the remaining 6 tablespoons granulated sugar and the cornstarch, being sure to break up any lumps. Whisk the remaining ¾ cup milk into the mixture. Add the egg yolks and whisk until the mixture is smooth.

▸ When the milk comes to a boil, gradually whisk the hot milk into the yolk mixture, taking care to not allow the eggs to scramble. Return the mixture to the pot and place over medium heat, whisking constantly, until the mixture boils and thickens, about 2 minutes. Remove the pot from the heat and whisk in the 1 tablespoon room-temperature butter. Slowly whisk in the melted chocolate. Pour the mixture onto a rimmed baking sheet. Allow to cool for about 15 minutes. Cover with plastic wrap, allowing the plastic to touch the pudding to prevent a film from forming, and chill in the refrigerator for at least 1 hour.

▸ To make the graham cracker crumble: Preheat the oven to 375°F. Put the 2 sticks of softened butter and the honey and brown sugar in the bowl of a stand mixer and cream the ingredients together. When the mixture is smooth, add the flour, ½ teaspoon kosher salt, the

continued

baking soda, and cinnamon. Refrigerate the mixture for 15 minutes to make it easier to manipulate. Line a rimmed baking sheet with parchment paper, pour the mixture onto the sheet, and roll it out to an even thickness of ¼ inch. Bake until lightly golden brown and set, about 15 minutes. Remove the sheet from the oven, allow to cool for about 1 hour, then break the graham cracker into a crumble.

▸ To serve, caramelize 8 marshmallows with a brûlée torch. Place a generous smear of the chocolate pudding on each of 4 dessert plates, and sprinkle graham cracker crumble over the plates. Top with a scoop of sorbet and sprinkle sea salt on the sorbet. Finish by placing 2 caramelized marshmallows on each plate.

Homemade Marshmallows

Homemade marshmallows are a cut above any that you will buy in the supermarket: pleasingly dense with a more understated sweetness. Use them in ice cream sundaes; to top candied yams; in place of store-bought varieties for your favorite Rice Krispies treat recipe; blended into an ice cream base to make marshmallow ice cream; or in a fried fluff sandwich along with peanut butter and banana, coating the sandwich in flour, egg wash, and panko bread crumbs, and pan-frying it. For cocoa marshmallows, toss with cocoa powder instead of cornstarch at the end.

MAKES ABOUT 80 (1 INCH) MARSHMALLOWS

2 tablespoons unflavored powdered gelatin

1¼ cups granulated sugar

3 tablespoons liquid glucose

2 large egg whites

1 teaspoon pure vanilla extract

Nonstick cooking spray

¼ cup cornstarch

¼ cup 10-X sugar

Put 1 cup cold water in a small pot and sprinkle the gelatin over it, but do not stir. Allow the gelatin to soften for about 5 minutes. Meanwhile, put the granulated sugar, glucose, and 5 tablespoons water in a separate small pot over medium heat. Put the egg whites in a mixer fitted with the whisk attachment and whip on medium speed until soft peaks form, about 7 minutes. Turn low heat on under the gelatin to melt it, then gradually add to the whipping whites.

▶ Raise the heat under the sugar mixture and continue cooking until it reaches 240°F when measured with a candy thermometer. Turn the mixer back on high and slowly pour the sugar mixture into the egg whites, then add the vanilla extract. Continue mixing until the bottom of the mixing bowl is lukewarm.

▶ Spray the bottom and sides of a 9 by 9-inch or similarly sized baking pan with nonstick cooking spray. Put the cornstarch and 10-X sugar in a bowl and stir to combine. Sprinkle some of the cornstarch mixture in the pan and turn to coat the bottom and sides, pouring any excess back into the bowl. Pour the marshmallow mixture into the pan and use a rubber spatula to spread it in an even layer. Sprinkle the top of the mixture generously with about half of the 10-X-cornstarch mixture. Allow the marshmallow to set, uncovered, at room temperature, until springy to the touch, at least 4 hours, or up to 12 hours. Cut the marshmallows into 1-inch cubes (you will have about 80 marshmallows), and dust with the remaining 10-X–cornstarch mixture. Store in an airtight container at room temperature for up to 3 days.

Ice Creams, Sorbets, and Sherbets

Dark Chocolate Sorbet

MAKES ABOUT 3 CUPS

½ cup granulated sugar

⅓ cup cocoa powder

1 shot espresso

3 ounces bittersweet dark chocolate, coarsely chopped

1 teaspoon pure vanilla extract

Whisk together ¾ cup water with the sugar, cocoa powder, and espresso in a large saucepan over medium-high heat. Bring to a boil, whisking frequently, and continue to whisk for 45 seconds. Remove the pan from the heat. Stir in the chocolate until it's melted, then stir in the vanilla extract and ¼ cup water. Transfer the mixture to a blender and blend for 15 seconds. Pour the mixture into a large bowl and chill in the refrigerator until cold, at least 3 hours or up to 24 hours. Freeze the mixture in an ice cream maker according to the manufacturer's instructions.

Buttermilk Sherbet

MAKES ABOUT 1 QUART

2¾ cups buttermilk

¾ cup granulated sugar

¾ cup plain yogurt

¼ cup honey

½ vanilla bean, split and scraped

Fill a large bowl halfway with ice water. Put the buttermilk, sugar, yogurt, honey, and vanilla bean pod and seeds in a large saucepan set over high heat. Cook, stirring constantly, until the sugar dissolves, being sure the mixture doesn't boil. Strain the custard through a fine-mesh strainer set over a bowl set over the ice bath. Cool, stirring constantly, until chilled, about 12 minutes. Freeze the mixture in an ice cream machine according to the manufacturer's instructions.

Buttered Popcorn Sherbet

MAKES ABOUT 1 QUART

2 cups whole milk

9 tablespoons (1 stick plus 1 tablespoon) unsalted butter

½ teaspoon kosher salt

½ bag popped unsalted buttered microwave popcorn

¼ cup glucose syrup

¼ cup plus 1 tablespoon light corn syrup

Bring the milk to a boil in a large saucepan over high heat. Add the butter, salt, and popcorn, remove the pan from the heat, and set aside to infuse for 1 hour. Strain through a fine-mesh strainer set over a large bowl and refrigerate until chilled completely and the butter separates and rises to the top of the mixture, at least 2 hours or overnight. Use a tablespoon to skim off as much of the butter as possible and discard it. Heat the glucose and corn syrup in a small saucepan over medium heat just until warm, then stir into the chilled milk mixture. Return to the refrigerator until cold, at least 3 hours or up to 24 hours. Freeze the sherbet in an ice cream machine according to the manufacturer's instructions.

Vanilla Bean Ice Cream

MAKES ABOUT 1 QUART

2 vanilla beans, split and scraped

3 cups heavy cream

1 cup whole milk

1½ cups granulated sugar

4 large eggs

Put the vanilla beans, heavy cream, milk, and sugar in a large saucepan over medium heat and whisk together. Bring the mixture just to a boil, whisking occasionally, then remove the pan from the heat.

▸ Put the eggs in a large bowl and beat them lightly. Slowly pour the hot cream mixture into the eggs in a thin stream, whisking constantly to keep the eggs from scrambling. Return the custard to the pan and set over low heat. Cook, stirring constantly, until the mixture reaches a temperature of 170°F. Do not allow it to boil.

▸ Strain the custard through a fine-mesh strainer set over a large bowl and let cool to room temperature, about 15 minutes. Press waxed paper directly on the surface of the custard to keep a film from forming, then chill in the refrigerator until cold, at least 3 hours or up to 24 hours. Freeze the custard in an ice cream machine according to the manufacturer's instructions.

Maple-Bacon Ice Cream

MAKES ABOUT 3 CUPS

1 cup heavy cream

¼ teaspoon kosher salt

½ cup whole milk

½ cup maple syrup

2 egg yolks

2 tablespoons granulated sugar

¼ cup chopped well-done bacon

Put the cream, salt, milk, and maple syrup in a large, heavy saucepan and cook the mixture, stirring occasionally, over medium-high heat. When the mixture just begins to boil, about 5 minutes, remove the pan from the heat. Beat the egg yolks and sugar in a medium bowl. Whisk the hot cream mixture into the eggs in a slow, thin stream, taking care to not allow the eggs to scramble. Pour the custard into a clean pan and cook over low heat, stirring constantly, until the mixture reaches 170°F. Do not allow it to boil. Pour the custard through a fine-mesh strainer into a clean bowl and allow it to cool for 15 minutes. Cover the surface of the custard with plastic wrap to prevent a film from forming and chill in the refrigerator for at least 3 hours or up to 24 hours. Fold in the bacon bits, and freeze the custard in an ice cream machine according to the manufacturer's instructions.

Peanut Butter Ice Cream

MAKES ABOUT 1 QUART

¾ cup creamy peanut butter

1½ cups heavy cream

½ cup whole milk

¾ cup granulated sugar

2 large eggs

Put the peanut butter, cream, milk, and sugar in a large, heavy saucepan over medium heat, whisking to incorporate. Bring the mixture just to a boil, stirring occasionally, then remove the pan from the heat. Put the eggs in a large bowl and lightly whisk them. Slowly pour the hot cream mixture into the eggs, whisking constantly and taking care to not let the eggs scramble. Return the mixture to the saucepan over medium-low heat. Cook the custard, stirring constantly, until it reaches a temperature of 170°F. Do not allow the custard to boil. Strain the custard through a fine-mesh strainer set over a large bowl and allow to cool to room temperature. Press plastic wrap directly on the surface of the custard to keep a film from forming, and chill in the refrigerator until cold, at least 3 hours or up to 24 hours. Freeze the custard in an ice cream machine according to the manufacturer's instructions.

Vanilla Bean–Caramel Ice Cream

MAKES ABOUT 1 QUART

½ cup granulated sugar

1 cup whole milk

1 cup heavy cream

1 vanilla bean, split and scraped

10 large egg yolks

Heat the sugar in a heavy saucepan over medium heat, stirring, until it begins to turn amber and caramelize, about 8 minutes. Carefully pour in the milk and cream, and add the scraped vanilla bean and seeds. Whisk thoroughly and bring to a boil. Slowly add the egg yolks, whisking constantly to ensure that they don't scramble, and continue to cook and whisk until the mixture is thick and ribbony, about 5 minutes. Strain the mixture through a fine-mesh strainer set over a large bowl. Set a piece of plastic wrap directly on the surface of the custard to keep a film from forming, and chill in the refrigerator for at least 3 hours or up to 24 hours. Freeze in an ice cream machine according to the manufacturer's instructions.

BASIC TECHNIQUES AND RECIPES

Certain basic techniques and recipes are called for repeatedly throughout the book and are quite common in cooking overall. Here are instructions for many of them.

BASIC TECHNIQUES

PEELING LEMONGRASS To access the edible part of lemongrass, slice off and discard the root end and the upper portion of the aromatic. Peel off a layer or two of its woody exterior, either by hand or with the help of a paring knife, then slice the lemongrass or crush it with the side of your knife as called for in individual recipes.

CHIFFONADE To cut basil or other herbs into chiffonade (ribbons), stack a few leaves, roll them into a cigar shape, then slice them crosswise with a sharp knife. Then unfurl.

ROASTING PEPPERS Impale peppers on a meat fork or other long, heatproof implement and roast in the open flame of a gas jet or over a grill until charred and blistered all over, about 6 minutes. Remove from the fork, transfer to a heatproof bowl, cover with plastic wrap, and allow to steam until the skin loosens, about 5 minutes. Remove the plastic, allow to rest until warm enough to handle, then remove the skin with a paring knife (it should come right off), seed if desired, and slice or chop as called for in individual recipes.

BLANCHING VEGETABLES AND GREENS Fill a large pot two-thirds full with salted water and bring to a boil over high heat. When the water is boiling, add the vegetable or greens and blanch; in the case of green vegetables, just until bright green. Blanching time will range from 1 to 3 minutes based on the size and thickness of vegetable.

Drain the vegetable in a colander. For green vegetables, transfer to a bowl filled halfway with ice water to "shock" them, stopping the cooking and preserving their bright color. Drain again.

CLEANING MUSHROOMS When I was learning to cook, the universal instruction was to brush rather than soak mushrooms to clean them because they have a tendency to take on liquid. It's true, but brushing delicate mushrooms can bust them up, and some mushrooms, such as the honeycombed morel, have textured surfaces or cavities where grit can hide. While most cultivated mushrooms have a durable texture and an easy-to-brush shape, many wild mushrooms need to be soaked to really get clean. For mushrooms such as morels, black trumpets, hedgehogs, and chanterelles, place them in a bowl of room-temperature water, agitate briefly to help loosen any grit, then lift them out of the water and allow them to dry on paper towels or clean kitchen towels at room temperature.

TOASTING NUTS, SPICES, SEEDS, AND COCONUT Place nuts, spices, seeds, or coconut in a wide sauté pan over medium-high heat and cook until lightly toasted and fragrant, 2 to 3 minutes. If you are toasting multiple spices for the same recipe and they will be ground together, you can toast them together.

BASIC RECIPES
Simple Preparations

TEMPURA BATTER Makes about 2 cups. Put 2 cups soda water and 1 cup all-purpose flour in a medium bowl and whisk together until smooth. Strain the batter through a fine-mesh strainer set over a wide, shallow bowl and dip ingredients into it as called for in recipes. If you are not using the batter immediately, refrigerate it, but for no longer than 1 hour; rewhisk it before using. To make more or less batter, simply multiply or divide the amounts of soda water and flour.

PORCINI MUSHROOM POWDER Preheat the oven to 275°F. Arrange a package of dried porcini mushrooms in an even layer on a baking sheet and dry thoroughly in the oven, 10 to 12 minutes. Transfer to a coffee or spice grinder and grind to a fine powder. (Remove the grinder's lid slowly to prevent the powder from spraying.) Alternatively, porcini mushroom powder may be purchased; see Sources, page 370.

CROUTONS Heat olive oil in a sauté pan over medium-high heat. Add cubed bread, preferably sourdough, season with salt and pepper, and cook, tossing to coat the bread, until golden brown, about 4 minutes. Drain the croutons on paper towels and use as directed in the recipe.

SIMPLE SYRUPS To make simple syrup, cook equal amounts sugar and water in a pot over medium-high heat, whisking until the sugar is dissolved, about 5 minutes. For the cocktails on pages 266–67, infuse with the herbs that are called for: for 1 quart syrup, use 20 perilla (shiso) leaves, 1 bunch mint, or ½ bunch sage. Strain the syrup before using.

Pastas
Basic Pasta Dough

MAKES ABOUT 3 CUPS PASTA (ENOUGH FOR 6 APPETIZER SERVINGS OR 4 MAIN COURSE SERVINGS)

Use this recipe to produce pasta to be cut into strands such as spaghetti, linguine, and fettuccine.

2¼ cups all-purpose flour, plus more for flouring a work surface
1 tablespoon kosher salt
4 large eggs

Put the flour and salt in the bowl of a mixer fitted with the hook attachment and blend them together. Slowly add the eggs and mix on low speed until blended, about 5 minutes. Turn the dough out onto your work surface and knead by hand until smooth and slightly elastic, about 1 minute, adding more flour if the dough feels too tacky. Wrap the dough with plastic wrap and refrigerate for 20 minutes. Using a pasta extruder, follow the manufacturer's directions to create your desired shape. The cut pasta can be coiled in small batches, dusted with cornmeal to prevent sticking, and refrigerated in plastic bags for up to 2 days.

Filled-Pasta Dough

MAKES ENOUGH PASTA FOR 6 APPETIZER SERVINGS OR 4 MAIN-COURSE SERVINGS

Use this recipe to produce filled pasta such as ravioli or agnolotti.

2 cups all-purpose flour, plus more for rolling
Kosher salt
Freshly ground black pepper
8 large egg yolks, plus 1 whole egg

Put the flour in a large mixing bowl. Season with salt and pepper and whisk to incorporate. Use clean hands to create a well in the center of the flour and add the egg yolks and whole egg to the center of the well. Use a fork to whisk the eggs, incorporating the flour a little at a time until a cohesive dough forms. Cover the bowl with a damp towel and set aside to rest at room temperature for 30 minutes.

▸ Divide the dough into 4 pieces and use your hands to form each piece into a rectangle. Dust with flour and use a pasta machine to roll out the pasta dough into very thin sheets. Use a pizza cutter, pasta mold, or ring mold to cut into desired shapes.

NOTE: To produce the cannelloni on page 141, use ½ cup flour and 2 large egg yolks plus 1 whole egg to produce a single 12 by 24-inch pasta sheet. Line a baking sheet with parchment paper and brush to lightly coat with olive oil. Bring a large pot of salted water to a boil. Add the pasta and cook until tender, about 2 minutes. Draining the large sheet can be challenging: If you own a spider, use it to remove the pasta from the pot; otherwise, gently pour the contents of the pan into a large colander, taking care not to tear the pasta. Transfer the pasta to a baking sheet and rub with olive oil. Set aside until ready to use.

Stocks

Vegetable Stock

MAKES 1 GALLON

You can use any vegetable scraps to make this stock, but this is my preferred mix.

¼ cup olive oil

2 carrots, peeled and coarsely chopped

2 Spanish onions, coarsely chopped

1 lemongrass stalk, peeled (see page 362) and coarsely chopped

5 garlic cloves, coarsely chopped

4 celery stalks, coarsely chopped

1 cup coarsely chopped button mushrooms

4 plum tomatoes, coarsely chopped

1 cup dry white wine

Heat the oil in a stockpot over high heat. When the oil is shimmering, add the carrots, onions, lemongrass, garlic, celery, mushrooms, and tomatoes and cook, stirring until softened, about 5 minutes. Pour in the white wine, bring to a boil, and continue to boil until reduced by half, about 10 minutes. Pour in 1 gallon water, return to a boil, then lower the heat to medium so the liquid is simmering, and allow to simmer gently for 40 minutes.

▶ Strain the stock through a fine-mesh strainer set over a large bowl, pressing down on the solids with a rubber spatula or the bottom of a ladle to extract as much stock as possible. Use right away, refrigerate in an airtight container for up to 3 days, or freeze for up to 2 months.

Mushroom Stock

MAKES 1 GALLON

1 cup olive oil

3 pounds mushrooms of your choosing (stems, trimmings, and/or dried mushrooms), coarsely chopped

2 carrots, peeled and chopped

2 Spanish onions, coarsely chopped

5 garlic cloves, coarsely chopped

4 celery stalks, coarsely chopped

4 plum tomatoes, sliced

1 cup ruby port

Heat the oil in a large pot over medium-high heat. When the oil is shimmering, add the mushrooms and cook, stirring, until lightly golden brown, about 8 minutes. Add the carrots, onions, garlic, celery, and tomatoes and cook for 5 minutes. Add the port, stir, and bring to a simmer, then lower the heat and continue to simmer until reduced by half, about 10 minutes. Add 1 gallon water. Return to a simmer and continue to simmer for 40 minutes. Strain the stock through a fine-mesh strainer set over a large bowl, pressing down on the solids with a rubber spatula or the bottom of a ladle to extract as much stock as possible. Use right away, refrigerate in an airtight container for up to 3 days, or freeze for up to 2 months.

Chicken Stock

MAKES 1½ QUARTS

1 whole chicken, about 2½ pounds

1 carrot, peeled and coarsely chopped

1 Spanish onion, coarsely chopped

2 celery stalks, coarsely chopped

1 thyme sprig

Heat a large, heavy saucepan or soup pot over high heat. Add the chicken, carrot, onion, celery, thyme, and 1 gallon water and bring to a boil. Reduce the heat and simmer for 30 minutes. Remove the chicken from the pot and set aside to cool slightly. Strain the broth through a fine-mesh strainer set over a large bowl, pressing down on the solids with a rubber spatula or the bottom of a ladle to extract as much stock as possible. Return the strained broth to the pot and continue to simmer until reduced to 6 cups, 35 to 40 minutes. Allow to cool, then skim the fat from the surface using a ladle. Use right away, refrigerate in an airtight container for up to 3 days, or freeze for up to 2 months.

▸ If you are using the chicken in a recipe, remove the meat from the bones and cut or shred as needed. You will have about 1 quart of meat; save what you don't use immediately for soups, salads, and chicken salad. You can also use it in recipes such as the *khao soi* on page 255.

Lobster Stock

MAKES 2 QUARTS

2 Maine lobsters, about 1 pound each

2 tablespoons white wine vinegar

1 tablespoon extra-virgin olive oil

1 Spanish onion, coarsely chopped

1 cup chopped plum tomato, with its seeds

½ cup coarsely chopped celery

¼ cup brandy

Kill the lobster by impaling it between the eyes with a chef's knife and pulling the knife forward like a lever.

▸ To cook the lobster: Fill a large bowl halfway with ice water. Remove the claws, knuckles, and tails from the lobsters and reserve the bodies. Bring 2 gallons water and the vinegar to a boil in a Dutch oven or large, heavy stock pot over high heat. When the water is boiling, add the claws and knuckles and cook until bright red, about 7 minutes. Use tongs or a slotted spoon to transfer the claws and knuckles to the ice water to stop the cooking. Add the tails to the boiling water. Cook the tails until bright red, about 5 minutes. Transfer the tails to the ice water. Reserve the lobster cooking water in a large bowl. When the lobster has cooled, in about 20 minutes, remove the meat from the shells and coarsely chop it. Reserve the meat and shells separately.

▸ To make the stock: Carefully wipe out the pot, set it over high heat, and add the oil. When the oil is shimmering, add the lobster shells and cook, stirring, until the shells are roasted and deep red, about 7 minutes. Add the onion, tomato, and celery and lower the heat to medium. Cook, stirring, until the vegetables are browned and tender, about 10 minutes. Carefully pour in the brandy and cook until it completely evaporates, about 1 minute. Add the reserved lobster water and simmer over medium heat, stirring occasionally, until the liquid is reduced by three-quarters, about 2 hours. Strain the liquid through a fine-mesh strainer set over a medium bowl, pressing down on the solids with a rubber spatula or the bottom of a ladle to extract as much stock as possible. Use right away, refrigerate in an airtight container for up to 3 days, or freeze for up to 2 months.

Shellfish Stock

MAKES 1 GALLON

½ cup olive oil

4 pounds crab, shrimp, and/or lobster shells

1 fennel bulb, thinly sliced

2 Spanish onions, coarsely chopped

4 plum tomatoes, coarsely chopped

1 bunch celery, coarsely chopped

1 quart dry white wine

Heat the oil in a stockpot over high heat. When the oil is shimmering, add the shellfish shells and cook, stirring, until the shells turn bright red, about 7 minutes. Add the fennel, onions, tomatoes, and celery and cook, stirring, until softened, about 4 minutes. Pour in the white wine, stirring to loosen any flavorful bits from the bottom of the pot. Bring to a boil and continue to boil until reduced by half, about 10 minutes. Pour in 1 gallon water, return to a boil, then lower the heat so the liquid is simmering, and allow to simmer gently for 1 hour.

▸ Use tongs to remove and discard the shells, then strain the stock through a fine-mesh strainer set over a large bowl, pressing down on the solids with a rubber spatula or the bottom of a ladle to extract as much stock as possible. Use right away, refrigerate in an airtight container for up to 3 days, or freeze for up to 2 months.

Duck Stock

MAKES 1 GALLON

6 pounds duck bones

1 bunch celery, coarsely chopped

5 plum tomatoes, coarsely chopped

2 Spanish onions, coarsely chopped

1 quart ruby port

Preheat the oven to 425°F.

▸ Arrange the duck bones in an even layer in a roasting pan and roast until golden brown, periodically shaking the pan to ensure even roasting, about 30 minutes.

▸ Transfer the bones to a stockpot and add 5 quarts water. Set the pot over high heat and bring the liquid to a boil.

▸ Meanwhile, arrange the celery, tomatoes, and onions in an even layer in the roasting pan and roast in the oven for 10 minutes. Transfer the pan to the stovetop over two burners on medium-high heat. Pour in the port, bring to a simmer, and continue to simmer until reduced by half, about 10 minutes. Use a wooden spoon to loosen any flavorful bits from the bottom of the pan, and pour the contents of the pan into the stockpot. If the water is not already boiling, return it to a boil, then lower the heat so the liquid is simmering. Allow to simmer gently for 5 hours.

▸ Use tongs to remove and discard the bones, then strain the stock through a fine-mesh strainer, pressing down on the solids with a rubber spatula or the bottom of a ladle to extract as much stock as possible. Skim the fat from the top of the stock using a ladle. Use right away, refrigerate in an airtight container for up to 3 days, or freeze for up to 2 months.

Veal Stock

MAKES 1 GALLON

8 pounds veal bones

1 bunch celery, coarsely chopped

5 plum tomatoes, coarsely chopped

2 Spanish onions, coarsely chopped

1 quart dry red wine

Preheat the oven to 425°F.

▸ Arrange the veal bones in an even layer in a roasting pan and roast until golden brown, periodically shaking the pan to ensure even roasting, about 40 minutes.

▸ Transfer the bones to a stockpot and add 5 quarts water. Set the pot over high heat and bring the liquid to a boil.

▸ Meanwhile, arrange the celery, tomatoes, and onions in an even layer in the roasting pan and roast in the oven for 10 minutes. Transfer the pan to the stovetop over two burners on medium-high heat. Pour in the red wine, bring to a simmer, and continue to simmer until reduced by half, about 10 minutes. Use a wooden spoon to loosen any flavorful bits from the bottom of the pan, and pour the contents of the pan into the stockpot.

▸ If the water is not already boiling, return it to a boil, then lower the heat so the liquid is simmering. Allow to simmer gently for 6 hours.

▸ Use tongs to remove and discard the bones, then strain the stock through a fine-mesh strainer, pressing down on the solids with a rubber spatula or the bottom of a ladle to extract as much stock as possible. Skim the fat from the top of the stock using a ladle. Use right away, refrigerate in an airtight container for up to 3 days, or freeze for up to 2 months.

SPECIALTY INGREDIENTS AND MAIL-ORDER SOURCES

Some of the recipes throughout this book call for Asian ingredients that are relatively uncommon and may not be easy to find, depending on where you live. Here is a glossary with brief descriptions of these ingredients and how to use them. Many can be found in Asian markets and gourmet or specialty shops, or you can order most of them on the Internet from the sources listed.

SPECIALTY INGREDIENTS

Black vinegar: A strong, pungent vinegar that I use in Asian cuisine the way you might use balsamic vinegar in Italian cooking (i.e., as a marinade for tomatoes, or reduced and used as a sauce).

Dried shrimp: A crispy garnishing element that delivers a potent hit of salt.

Fermented yellow bean sauce (or fermented yellow bean paste): An additive that brings flavor-enhancing salinity to vegetable-based sauces.

Fried garlic: A store-bought garnish of minced, fried garlic that adds crunch and punch to soups and other dishes. Despite the name, this isn't one to make at home.

Fried shallots: Just what the name says: a crunchy, oniony garnish. As with fried garlic, this store-bought garnish is a fine substitute for homemade.

Garam masala: A complex Indian spice blend.

Korean pepper paste: A sweet pepper paste that's best

employed with shellfish and pork.

Oyster sauce: A stir-fry sauce that turns up a lot in Asian cooking. It's *not* just for seafood but is also terrific for vegetables and beef; a little can go a long way in marinades.

Palm sugar: One of the workhorse aromatics of Thai cuisine, adding a subtle sweetness to all types of dishes.

Pickled green peppercorns: Tart and pungent peppercorns, used in Thai curries and salads.

Plum vinegar: A sweet and tart vinegar that I especially like in salad dressings.

Sambal (often sold as "sambal oelek" or "chili-garlic sauce"): A thick, chili-garlic condiment that knows no boundaries.

Shiro dashi: Dashi with soy sauce that brings a big umami flavor to raw fish and is also delicious tossed with spaghetti squash.

Shrimp paste: There are two types of shrimp paste: shrimp paste in oil, which is used to bring a burst of shellfish flavor to dishes; and fermented shrimp paste, which is dried and used in curry pastes.

Soy sauces: There's much more to soy sauce than many Western cooks realize. Explore beyond the supermarket aisles and you'll discover a world of exquisite soy sauces out there that rival the complexity of, say, balsamic vinegars. Some brands that I like include Yamasa (perfect for sushi); KHS (for stir-frying); and Kikkoman ponzu sauce (for raw fish or dumplings). There are also white soy sauces that I like for lighter dishes such as those featuring vegetable curries, and mushroom soy sauces that I like for mushroom-focused dishes. Sweet soy sauce is a darker concoction that I like for stir-fries; specifically, I make a stir-fry sauce by combining sweet soy sauce, light soy sauce (fermented for less time than regular soy), and fish sauce (see page 245); it's also delicious tossed with Asian-style noodle dishes.

Sriracha: My favorite condiment, a blend of sun-ripened chiles and garlic that adds an addictive heat to just about any kind of dish.

Tamarind: The tart pulp of tamarind fruit, especially at home in curries. The recipes in this book call for tamarind concentrate.

Toasted rice pearls: Cereal-like Japanese crisps used to garnish a variety of dishes. If you cannot find them, whole grain rice cereal is a fine substitution.

XO sauce: A dry Chinese shellfish condiment.

Yuzu: A Japanese citrus fruit that has a terrific affinity with raw fish.

SOURCES

Amazon.com
www.amazon.com
Black truffle peelings, CO_2 canisters and chargers, dried shrimp, fermented yellow bean paste/sauce, fried garlic, fried shallots, Korean pepper paste, sausage casings, squid ink

Asian Food Grocer
www.asianfoodgrocer.com; 888-482-2742
Shiro dashi

Catalina Offshore Products
www.catalinaop.com
Sea urchin

D'Artagnan
www.dartagnan.com; 800-327-8246
Duck fat, foie gras, game birds

Kalustyan's
www.kalustyans.com; 800-352-3451
Banyuls vinegar, black vinegar, garam masala, mustard oil, oyster sauce, palm sugar, plum vinegar, porcini mushroom powder, preserved lemons, rice wine vinegar, sambal, shrimp paste, sriracha, soy sauces, tamarind, XO sauce, yuzu juice

La Quercia
www.laquercia.us; 515-981-1625
Cured and aged meats such as *guanciale* and speck

Marx Foods
www.marxfoods.com; 866-588-6279
Shiso leaves

ACKNOWLEDGMENTS

My great thanks to the following people:

My collaborator, Andrew Friedman. Back when I was a sous chef at The Harrison we made a pact that we'd write a book together one day, and here it is. Nothing like working with old friends.

Our original editor, Amanda Englander, for snapping up the concept based on a couple of early blog posts, and for helping us see it through to reality with patience and diligence. It was fun working with you.

Editor Karen Murgolo, who shepherded the book down the homestretch, taking it under her wing with great care.

David Black, agent extraordinaire, and a great dinner companion, for his involvement in every step of the process.

Daniel Krieger, our photographer, for his beautiful images and NSFW background music.

Eve Hammer, for her brilliant illustrations that bring the Notebook entries to life.

Denise Canter, for her prop selection and styling.

Douglas Riccardi and his team at Memo, for the book's design.

Publisher Jamie Raab and the entire Grand Central Publishing team, for their belief and support.

Joshua Del Valle and Stephanie Koptya, for testing the recipes.

My business partner Alicia Nosenzo, for sharing this incredible adventure with me.

Mom and Dad…I love you guys. Thanks for showing me the ropes.

My team of chefs: Garett McMahan, Mike Cain, Evelyn Garcia, Erik Rentz, Ben Singleton, and Steve Lopin. You guys rock.

The entire HAND restaurant group team, for minding the stores and treating our customers right.

And, finally, a huge, heartfelt thanks to our restaurant guests and regulars. It might sound like a cliché, but it is an honor to serve you.

NOTEBOOK SUBJECT INDEX

INDEX